W9-BUL-095

THE WORLD'S RELIGIONS

THE
WORLD'S RELIGIONS

Edited by

J. N. D. ANDERSON, O.B.E., M.A., LL.B.

Sometime Senior Scholar, Trinity College, Cambridge
Professor of Oriental Laws in the University of London

ANIMISM

·

JUDAISM

·

ISLAM

·

HINDUISM

·

BUDDHISM

·

SHINTO

·

CONFUCIANISM

WM. B. EERDMANS PUBLISHING COMPANY
GRAND RAPIDS, MICHIGAN

First Edition	June, 1950
Second Edition	November, 1951
Reprinted	November, 1951
Third Edition	August, 1955
Reprinted	August, 1957
Reprinted	February, 1960
Reprinted	August, 1962
Reprinted	October, 1963
Reprinted	June, 1966
Reprinted	September, 1968

PHOTOLITHOPRINTED BY GRAND RAPIDS BOOK MANUFACTURERS, INC.

GRAND RAPIDS, MICHIGAN, UNITED STATES OF AMERICA

1968

CONTENTS

8685

FOREWORD

IN the following pages an attempt has been made to summarize the origin and teaching of the most important of the non-Christian religions and to give some appreciation of what they mean in the thought and lives of their adherents. For this purpose six such religions have been chosen—Judaism, Islam, Hinduism, Buddhism, Shinto, and Confucianism, together with those pagan beliefs and practices which are now commonly grouped together under the title of 'Animism'.

The choice of these seven is, of course, open to criticism, and it was largely considerations of space which prevented the inclusion of certain others. Islam and Hinduism were automatic choices, since each claims some three hundred million followers. Modern Judaism has incomparably less adherents, but demanded inclusion as one of the three great monotheistic faiths. Animistic beliefs and customs underlie and permeate the practices, if not the precepts, of so many other religions (quite apart from the widespread theory which sees in them the origin of all religion) that Animism could not be excluded. For the rest, Buddhism, Shinto and Confucianism were selected as probably the most important of the other great religions which challenge men's allegiance. Some reference to Taoism will be found included in the section on Confucianism.

It may well be asked why Christianity finds no place among the religions treated in this book. These studies, however, are intended primarily for students of religion in English-speaking countries, and aim at providing factual information which they might otherwise find difficult to obtain. The majority of readers will at least be in daily contact with those who profess the Christian faith and should therefore have no difficulty in acquainting themselves with the main outline of Christian belief and practice. In the Epilogue, moreover, some reference is made to the distinctive teaching of Christianity, and to the Christian's attitude to other religions.

Each of the following articles has been contributed by one who has not only studied in the abstract the religion of which he writes, but has had direct contact with its devotees. The contributors have attempted to treat each religion objectively, the purpose being to provide material which is factual without being wearisome, and scholarly without being technical. They have tried to be scrupulously fair to their subject and rigidly to avoid the temptation to overemphasize weaknesses or to make adverse comparisons with Christianity. No attempt has been made to unify the different styles of individual contributors, and no rigid control has been imposed on the length of the different articles. Such a method has certain obvious defects, but it is hoped that these will be outweighed by the advantages of variety and individuality of treatment.

J.N.D.A.

THE WORLD'S RELIGIONS

CHAPTER I

ANIMISM

THE use of the term 'Animism' to describe the religion and the philosophy of primitive peoples dates only from the publication of Sir Edward Tylor's *Primitive Culture* (1871), when he coined the word to sum up his account of the origin of religion.

'Animism is the doctrine which places the source of mental and even physical life in an energy independent of, or at least distinct from, the body. From the point of view of the history of religions, the term is taken, in the wider sense, to denote the belief in the existence of spiritual beings, some attached to bodies of which they constitute the real personality (souls), others without necessary connection with a determinate body (spirits).'[1]

Derived from the word 'anima' (breath), Animism can be more simply and popularly defined as 'Spirit Worship', as distinguished from the worship of God or gods.

The extent of its ramifications in primitive religious thought shows how basic it is to natural, as opposed to revealed, religion. It includes Necrolatry, a term which conveniently describes the worship of the souls of men and animals, especially of the dead; Spirit Worship, involving the worship of spirits not particularly associated with bodies or objects; and Naturism, which sums up the worship of spiritual beings who direct the phenomena of nature. As such, it is not only the religion of wild and savage tribes before contact with civilization, but the background of the religious philosophy of the Hindu, the Buddhist, the Shintoist, the Confucianist, and the Muslim, and is at the bottom of all the folklore of Christendom in Europe, as well as of the mythology of Egypt, Babylonia and Assyria, Greece, Rome, and Scandinavia. In America, before the conquests by Spain and Portugal, we find Animism in a highly developed form as the religion of the Aztecs of Mexico and the Incas of Peru.

Its ramifications are worldwide, so that every continent, and the islands of every sea, reveal their close relationship with animistic belief

[1] Article by Goblet d'Alviella in Hastings's *Encyclopaedia of Religion and Ethics*.

and custom, whether it be among the aborigines of Australia, the tribes of Africa, or the Eskimos of the Arctic belt.

Many of the writers and investigators of Animism have attempted to assign its chronological place in the history of religion. Sir J. G. Frazer, in his monumental work of nine volumes, *The Golden Bough*, has amassed evidence to prove that in his opinion Magic is the origin of all religion. Frazer provided, in his one-volume abridgment of his own work, a convenient means of seeing the picture of his worldwide investigation as a whole, and in less detailed form.

He states: 'An Age of Religion has thus everywhere, as I venture to surmise, been preceded by an Age of Magic,' and that 'the universal faith . . . is a belief in the efficacy of magic. While religious systems differ not only in different countries, but in the same country in different ages, the system of sympathetic magic remains everywhere and at all times substantially alike in its principles and practice. Among the ignorant and superstitious classes of modern Europe it is very much what it was thousands of years ago in Egypt and India, and what it now is among the lowest savages in the remotest corners of the world.'[1]

On the other hand, H. Spencer, in his *Principles of Sociology*, regarded Ancestor Worship, including the hero cult, as the basis of human religion: he says 'we conclude that Ancestor Worship (in its broadest sense) is the root of every religion'. F. B. Jevons, in his *Introduction to the History of Religion*, tried to prove that Totemism was precedent to all other forms of religious belief and practice. Andrew Lang, however, in his work *Myth, Ritual and Religion*, scoffed at the idea that gods were originally departed human souls (which would account for a belief in Ancestor Worship as basic to all religion). He contended that in all known savage philosophy the Maker is regarded as a being in existence before death came into the world.

We must return to this argument later, but meanwhile it is safe to say that, apart from revealed religion, some form of animistic belief has preceded all other human and historical religions.

As Frazer says: 'The view of nature as animated by indwelling spirits appears to have generally preceded the view of it as controlled by external deities; to put it shortly, Animism precedes Deism.'[2]

As we briefly look at the content of animistic belief under the three

[1] *The Golden Bough* (one volume), p. 56.
[2] Op. cit., p. 422.

heads of Necrolatry, Spirit Worship, and Naturism, an explanation
may be required of the frequent illustrations drawn from one particular
tribe—the Kachins (or Jinghpaw, as they call themselves) of Northern
Burma. A comparative study of animistic belief and practice needs
firsthand knowledge to give flesh to the skeleton outline, and any such
knowledge, in the writer's experience, is largely due to living for fifteen
years among this one particular tribe, whose beliefs and customs find
their counterpart among similar tribes all over the world.

NECROLATRY

It is a remarkable fact that no people have been discovered who do
not believe in the existence and survival of human souls. Not only does
the savage possess an instinctive knowledge of the survival of the soul
after death, but his primitive observation and reasoning would lead
him to such a conclusion. He wakes from a dream, and finds that
though his body is in the same place where he lay down to sleep, part
of him has been travelling to distant places, or taking part in exciting
activities. Obviously there must be some part of him which is free to
come and go from the house of his body. He observes others when
asleep, sees that their bodies lie still, and that they themselves are not
conscious of the world around them. The soul has made a temporary
exit, and the bewilderment seen on the face of someone awakened too
suddenly shows the danger that may be involved in too sudden action
for the soul in process of returning to the body.

Death is a permanent prolongation of this process of the departure
of the soul from the body. The Eskimos believe that the soul is of the
same shape as the body to which it belongs, but of a more ethereal
nature. The common belief of many primitive tribes is that the soul is
a little man or animal inside the body, who indicates his presence by
the movements of that body. When the body lies still in sleep, the
soul has temporarily left it; and when death ensues, the soul has
departed for ever, unless it can be coaxed back.

The illness and delirium of someone in a fever may be a sign of the
conflict that is going on between the soul and the body, and every
possible step must be taken to prevent the soul departing. If it is
thought that the soul regularly takes one particular route out of the
body, appropriate measures must be taken to bar the exit. So most
of the peoples of Burma will tie a string round the wrist of a patient
to prevent the soul from departing by this usual route.

As the souls of the dead survive their departure from the body, much speculation ensues in the primitive mind as to what has happened to these innumerable souls, and where they have gone. Are they still capable of exercising an influence over the living, and is that influence friendly? If, as most believe, the soul roaming apart from the body constitutes a danger to the living, what measures can be taken to ensure that the soul is removed as far as possible, and made secure in that land of departed spirits from which there is no return?

1. *Ancestor Worship*

With a high mortality rate among primitive peoples, it is natural that death should assume great terrors, and that much time and thought should be given to the security of the living in relation to the souls of the departed. This leads to Ancestor Worship, or the Worship of the Dead. We are not concerned here so much with that form of Ancestor Worship largely associated with the philosophy of Confucius; while this was no doubt a survival of primitive Animism, Confucius made use of it to emphasize his teaching on filial piety, and the supreme reverence, therefore, that should be paid to parents after death. In this case the dead are generally regarded as friendly, although the element of fear is sometimes present. But in much animistic belief the savage mind is torn between the love of those who have just passed on, and the fear of the potential danger they may prove to be to those who survive. On the whole, the balance seems to come down on the side of the dead being regarded as unfriendly and calculated to do harm.

This is especially true in the case of those who die in a particular way. For instance, the Jinghpaw has a terrible fear of the spirit of a woman who has died in childbirth; of the spirit of one who has been murdered, or slain by a wild beast; or of one who has met with sudden death by accident. No amount of love for a living individual will, if he or she has died from any such cause, prevent the living from taking urgent measures to rid themselves of the malevolent influences likely to be exerted by these departed souls.

Among the Battaks of Indonesia, 'if a woman dies in giving birth to a child, it is a sign that the soul of the mother refuses to accept the child. This, therefore, is a death that is regarded as extremely disgraceful. The corpse of the woman is thrown beneath the house, and there buried.'[1]

[1] Warneck, *The Living Forces of the Gospel*, p. 52.

The Jinghpaw believes that the souls of all those who die violent deaths become 'nats' (spirits) and do not go to Kătsan Ga (the land of the departed), but remain to bring misfortune on the inhabitants of their former village.

When a Jinghpaw dies a natural death, the soul is supposed to wander aimlessly about the vicinity of the house until the appropriate ceremonies have taken place. These are on three distinct occasions. The first ceremony is the actual burial, with sacrifices offered to the spirits, but this deals only with the inanimate corpse, although at the graveside the mourners will call out to the soul of the departed to come home again, offering all sorts of comforting inducements to that end. Some weeks later there takes place the ceremony of collecting the soul and securing it at the household shrine until it is ready to be sent to Kătsan Ga. The nat priest is called in for this purpose, and by his incantations wheedles the soul of the departed to come from his hiding-place underneath, or in the neighbourhood of, the house, and after entering the house by the log stairway, to settle at the shrine inside the doorway.

There the soul will stay until the family are able to afford the large number of sacrifices (of pigs, bullocks, etc.) required to waft the spirit safely to the land of the departed. This ceremony may take place a year later, or after an even longer lapse of time. At the final ceremony the priest informs the spirit of the route which must be taken across mountains and rivers to the unknown land where the spirit will be at rest. So, too, the Yoruba sorcerer of Southern Nigeria wishes a safe journey to the soul, and adjures it to depart, and not to haunt the dwellings of the living. In West Africa two distinct funeral ceremonies take place, the second from forty days to a year later.[1]

Though the Jinghpaw seems to regard most nats as malevolent spirits, there are two, Duwa (chieftain) and Dujan (chieftainess), who seem to be regarded as exercising a benevolent influence, like the Penates, the household gods of the Romans. The interesting fact, which has its counterpart in other lands, is that although they are said to be the souls of departed humans, they are worshipped, and their aid invoked.

2. *Totemism*

The totemistic school of thought would emphasize any indications which show that the dead are regarded as friendly. The argument was

[1] Dr. Geoffrey Parrinder, *West African Religion*, p. 121.

developed by F. B. Jevons in his book, *Introduction to the History of Religion*, where he maintained that the primitive savage would naturally try to keep on friendly terms with the spirits of deceased members of the same clan, who might be reincarnated in living animals.

The word 'Totemism' is derived from a word in the Ojibwa dialect of North America, which means 'brother-sister-kin', and was first used at the end of the eighteenth century. It has had its fullest development in North America and Australia, but traces of it can be found in almost every part of the world where Animism has prevailed, including the whole continent of Africa. Clans are united by a professed relationship with some animal or plant, which thereby becomes sacred.

F. B. Jevons noted two characteristics of all those who are bound by Totemism: that they are exogamous, that is, members must not marry partners within the same totem clan; and that at long intervals members partake of the totem animal (normally taboo) at a special ceremonial feast, when a mystic relationship is established.

Jevons went so far as to suggest that the domestic animals in Europe, such as the horse, dog, etc., were originally the totem animals of certain clans, and therefore taboo, and not liable to be killed. In the same way it might be suggested that the cow and the monkey, sacred among Hindus, might originally have been totem animals in India. Whether this be true or not, traces of Totemism are found in every continent, and though the Jinghpaw of Northern Burma are not normally regarded as totemistic in practice, the two main marks of Totemism tend to survive among them. Members of the five clans of this tribe never marry within their own clan, but a member of one clan has to seek a wife from a particular clan or choice of clans outside his own. Similarly, on certain occasions when a communal sacrifice of a buffalo (the most prized animal) takes place, the blood of the sacrifice is ceremonially drunk, and the participants believe that by so doing they are in communion with the nat to whom the sacrifice is offered, for 'the life is in the blood'. Dr. Geoffrey Parrinder shows that the practice of communion with the spirit through sacrifice is equally true in Africa: 'Communion meals form part of very many sacrifices; the blood only is poured out to the god, the carcass being eaten by the worshippers.'[1]

It is said that the initiatory rites at puberty, common among tribes in Central Africa, are a survival of a decadent form of Totemism. Tattooing, ritual murders, and secret names may have the same mystic

[1] *West African Religion*, p. 197.

origin. A Jinghpaw child at birth is given a nat name that is never used in public, and is known only to the priest who gives the name and to those immediately connected with the child.

SPIRIT WORSHIP

Spirit Worship is regarded as a stage in human reasoning beyond that of the worship of the dead, for it suggests not only the survival of the souls of human beings after death, but the existence of spirits or powers independent of human spirits who exercise a power outside man's control. Just as man realized the possession of a soul apart from his body, so he credited animals, trees, rocks, and rivers, with similar powers.

1. *Magic*

It may be that, before these spirits were differentiated, there was a stage in which magic summed up the contents of the savage mind, as Sir J. G. Frazer contends. He describes magic under two heads, that of homœopathic and that of contagious magic. Homœopathic, or imitative magic, covers those many instances where it is thought that harm can be inflicted on an enemy by attacking a picture or representation of him. Similarly, contagious magic concerns the kinship between an individual and something severed from him, such as a lock of hair, nail parings, etc.; if such things can be obtained from an enemy, they may be used for revenge without even going near him. Shortly before the second world war there was a big court case in Burma arising out of the attempt by a usurper to the throne of one of the Shan States to use such magic to bring about an early demise of his rival in the State. It was obvious from the evidence that the Buddhist witnesses fully believed in the efficacy and criminality of such attempts on the life of the ruler.

Magic can, however, be used for a beneficent end, to strengthen an individual, or bring good fortune. Such is the reason for drinking the blood of a lion or tiger, or eating meat to acquire the strength of the animal slain. Cannibalism is only an extension of this idea. In an insurrection in Burma some years ago, rebels could be identified by certain tattoo marks on the chest; they believed that these tattoo marks rendered them impervious to bullets.

While conveniently grouped under the head of Spirit Worship, magic needs to be clearly differentiated, for in Africa, where the clearest and most detailed evidence is found, magic may be said to correspond to the African's science rather than to religious belief. Dr. Vernon Anderson, in an article on *Magic and Witchcraft among the Baluba of Central Africa*, writes: 'Magic . . . is not his religion. It is rather a para-religious phenomenon. In religion man prays and implores, and in magic he commands and rules. . . . Some have been known to beat their charms in order to coerce them to do their possessor's bidding. One does not so approach a deity.'

So in connection with magic the analogy of electricity has been used. Just as electricity can be used in countless ways, both for destruction and for healing, so the African regards every being as having been endowed with a certain force, so that some are to an extraordinary degree magnetized with magic. When magic is used for beneficent purposes it is called 'White Magic', and for destructive purposes 'Black Magic'.

Dr. Edwin Smith, a modern authority on African religion, has employed the word 'Dynamism' to express more aptly what has been connoted by the term magic—'the belief in, and the practices associated with the belief in, impersonal, pervasive, mysterious forces acting through charms and amulets, spells, divinations'.[1]

This belief has been by no means confined to Africa: the Polynesians, who used the term 'Mana' to describe it, and the Red Indians, who asserted that this force existed in innumerable plants as well as human beings, are notable examples.

2. *Taboo*

It is obvious that where a belief in magic exists, the utmost caution will be used in securing protection from invisible attacks of one's enemies, and this gives rise to the common practice of taboo. It is not too much to say that the life of the primitive savage is governed by taboo from birth to death, by day and night, and it is all due to his belief in the efficacy of magic.

In a Burmese village a grave had been dug so that the feet would point in the direction of the village, and the headman insisted that the grave must be abandoned, because it would result in the outbreak of some disease in the village. The Jinghpaw father, however, who was burying his child, declared that it was taboo for him, having begun a grave, to abandon it and dig another. A compromise was made by

[1] Foreword to *West African Religion*.

using the length of the grave as the width, so that the coffin would be at right-angles to the village.

Many taboos are associated with women in childbirth, with infants when born, with every crisis in the life of a household or village, with seasons of sowing, planting and harvesting, with housebuilding, and especially with funerals. The sight of a nightbird, called the hkam-hkam, is taboo to the Jinghpaws; no harm can result from hearing the call of the bird at night, but if the call is heard in the day-time, or if the bird is seen in the jungle, death will ensue. The case was reported of a strong, healthy Jinghpaw man who returned home to his village trembling with fear, having seen the hkam-hkam in the forest; within a few hours he had expired from sheer fright. Such is the hold that taboo has on primitive people.

3. Fetishism

Closely related to this subject of magic and taboo is fetishism. The term itself, however, is tending to be discarded. Its Portuguese origin is associated with a superficial understanding of what it really is, for it has often been confused with spirit and ancestor worship, whereas it really concerns charms, amulets or talismans, with which 'lucky mascots' in the western world may be compared. West Africa is the main habitat of this cult, but it has been found in North and South America, and in India, too.

The African does not say that his charm is inhabited by a spirit, but that it is the container of a harnessed, pervasive energy. Such a charm will be venerated as long as its owner regards it as the purveyor of good fortune, but if his luck changes he may break and curse or abandon his charm, in the belief that it has become powerless.

To return to the subject of Spirit Worship proper, we find that the Animist lives in a world peopled by spirits, which are generally regarded as malevolent and bringing misfortune. These are to be found in the earth, air, fire and water, in rocks, trees, mountains, and in animal life. There is no attempt at material representation of these spirits, and therefore idolatry is excluded.

The whole aim is to keep on the right side of the spirits, and thus avoid misfortune and disaster. This is done by seeking the aid of an expert mediator, able to divine and influence offended spirits, and the means of propitiation is usually by animal sacrifice.

B

To take the Jinghpaw as an example. He describes his religious practice as 'nat jaw' (giving or sacrificing to the nats or spirits). The ordinary tribesman cannot protect himself, but when illness or misfortune threatens his household, he calls in the aid of a dumsa (priest); the latter has a sacred language which he has acquired (probably an obsolete form of the same language), and, having set up a bamboo shrine, he squats in front of it, waving a sheaf of grass and muttering his incantations. His object is first of all to divine which of the many hundreds of nats is offended. This is frequently done by taking short lengths of bamboo and holding them over a fire; when some of the fibres pop in the fire, and split, the direction in which they point is said to indicate the nat concerned. Eventually, after muttering many incantations in a singsong staccato voice, the dumsa will announce that such and such a nat is offended, and can be appeased by the sacrifice of a chicken, a pig, a dog, a buffalo, etc.

If the sick inmate of the house does not recover, further shrines will be made and sacrifices offered, and when a horned animal is sacrificed the horns will be set up over the portals of the house.

On the outskirts of every village is a communal shrine, where many different shrines are established, representing the major nats—the earth spirit, water spirit, mountain spirit, nat of the thick forest, of thunder and lightning, etc. Communal sacrifices may take place at a time of illness affecting the whole community, at funerals, and especially when the ground is cleared of trees for the annual sowing of rice, and at harvest-time.

Among a people who live amidst forest-clad mountains it is not surprising that Jăhtung Wa (the nat of the thick forest) is most dreaded. Dogs are often offered in sacrifice to this spirit, and the carcass hung on a tree in a bamboo casing, for it is not eaten as the other sacrifices are.

Climbing up the thickly wooded slopes of a mountain peak, a well-built Jinghpaw youth was seen to draw his sword from the scabbard and make violent passes in the air. 'Jăhtung Wa,' he muttered, and his companion could well understand the evident fear which gripped him at this interpretation of some unexpected sound.

Never at any waking moment of day or night is the animist parted from consciousness that he is surrounded by a host of evil spirits who may ruin his crops, or inflict other misfortunes, unless he walks warily and observes the necessary taboos.

NATURISM

It is in the worship of the phenomena of Nature that the savage begins to pass beyond the realm of spirit worship to the personification of those major powers—the sun, the moon and the stars. But at the outset he is content to pay homage to the sun which warms him and gives him light, without going beyond that conception.

Historically, the best examples, perhaps, are the developments of the nature gods of Greek and Roman mythology. As animism passes into deism, and the invisible spirits become visible gods whose features can be portrayed in images and idols, there is no tendency to rise upwards to monotheism; but polytheism, the worship of innumerable and greater and lesser deities, engrosses the human mind.

It is the Corn Spirit which, in many forms and under many titles, can be most easily traced wherever man is found. Seed-time and harvest, and the recurring phenomena of new life in spring, leading on to the full bloom of summer, the gradual decay of autumn and the seeming death of winter, have all been associated with this cult.

Sir J. G. Frazer traces this development in many lands in a masterly way in *The Golden Bough*. The animal and plant gods, which at one time formed the object of worship, tend at a later stage to become humanized, until at a later stage still the complete god emerges, but accompanied by, or associated with, the plant or animal from which he originally emerged.

The yearly cycle of death and resurrection enacted in the world of nature becomes embodied in the gods in human form, around whom the myth grows. Dionysus, of Greek mythology (corresponding to the Roman Bacchus), was regarded as the god of agriculture and corn, but later as the personification of the vine. Dionysus was believed to have died a violent death, but to have risen again. He was often represented in the form of a bull, and a live bull was torn to pieces by his devotees, which seems to point to an earlier animal cult before the humanized form of the god developed. This is just one example of a cult in similar form to be found at some time all over the world, including Europe and the British Isles.

The offering of human sacrifice can often be traced to this source, and is closely associated in the mind of the savage with the mystery of life and death as seen in the seasons of the year, and the provision by that means of his daily food.

It might be thought that the wild Nagas of North-West Burma were far more brutal and savage than tribes among whom human sacrifice is entirely unknown. But while we would not attempt to minimize the horror of this degrading practice, it is clear that here the sole purpose was to secure good crops by propitiating the spirits in this manner. It was customary for a household or an individual to make a vow to offer a human sacrifice, and if in the lifetime of the individual concerned sufficient money had not been saved to procure a victim, the vow devolved upon the relatives to fulfil. A captive would be purchased from a neighbouring tribe who specialized in raids on other tribes, and the victim would be well treated and fattened up until the day when the supreme sacrifice was offered to propitiate the nats. When British administration attended to this area, and orders were given that human sacrifice must cease, the first bewildered question of the people was—what would happen to the crops? So fearful were they of the consequences that the first Naga chief who promised to obey the order was murdered by his own people. It would appear that in Africa human sacrifices have been more associated with cannibalism, where the partakers of human flesh have been desirous of absorbing the magic and strength which their victim possessed.

THE EFFECT OF ANIMISM ON PRIMITIVE PEOPLE

Dr. William Paton, in his book *Jesus Christ and the World's Religions*, has suggested four characteristics of spirit worshippers: (1) The prevalence of fear, (2) the absence of anything in the nature of religious consolation, (3) no differentiation between good and evil, and (4) a fatalistic outlook on life.

Fear is certainly the outstanding and most noticeable characteristic of every primitive tribe. In answer to the question put to a Jinghpaw, 'Why do you give to the nats?' the invariable answer is 'Because we are afraid.' 'Would you give to the nats if you had no cause to fear?' 'Of course not,' is the scornful reply. Warneck[1] gives a vivid picture of the fear which haunts the Battak tribesmen of Indonesia, typical of this characteristic found among animistic peoples all over the world. He says: 'Animism seems devised for the purpose of tormenting men, and hindering them from enjoying life. To that must be added fear of the dead, of demons, of the thousand spirits of earth, air, water, mountains and trees. The Battak is like a man driven in frenzied pur-

[1] *Living Forces of the Gospel*, p. 109.

suit round and round. Ghosts of the most diverse kind lurk in house and village; in the field they endanger the produce of labour; in the forest they terrify the woodcutter; in the bush they hunt the wanderer. From them come diseases, madness, death of cattle and famine. Malicious demons surround women during pregnancy and at confinement; they lie in wait for the child from the day of its birth; they swarm round the houses at night; they spy through the chinks of the walls for their helpless victims. Gigantic spirits stride through the villages, scattering epidemics around them; they lurk in the sea and rivers with the view of dragging travellers into the depths . . . the dead friend and brother becomes an enemy, and his coffin and grave are the abode of terrors. It is fear that occasions the worship of the departed, and the observances of their mourning usages in its smallest details; fear decides that host of prohibitions which surrounds every movement of their daily life. Fear is the moving power of animistic religion, in Asia as in Africa.'

The complete absence of any conception of love on the part of the spirit world or the spirit-worshipper deprives the individual of any of the consolations of religion. 'You may go through heathendom anywhere, in the Indian Archipelago, in New Guinea, in the South Seas, and in Africa, and you will nowhere find humanity, mercy, kindness and love. Selfishness reigns nakedly everywhere, and self-complacency is boasted of as a virtue.'[1] For the old and infirm life has few comforts; once they have become useless to the tribe, their existence is only just tolerated, and nothing is done for their comfort in sickness. Death holds only terror for the living, for it is a passing into the darkness of the unknown. A vague and shadowy, dismal existence is envisaged without any certainty of meeting again the loved ones left behind on earth. The spirit-worshipper is without hope.

Some primitive tribes are remarkably free from lying and stealing as a general habit, and adultery is a crime often punished with death. Superficially, one might conclude that here is a clear differentiation between good and evil; but on closer examination one finds that practices which would tend to break up the social life of the family or clan are taboo for that reason, and are not a sign of intrinsic virtue. Adultery is not viewed on criminal or moral grounds, but because the wife is the purchased property of the husband and probably of the family into which she has married. Custom and taboos are the binding

[1] Warneck, op. cit., p. 124.

factors, but the idea of morals is entirely absent. While adultery among Jinghpaws is regarded as a heinous crime, promiscuous intercourse among the unmarried youth is not only condoned, but encouraged by the elders of the tribe. There is no sense of sin, and the very word used for sin, 'yubak', really means punishment—the consequences of misbehaviour. Misfortune may be regarded as a crime, for death in childbirth or by accident is treated with horror, as though the victim was responsible in some way for inflicting this manner of death on the community. Sin is offending against tribal custom or taboo, and what is morally evil may be regarded as good if it does not transgress tribal law.

Life beyond the grave and the manner in which it is spent bears no relation to life here on earth, whether good or evil. Misfortune in this life is due to offence given to one or more denizens of the spirit world, by a failure to observe the necessary taboos. This naturally leads to a fatalistic outlook on life. All the events of life are predetermined, and in no way dependent on the character of the individual concerned. The savage often appears to be lacking in imagination or emotion, but his stoical calmness is in reality due to an innate fatalism.

This fatalistic attitude induces laziness, for no effort can alter a predetermined fate. The Jinghpaw who saw the fatal nightbird in the day-time knew that he must die, and without any illness to sap his strength, accepted his fate, lay down, and died. Such fatalism prevents belief in a merciful God. And yet the primitive savage has always been found to possess the instinctive knowledge, not only that the human soul is immortal, but that there is a Creator, a Supreme Being, who is the maker of all things and holder of the key of life. Every tribe has a name for the Maker. The Jinghpaws refer to Him as Karai Kasang, the Self-Existent One. An invisible string connects Him with every individual; He holds 'the string of life' which, if severed, brings death.

But, though every known tribe recognizes the existence of a Creator, with varying mythological views of His character and the story of creation, there seems to have been a universal departure from the worship of the Creator. To the question, 'Why do you not worship Karai Kasang?' the Jinghpaw will answer: 'Why should we? He never did us any harm.' Or like his African brother, he will say: 'God is too far away, and we do not know what food He eats, so how can we offer to Him?' From the first European contacts with West Africa it was observed that they believed in a high God, though they did not worship Him. 'They have a faint idea of the true God, but they do not pray to Him, or offer any sacrifices to Him.'[1]

The very fact that this instinctive knowledge is found in the breast of every savage seems to point to a primeval worship of God as Creator, from which man has fallen. Though the Jinghpaw does not worship Karai Kasang, he will sometimes call out His Name in sudden fear, or in an oath. All the theories concerning the origin of religion which leave out of account this instinctive knowledge of a beneficent Supreme Being seem to break down before this stubborn fact.

As Warneck[2] says: 'If the spirit worship which prevails among the Animists were the oldest religion of mankind, from which every other religion was developed by a long and laborious process, how could these religions, which represent the initial stage of development, derive any nourishment in that initial stage from the idea of a Supreme God, who should be the last member of a long series of acquisitions, laboriously won? Why does the Indonesian, when in great distress, flee to God, of whom, according to that hypothesis, he should have no knowledge whatever? How is it that, in taking an oath, the Animist appeals to God? That is forestalling his development indeed. It is a fact that he has the idea of God; but the fact that this idea is but dimly apprehended proves that we are not dealing with a new idea, victoriously opening up new paths. . . . The Animism of today gives us the impression of a religion that carries the marks of a fall, of a worship no longer understood, and become an empty ceremony.'

As another writer has said: 'The common essence of heathenism is not a denying of God . . . but an ignoring of Him in the worship of natural powers and mysterious demonic powers through magic and magical sacrifices and ceremonies.' To the Animist, these demons are realities, to be ignored at his peril. A missionary speaking for the first time to the Jinghpaws in a village about the big nat Satan, who brought evil into the world, found his audience eagerly discussing, in an aside, the purport of his remarks. When he had finished speaking, some of the elders round the fire tackled the missionary on the subject of this Evil Spirit, for if he was so powerful they would like to know what sacrifices they should offer to propitiate him.

It is because the Animist has turned aside from the worship of the

[1] *West African Religion*, p. 19.
[2] Op. cit., p. 99.

Life Giver that he finds himself a slave, in bondage to fear of evil spirits. This leads to the development of human mediums, who become possessed with a demon, and proceed to convey his message to those around. The witch doctor and sorcerer, the wizard and magician are found among Animists everywhere. Among the Jinghpaws there are a class of mediums or clairvoyants called 'myihtoi' (enlightening the eye) who, when it is required, will fall into a trance and become devil-possessed. Foaming at the mouth and performing physical feats normally impossible, they shriek out the message of the demons. When the scene is over the myihtoi will lie like a log, weak and exhausted, and when he has recovered he will remember nothing of what has happened.

It would appear, therefore, that in forsaking the light he once possessed, the Animist has launched himself into a darkness of despair, from which he has no power to extricate himself.

This indeed is the argument of St. Paul, who in his day had the opportunity of studying at first hand Greek and Roman religions then extant, and delving into the primitive religions of Assyria and Babylon. In writing to the Christians at Rome, he says: 'The wrath of God is revealed from Heaven against all ungodliness and wickedness of men who by their wickedness suppress the truth. For what can be known about God is plain to them, because God has shown it to them. Ever since the creation of the world His invisible nature, namely, His eternal power and deity, has been clearly perceived in the things that have been made. So they are without excuse; for although they knew God they did not honour Him as God or give thanks to Him, but they became futile in their thinking and their senseless minds were darkened. Claiming to be wise, they became fools, and exchanged the glory of the immortal God for images resembling mortal man or birds or animals or reptiles.

'Therefore God gave them up in the lusts of their hearts to impurity, to the dishonouring of their bodies among themselves, because they exchanged the truth about God for a lie and worshipped and served the creature rather than the Creator.'[1]

[1] Epistle to the Romans, i. 18-25 (Revised Standard Version).

CHAPTER II

JUDAISM

IT would not do justice to the unique position occupied by Judaism among the religions of the world to start this article with the statement found in the *Jewish Encyclopædia*, 'Judaism is a mode of life based on the Fatherhood of God and on Revelation.'[1] Somewhat similar claims are made by the other two monotheistic religions which are often described as 'daughters of Judaism'.[2] But their adherents would not maintain that the Old Testament, a treasure common to all three of them, calls any one but Israel 'the Chosen People', or 'the property' of the very God in whom they all believe. It must, therefore, be stated *a priori* that Judaism is not just another non-Christian religion but a system of faith and worship inseparably linked, on the one hand, with the idea of God as accepted (to some extent) by Christians and Muhammadans and, on the other hand, with the existence of a particular people. Not only the Jew but the followers of Jesus and Muhammad as well would assert that the Old Testament was somehow a way of life and an approach to God, but only the Jew will make it the centre of his doctrinal edifice.

For all that, it would be incorrect to identify Judaism with Old Testament religion, and overlook the rabbinical teaching which forms a large part of present-day Jewish religion. Again, it would be equally fallacious to assume that rabbinical or orthodox Judaism was the kind of religion most widely practised among Jews. Judaism is a conglomeration, the result of a long process of religious development. It has been influenced by ideas which cannot be traced back to the Old Testament, and has also appropriated some teaching which cannot be found in the literature of the Talmud, that encyclopædic body of Jewish religion and mentality compiled between the third and the sixth centuries of the Christian era, whose instructions are accepted as scarcely less important than those of the Old Testament.

There is another basic difficulty which faces the student of Judaism. Christianity has its Apostles' and Nicene Creeds; Islam has its Kalima. But there is no such formal summary of Jewish doctrine that would be recognized as absolutely binding by all and sundry. This does not

[1] Shapiro, Vallentine & Co., London, 1938.
[2] Although the concept of the Fatherhood of God is absent in orthodox Islam.

mean that no attempts have been made to systematize and formulate the tenets of Jewish religion. Scholars and philosophers have endeavoured repeatedly to work out a confession of faith and their products are occasionally used to this day. But none of them has ever enjoyed the official sanction of a supreme ecclesiastical organization. This absence of an authoritative creed will become understandable only as we proceed to show that Judaism and Jewry, religion and people are partly identical, so that race and birth are of greater importance than the profession of certain dogmas.

ORIGIN AND EARLY DEVELOPMENT

It is almost impossible to say when monotheistic Judaism as originally revealed was first consistently and generally practised, but one can safely assume that this did not happen until after the Babylonic captivity, when a small proportion of the Jewish nation returned to Palestine. It was then that they founded a new theocratic society in which the God of Abraham, Isaac and Jacob was the only God. The reason for dating Jewish monotheism so late is that, up to that time, we constantly read in the Old Testament of idolatry among Israel and Judah.[1] Only now did the references to the worship of Baal and others cease. Ezekiel and the teachers of the Law gave the new community its theocratic constitution. The real monotheism and the exclusiveness of the worship of the one God find their most perfect expression in the second part of Isaiah. All other gods are false. There is only one God in the universe, and He is the God of Israel. Israel's suffering is not merely punishment; it is sermon and object lesson, and it is a means of redemption to the whole world. Again, it was in the post-exilic Jewish community that the individual assumed a place of ever-growing importance. Even the ideas of life after death, and the love of God that could not possibly stop at the end of material life but would have to continue on the other side, only now matured. Similarly, the hope of the coming of the Messiah, the conception of the Day of the Lord, and similar trends only now became dominant ideas. And while it is true that during the time between the last of the prophets and the appear-

[1] Cf. 2 Ki. xxi. 2-6, where we are told that king Manasseh erected altars to other gods in the very Temple of God, the nation taking up such idolatry quite eagerly (verse 9); and also 2 Ki. xxxiii. 22, which shows that the Passover festival had been completely neglected.

ance of John the Baptist no major work of religious literature was produced, we must understand that it was centuries before the spirit of the prophets had really permeated all strata of society and had become the common property of the people. In those days the so-called 'Men of the Great Synagogue' that had originated under Ezra[1] and the Scribes were the recognized authorities on the text and inter-pretation of the Scriptures, and began to formulate the Oral Law which often differed from, and modified as well as exceeded, the written Law as laid down in the Pentateuch.

It was during that same period that Judaism came in contact with the other parts of the world, its religions and peoples, and especially with Greek thought. But it would be a mistake to attribute the 'Wisdom Literature', largely contained in the Apocrypha, to Hellenistic origins only. While the Hellenistic element is undoubtedly present in those books, the majority of its material is essentially Jewish. Yet during this period of intensification of Judaism and onwards the Jews still had to fight the danger of polytheism. This is shown, for example, by the two Books of the Maccabees. To this day one can see the mosaic floor of a synagogue in Beth Alpha in the Emek, that dates back to the fourth century after Christ, with a design representing the sun god in his chariot.

The unique feature of Jewish monotheism as displayed in Judaism just before the birth of Jesus Christ is that the national God becomes the expression of the highest, purest and most sublime thought as well as of the most intimate religious sentiment, without in the least losing His personal qualities. Only in a nation which in its history had experienced the power of that God as Deliverer, Lawgiver, and Father, was such a development possible. But even the best and loftiest pro-phet could not attain to a universalism that would overcome all barriers of nationality. What the Jews presented to other nations was not so much an individualistic and universal religion that thought little of all national and tribal frontiers, but rather their own national religion which had achieved an ethical and theological summit. They hoped that others would turn to that type of religion and thereby acknow-ledge the sovereign reign of their own national God by whom they had been chosen as a peculiar people, as privileged priests, and as a holy nation.

The time between the Alexandrian conquest and the beginning of

[1] See Ne. ix and x.

the Christian era saw the rise of Rabbinic Judaism, most clearly represented by a group of men who saw in the strictest observance of both written and oral Law the only hope for survival, and separated themselves from all others in order to carry out their hard task. They were soon called Pharisees (from the Hebrew 'Perushim', i.e. the Separated) and had the largest following among the democratic, urban laity, whereas the opposite body of aristocratic people of the ecclesiastical party came to be known as Sadducees (from Zadok, Solomon's High Priest). The Pharisees not only produced a school of famous rabbis like Hillel and Shammai (who lived just prior to the birth of Jesus), but developed the doctrine of immortality, introduced those translations of the Scriptures into the vernacular Aramaic which are known as *Targumim* (from 'Targum', i.e. translation), and fostered the establishment of synagogues wherever Jews had settled in the wide dispersion of the Mediterranean civilization.

It is noteworthy that the synagogue was both a place of worship and a communal centre. It was designed to bring religion to the masses of the people, and was accordingly called the 'House of Prayer' as well as the 'People's House'. It proved to be one of the principal means of keeping Judaism alive when both the Temple and the national life of the people were lost. With the destruction of the Temple the system of sacrifices came to an end and the Sadducees disappeared, thus leaving the field to their opponents, which meant that henceforth the Law became the pivot of Jewish religion. Its 613 commandments were divided into 248 positive injunctions and 365 prohibitions, and surrounded by a large number of interpretative regulations. This oral Law gradually became recognized as divinely inspired.

The whole body of written and oral Law is known as the *Torah*, and represents to the Jew the whole mystery and tangible expression of God. That is to say that, quite apart from its manifold connotations, the application of the Torah extends to the deepest emotions, the very heart of the Jew. Rabbi Dr. Isidore Epstein, of the Jews' College, London, a well-known Rabbinic authority, says of the Torah: 'It is more than a mere collection of commands and precepts which are comprised in what are known as the Five Books of Moses. Torah connotes the whole body of Jewish teaching, legislation, practices, and traditions that have proceeded from the interpretation and re-interpretation of the laws of the Bible according to the light of reason, and the principles of righteousness, justice, and equity, as well as any adaptations or modifications made by the spiritual leaders of the people applicable to changed conditions of life—economic, domestic, social.'[1]

The discussions and decisions of scholars and rabbis in the matter of Torah, covering not only legal and ethical but also homiletic and didactic questions, were eventually gathered up in that monumental work called *Talmud*. There is an earlier compilation, the Palestinian Talmud, and a later recension, the Babylonian, published about 500 years after the crucifixion. The influence of the Talmud upon Jewish life can hardly be overestimated. It has kept the Jew mentally and theologically alert, it has been his refuge in the long and dreary centuries of persecution and Ghetto life when he was debarred from secular studies, and it still exerts considerable influence upon Jewish teaching today, although it is *terra incognita* to the average Jew. Its vast dimensions can be gauged from the fact that translations take up from eleven to sixteen volumes.

But not even the Talmud tried to summarize Judaism in a creed or confession of faith. The first definite attempt to produce a formula against which doctrines and principles could be measured was made by Moses Maimonides in the twelfth century. He worked out Thirteen Articles which are listed to this day in the Authorized Prayer Book of most Jewish congregations, and laid down the following fundamental axioms, the denial of which cuts a man off from Israel: (1) Belief in the existence of a Creator and Providence. (2) Belief in His unity. (3) Belief in His incorporeality. (4) Belief in His eternity. (5) Belief that to Him alone is worship due. (6) Belief in the words of the prophets. (7) Belief that Moses was the greatest of all prophets. (8) Belief in the revelation of the Law of Moses at Sinai. (9) Belief in the immutability of the revealed Law. (10) Belief that God is omniscient. (11) Belief in retribution in this world and the hereafter. (12) Belief in the coming of the Messiah. (13) Belief in the resurrection of the dead.[2]

The creed as sketched out by Maimonides came in for severe criticism by many Jewish authorities in the following centuries. Among the more interesting attacks was one by Rabbi Joseph Albo, who pointed out that even within the body of the Law there were certain contradictions and discrepancies, so that it was not safe to claim, as

[1] *Judaism*, Epworth Press, 1939, p. 33.
[2] *The Authorized Daily Prayer Book*, London, 1935, p. 89.

Maimonides had done in his ninth article, that the Law will never be changed. In the course of the last five or six centuries various and often differing doctrinal statements have been issued by leaders of the different groups in Judaism, and if all of these formal summaries were put down as authoritative explanations of what Judaism means, the average reader would be completely at sea. But as all of them refer to the Talmud, we may take some of the doctrinal utterances of the Talmud to guide us in our search for the essence of Judaism.

One of the basic parts, the 'Sayings of the Fathers', begins with the words: 'Moses received the Torah on Sinai, and handed it down to Joshua; Joshua to the Elders; the Elders to the Prophets; and the Prophets handed it down to the men of the Great Synagogue. They said three things, Be deliberate in judgment, raise up many disciples, and make a fence round the Torah. Simon the Just used to say, Upon three things the world is based, upon the Torah, upon the Temple services, and upon the practice of charity.'[1] Again we read: 'The more Torah the more life. . . . He who has acquired for himself words of Torah has acquired for himself life in the world to come.'[2] 'If three have eaten at a table and have spoken there no words of Torah, it is as if they had eaten of sacrifices to dead idols. . . . But if they have spoken words of Torah, it is as if they had eaten at the table of the All-Present.'[3] The sixth chapter is an addition to the tractate and is known as 'The Chapter on the Acquisition of the Torah'. It says: 'Whosoever labours in the Torah for its own sake merits many things . . . he is called a lover of the All-Present, a lover of mankind. It clothes him in meekness and reverence, fits him to become just . . . it keeps him far from sin . . . he is made like a never-failing fountain . . . and it magnifies him and exalts him above all things.'[4] In brief, it is to the Torah that the work of grace is ascribed, and the strict observance of the Torah is one of the most distinct features of Judaism, making for the separation of the Jew from his fellow men.

THE CENTRAL DOCTRINES

Bearing in mind the difficulty of finding authoritative statements which would be generally accepted as absolutely binding, we must examine the Jewish teaching on certain central doctrines of religion.

[1] Dr. A. Cohen, *Everyman's Talmud*, London, 1943, I. 1-2.
[2] II. 8.   [3] III. 4.   [4] VI. 1.

1. *God and Man*

To the Jew, God is a full personality, free from all limitations and imperfections, pure Spirit, and the life of the universe. While Judaism admits that nature and all its phenomena point to the existence of a Creator, and that philosophy and science may provide an indirect knowledge of God, it insists with noteworthy emphasis that only religion reveals a direct, personal, and complete knowledge of the divine character, will, and purpose. Though the revelation to Moses, which means the Torah, is the foundation stone on which Judaism rests, revelation has not reached its completion at any particular point of history, but is considered to be progressive. 'There is a constant equipoise of tradition and progress. Custom adjusts law to changed circumstances. Revelation has room for varieties of thought,' states Herbert Loewe, Reader in Rabbinics in the University of Cambridge, in *The Jewish Encyclopædia* (p. 335).

Man is to see in God his Heavenly Father and Companion who is concerned in his fate and does not leave him alone in an apparently friendless universe. As man is made in the image of God, it follows that all human beings are creatures of the same Creator and meant to live as brothers. All have a share in God's eternal spirit. Neighbourly love is stressed as an altogether Hebrew thought, for as nature knows only fear and defence, heathen religions are ignorant of divine revelation and cannot propagate the dignity of human relationship, nor can they postulate love as the basis of such relationship.

Any opposition between spirit and matter, body and soul, is looked upon as an altogether alien doctrine, for each man is a unity and totality, corresponding to the unity and totality of the Creator. Equally vehemently is the idea denied that there might be a cosmic force of evil. 'There is no loss of the God-likeness of man, or of his ability to do right in the eyes of God,' says the late Chief Rabbi of the British Empire, 'and no such loss has been transmitted to his latest descendants.'[1] Over against the doctrine of Original Sin, Judaism puts its emphasis on original virtue and righteousness which, according to the Jewish doctrine of 'the merits of the Fathers', are the common heritage of every member of the congregation of Israel. There is, however, the idea of 'Yezer-ha-Ra', an evil inclination or impulse, which is the source of man's rebellion against God, but cannot dominate him per-

---

[1] Dr. J. H. Hertz, *Genesis*, p. 60.

manently. Dr. Epstein explains the position as follows: 'Judaism rejects the idea of human proneness to sin. A natural tendency to evil would be a contradiction to the fundamental command of holiness, a contradiction to the holiness of God which man is called upon to reproduce in himself. . . . Sin lieth at the door, not within man himself, and this is followed by "and thou shalt rule over him" (Gn. iv. 7).'[1] And again: 'The divine relationship with man is indestructible. It can be strained or marred but cannot be severed entirely and broken beyond repair, not even by transgression and sin. . . . If by erring from the right path man yields to temptation and lapses into sin, regret and penitence can repair the ravages of his sin and restore perfect harmony to this relationship.'[2] Thus, while recognizing definite sins, Judaism does not acknowledge sin as such, and accordingly sees no cause for admitting a sense of personal unworthiness. This has a profound bearing on the question of atonement.

2. *Atonement*

There is but one teaching regarding atonement among all groups of theologians, however widely they may differ on other points. Repentance, prayer, and active kindness achieve perfect reconciliation. To quote from the writings of Dr. Hertz: 'Note that the initiative in atonement is with the sinner. He cleanses himself on the Day of Atonement by fearless self-examination, open confession, and the resolve not to repeat the transgressions of the past year. When our Heavenly Father sees the abasement of the penitent sinner, He sprinkles, as it were, the clean waters of pardon and forgiveness upon him.'[3] And again: 'On the Day of Atonement the Israelites resemble the angels, without human wants, without sins, linked together in love and peace. It is the only day of the year on which the accuser Satan is silenced before the throne of Glory, and even becomes the defender of Israel. . . . The closing prayer begins: "Thou givest a hand to transgressors, and Thy right hand is stretched out to receive the penitent. Thou hast taught us to make confession unto Thee of all our sins, in order that we may cease from the violence of our hands and may return unto Thee who delightest in the repentance of the wicked." These words contain what has been called "the Jewish doctrine of salvation".'[4]

[1] Op. cit., p. 82.   [2] Op. cit., p. 80.
[3] *The Pentateuch and Haftorahs*, 1938, p. 484.
[4] Op. cit., pp. 523-4.

As in the late Chief Rabbi's pronouncement, so elsewhere much prominence is given to the belief that human initiative takes the first step in the process which eventually leads to perfection. The second sentence of the Credo worked out by Prof. M. L. Margolis, an outstanding Hebrew scholar, underlines that basic doctrine: 'I believe that man possesses a divine power wherewith he may subdue his evil impulses and passions, strive to come nearer and nearer the perfection of God, and commune with Him in prayer.' There is a definite note of optimism implied in these statements. A hopeful view is taken of man and his progressive development. The student of Judaism will frequently be struck by the similarity that exists between Jewish teaching and the evolutionary theories, a phenomenon which is particularly obvious in the doctrine of the Messiah.

3. *The Messiah*

Few Jews of today would explicitly subscribe to the Twelfth Article of Maimonides' Creed, for the meaning of the term *Messiah* has undergone a radical change in the course of the centuries. There was a time when the idea carried with it the belief in a divinely appointed person who would deliver Israel and bring about the consummation of the divine plan with its corollary of peace, freedom, and justice. Thus the Authorized Prayer Book contains a prayer going back at least seventeen or eighteen centuries and closing with the words: '(Lord our God) Who rememberest the pious deeds of the patriarchs, and in love wilt bring a redeemer to their children's children for thy name's sake.'[1] But in modern Jewish thought this conception is as good as abandoned, and we read in *The Jewish Encyclopædia*, 'The doctrine of the Messiah is allied to that of physical evolution or Darwinism, and to that of political development, which looks forward to an omnipotent or just League of Nations that shall make peace universal,'[2] and also: 'What is called the doctrine of the Messiah is, in reality, the belief in progress and hope.'[3] In the terminology of the Talmudic writings, the doctrine of the Messiah was bound up with the other eschatological ideas of the divine retribution and the resurrection of the dead, both of which have gone through a long process of modification. While at times resurrection was confined to the just, or to Israel only, the belief in the survival of personality is now generally held and applied to all human beings.

[1] P. 44.   [2] Article, 'Judaism', p. 335.   [3] Article, 'Messiah', p. 423.

C

4. The Future Life

'In rabbinic teaching the wicked, save in exceptional cases, spend twelve months in Gehenna, after which they join the righteous in Gan Eden, where there is no eating or drinking, no begetting of children, no bargaining, no jealousy, no hatred and no strife, but the righteous sit with their crowns on their heads, enjoying the effulgence of the "Shechinah" (the divine Presence),' says Dr. Epstein,[1] and it will be noted that the quotation not only expresses the idea of a purgatory, but takes it for granted that all adherents of Judaism will eventually enter the realm of the blessed. This view is shared by all Jewish writers to this day: a Jew inherits heaven by right, through the divine Covenant with Abraham. Prof. Dr. H. J. Schoeps, of Erlangen, declares: 'In Isaac all Jews have become as the seed of Abraham (i.e. Children of the Promise), and they can all return to Abraham's bosom.'[2] As to the principles which are to guide retribution, and as to the mode of the judgment to come, very little is said in the textbooks, the matter being left to God in His infinite wisdom.

5. The Scriptures

When we come to study Jewish teaching on the authority and inspiration of Holy Scriptures, we must understand that not all parts of the Old Testament are considered to be of equal value. The arrangement of the books of the Hebrew Bible differs from that familiar to Christian readers. There is first of all the *Torah*, i.e. the Pentateuch, regarded as the most authoritative group. This is followed by the second group of books, the *Prophets*, which are divided into Former and Latter Prophets. The first division consists of the books of Joshua, Judges, 1 and 2 Samuel, 1 and 2 Kings; the second division contains Isaiah, Jeremiah, Ezekiel, and the so-called Book of the Twelve, known to Christians as the Minor Prophets. The last group bears the title *Writings* and is divided into three parts. Part one is composed of the Psalms, Proverbs, and the book of Job; part two consists of the 'Five Rolls', viz. Ruth, Song of Songs, Ecclesiastes, Lamentations, and Esther. Part three is made up of the remaining books, Daniel, Ezra, Nehemiah, and 1 and 2 Chronicles. The arrangement is all the more important as it reflects the varying degree of authority attached to the

---

[1] Op. cit., p. 83.
[2] *Juedisch Christliches Religionsgespräch in 19 Jahrhunderten*, p. 150.

different sections by Jews. The Torah is regarded as so absolutely and fully inspired that every letter and phrase bears the mark of its divine origin. Inspiration to a slightly lesser degree is attributed to the Prophets, and to a still lesser degree to the Writings, though it has to be stated emphatically that the authority of the Scriptures has never been seriously questioned in Judaism. The care with which they were passed on from generation to generation, the reverence and awe in which they were held, and the courage and sacrificial love with which they were defended, are without parallel in human history. This applies especially to the Torah, for whose sanctity innumerable martyrs have laid down their lives.

6. Religion and Morality

One of the main tenets of Judaism is the inseparable link between religion and morality. Faith is meaningless unless it is translated into action, and there are some specifically Jewish terms which require elucidating as they express ethical consequences of doctrinal beliefs. The word 'Tsedakah' (literally: righteousness) has gathered up the inter-relationship between faith and action in an utterly untranslatable way, covering, among many more meanings, charity, social justice, and the giving of tithes in support of the whole spiritual and social work of the synagogue. Relief is a matter of legal rightness, and kindness to those in need is at once presupposition and evidence of the correct attitude to the Law. Another Hebrew term, 'Rachmanut' (literally: mercy), has almost been raised to the level of a religious postulate demanding of the Jew very nearly indiscriminate charity towards those in distress.

JEWISH DISTINCTIVENESS

From the very outset it has been pointed out time and again that in Judaism the spiritual and national ideas coalesce. If the creation constitutes one focal point of Jewish doctrine the Exodus constitutes the other, and between them they have conditioned not merely the rigid monotheism of the Jew, but his distinctiveness among the nations of the world and his attitude to other peoples and religions.

When a Jewish boy reaches the age of thirteen he becomes a 'Son of the Commandment' (Barmitzvah) and is called up to the reading of the Torah on the Sabbath following his birthday. On that occasion he recites the words: 'Blessed art Thou, O Lord our God, King of

the universe, who hast chosen us from all peoples, and hast given us
Thy Law.' And every Jew is supposed to reiterate three times daily
the words of the following prayer: 'It is our duty to praise the Lord
of all things, to ascribe greatness to Him who formed the world in the
beginning, since He has not made us like the nations of other lands,
and has not placed us like other families of the earth, since He has not
assigned unto us a portion as unto them, nor a lot as unto all their
multitude. For *we* bend the knee and offer worship and thanks before
the supreme King of Kings, the Holy One.'[1] For while all peoples
and nations are God's creatures through Adam, the Jew only is His
elect child through Abraham, and continues, in the words of Prof.
Margolis, to be 'chosen by God as His anointed servant to proclaim
unto the families of mankind His truth . . . until there come in,
through him (that is, the Jew), the Kingdom of Peace and moral perfection.'[2] It follows that Israel and other people, be they Gentiles,
Muhammadans, or heathen, cannot be equals. The biblical records of
the missionary period in Israel's history (Isaiah, Jonah, Malachi) show
that even in those efforts to win the outsider, the national character
was retained, for Israel was to be the leader and master.

A mission to the Gentiles or heathen, therefore, would mean a contradiction of one of the principal dogmas, for neither of them could
become sons of Abraham. This explains why missionary efforts have
never been made on any large scale, not because it might run counter
to the Jewish idea of tolerance, but because it could not be reconciled
with the distinctiveness that goes with the idea of the 'Chosen People'.
Judaism looks upon itself as the redeemed community, its adherents
being the covenanting partners of God. That is the principle underlying its view, already described, of such doctrines as the atonement
and the life hereafter.

This physical character of Judaism has been expressed times without
number, but one of the clearest definitions has been provided in the
writings of Prof. Schoeps. 'The election of Abraham's seed brings the
result that he who has been born an Israelite is already in the Covenant
by his physical descent. So the seed of Abraham has become "holy
seed". . . . Jews have been elected by God ever since the day that
the reception of Abraham's complete devotion has been fixed in the
covenant with him, so that even a Jew who has turned away from his

---

[1] *Authorized Daily Prayer Book*, p. 68 and p. 76.
[2] *A Book of Jewish Thoughts*, p. 14.

faith requires, on his repentance, only to turn back into that relation to Abraham which he received by birth.'[1]

Judaism is at once a religion and a people, and the very core of all its doctrine is this conception of the 'bene Yisrael', the children of Israel, as the people of God who cannot withdraw His benediction given once for all. 'We are the priests, and ours is the blessing', reads the conclusion of the Sermon for the Week in the *Jewish Chronicle*,[2] the official organ of British Jewry, and the most important Jewish publication in the English-speaking countries. A Jew may be completely secularized, he may have embraced atheism, but he is and remains a son of the promise, because he is of Abraham's seed irrespective of his attitude to religion. This conviction is the ultimate reason for the rejection of a Messiah who not only claimed to be the Saviour of the Jews, but had come to admit the outsider on the same terms as the sons of the promise. Lk. iv. 16-30 is a striking illustration of that fact, for it shows that the preaching of Jesus was received without resentment until He began to point out the universality of God's redeeming love that does not stop at any racial or national frontier. In the most profound treatise ever written on the subject of Jesus by a Jewish authority, the author, a Professor in the Hebrew University of Jerusalem, says: 'Judaism is not only religion and it is not only ethics: it is the sum-total of all the needs of the nation, placed on a religious basis. It is a national world outlook with an ethico-religious basis . . . Judaism is a national life, a life which the national religion and human ethical principles embrace without engulfing. Jesus came and thrust aside all the requirements of the national life . . . he ignored them completely. In the self-same moment he both annulled Judaism as the life-force of the Jewish nation, and also the nation itself as a nation. For a religion which possesses only a certain conception of God and a morality acceptable to all mankind, does not belong to any special nation, and, consciously or unconsciously, breaks down the barriers of nationality. This inevitably brought it to pass that his people, Israel, rejected him.'[3] There is a logical consistency in that attitude which can hardly be questioned.

For the moment we are not concerned with the general attitude of Judaism to Jesus which will be the subject of a later paragraph. The matter under discussion is the national character of the Jewish religion

---

[1] Op. cit., pp. 149 ff.   [2] 18th June 1948.
[3] Joseph Klausner, *Jesus of Nazareth*, p. 390.

which determines the view Judaism takes of other peoples and religions. Once we realize the distinct superiority which Israel claims above all others, we must expect to find those others relegated to the position of spiritual subordinates, however carefully that position may be paraphrased in order to eschew the appearance of haughtiness.

The Jewish educational authorities published a few years ago a Guide Book for Teachers under the title *Man and his Creator*, in which Dr. Epstein set out some of the more important doctrinal beliefs of Judaism. In the article on Israel's contribution it is made perfectly plain that Israel (and that means Judaism) is to be the divinely appointed promoter of righteousness on earth, a kingdom of priests, a holy nation 'that is able to achieve a mastery over the senses . . . and thus make the highest contribution towards the realization of a divine purpose.' It follows that other nations and religions will be led by Israel towards the goal of righteousness, Judaism setting the task and supervising the development.

There are certain religious demands Judaism makes upon others as a prerequisite of their partnership in the realization of that plan. They cannot become children of Abraham. Judaism is out of reach for most of them, although individuals are admitted if there are good reasons, as, for example, where there has been a mixed marriage. The Religion of Humanity is, then, the condition upon which partnership is granted to others, and which constitutes the rôle assigned to the nations. It is based on the seven precepts which, according to rabbinical teaching, were given to the sons of Noah, and has been termed 'Noachism'. The Guide Book for Teachers, mentioned above, states the case as follows: 'A simple set of rules has been communicated by God to mankind; Abstention from (1) idolatry, (2) blasphemy, (3) incest, (4) murder, (5) theft, (6) the eating of a limb torn from a living animal, and finally (7) the command for the administration of justice. Such are the seven duties, purely ethical and moral in aim and scope, which constitute for all time the religion of humanity, the universal observance of which affords a guarantee of the development of mankind towards righteousness.'[1] This is the missionary programme of Judaism for the nations, whether they be Christians, Muhammadans, heathen, or adherents of some other creed. It is significant that in the forty-eight pages of the Guide Book neither Christianity nor any other religion is mentioned, which is, of course, absolutely consistent

[1] Op. cit., p. 41.

with the view held in Judaism that all other religions transgress at least against either the first or the second Noachitic precept. Nor can we overlook the eschatological implications of Noachism which the Guide Book is careful to underline by quoting, among the proof texts, this sentence from the writings of Maimonides: 'Whosoever accepts the seven precepts and is careful in the observance of them is of the pious among the nations of the world and has a share in the world to come.'

Observers of Jewish life are occasionally puzzled over the phenomenon that even a Jew who has turned a free-thinker is still regarded as a Jew, whereas one who has become a Christian is immediately looked upon as traitor and apostate. But there is nothing inconsistent in such an attitude as anyone, who has followed the argument, will easily understand. By accepting, through Jesus, the universal validity and applicability of redemption, election, grace, eternal life, etc., a Jew has left the Covenant, has deserted the host of the Chosen People, has thrown away his election, and cut himself off from the redeemed community.

THE PRACTICE OF JUDAISM

Official Jewish circles in Britain make no secret of the deplorable religious situation in which Judaism finds itself. In its issue of 10th June 1949, *The Jewish Chronicle* devoted an article of nearly 1,000 words to a discussion of the state of affairs. It was entitled 'The Banishment of God', and opened with the assertion, 'God hardly enters at all actively into the thought of the Jew today.' The external character of much that passes for religion is then criticized: 'Ceremonial, organization, financial prosperity, the virtue of numbers, all these matters are of vital importance in a Jewish group. But real concern for a lofty, moral conception of life and conduct, for a true worship of God, for an unshakable trust in Him in times of sorrow and disappointment, this is utterly and pathetically absent.' Finally the question is asked: 'Is it the fault of Rabbis and other religious leaders? The answer to this question is an alarming one. The shepherds are blind mouths, as Milton called them.' Judaism as such is undoubtedly declining as a religious force. A Jewish Psychic Society was formed in London quite recently to establish contact with friends and relatives who have passed over, and thus to help Jews to acquire knowledge of, and faith in, the fact of survival after death.

In America the situation is much worse as is evident from very many pronouncements by leading Rabbis. The President of the Union of American Hebrew Congregations, Dr. Maurice M. Eisendraht, stated in 1949 that not even one-quarter of the two and a half million Jews living in New York had any connection whatever with organized religion, and declared that there existed today a widespread 'paganization and demoralization of Jewish life'.

But although it is an undisputed fact that the observing of the practices, rites and religious customs of Judaism has most markedly declined, no survey of the Mosaic religion would be complete without a description of some of the more important features of that practice. It is true enough that only a small minority now observes what in the past would have been considered the barest minimum, but it is equally necessary to add that there are, and always will be, people of Jewish faith to whom the faithful attendance at public worship, the regular perusal of the Prayer Book, and the celebration of festivals and ceremonies mean everything.

Compared with the study of the Torah, prayer is of secondary importance to the Jew, although it is regarded as superior to the sacrifices once offered in Jerusalem. Prayer now takes the place of offerings, and the set times of morning, afternoon, and evening worship correspond to the hours of the Temple sacrifices. At morning prayers and on festivals the male worshipper wears the Tallit, a cloth of white silk or wool with blue or black stripes at the ends and fringes (cf. Nu. xv. 37 ff.). Another biblical injunction (Ex. xiii. 9) is observed by putting on, at morning prayers, the Tephillin (Phylacteries) which consist of two small leather boxes (containing passages from Scripture) and a long leather strap. A third custom going back to Mosaic legislation and most likely to be noticed by anyone visiting a Jewish home, concerns the Mezuzzah (Dt. vi. 9), a small case of wood or metal, containing the words of Dt. vi. 4-9 in Hebrew, which is affixed to the doors. The principal prayer at all services is the Amidah, which may well be as ancient as the books of Ezra and Nehemiah, and is made up of eighteen blessings expressing, in turn, eulogy, petitions, and thanksgiving. The Amidah is preceded by the Shema, often considered the most significant part of the Jewish liturgy as it contains the whole dogma in the opening sentence: 'Hear, O Israel, the Lord is our God, the Lord is *one*!'

The services are conducted by the Reader ('Chazzan', i.e. Overseer), as distinct from the Rabbi who gives a discourse and is the head of the community. The Reader also attends to the public recitation of the Pentateuch, which is divided into a large number of portions to make up an annual or triennial cycle. The Reading from the Law is a conspicuous part of the service and it is followed by a supplementary portion from the Prophets, including certain passages from Isaiah, but leaving out lii. 13-15 and the whole of chapter liii. A fixed selection of Psalms is embodied in the Prayer Book, but does not contain, among others, Psalms ii, xxii, xxxi, xlv, lxix, and cx.

There are more elaborate services on the Sabbath, which is celebrated in memory of the creation as well as of the Exodus, both of which form the central idea of the Kiddush, a series of prayers and blessings read in the home by the master of the house. A cup of wine and two loaves are partaken of to symbolize joy and plenty, and hymns and table songs are prescribed which show the twofold character of the Sabbath as a religious and socio-ethical festival with a definite Messianic connotation as it typifies peace and brotherhood to come.

Three feasts serve to keep alive the memory of the pilgrimages that used to be undertaken three times a year in order to offer sacrifices in Jerusalem. They coincided with the three main crops of the Holy Land: Passover being held at the time of the barley harvest, Pentecost at the gathering of wheat, and Tabernacles at the season of fruit. Passover (Hebrew: 'Pessach') is by far the most important of the three, for it commemorates God's intervention on behalf of His People, the exodus from Egypt. All traces of leaven must be removed from Jewish homes as this is the Feast of the Unleavened Bread, the 'Matzot', and the most significant part of the service is held in the home. The story of the divine deliverance from Pharaoh is related in all its details, and accompanied by many symbols, e.g. a roast shank bone to remind the participants of the paschal lamb which was slain and whose blood was sprinkled on the doorsteps so that the angel of death, walking through the country and killing the first-born of the Egyptians, would recognize the Jewish homes and 'pass over' them. At one point the master of the house breaks a cake of unleavened bread and says: 'This is the bread of affliction which our ancestors ate in the land of Egypt. Let all those who are hungry enter and eat thereof, and all who are in distress, come and celebrate the Passover. At present we celebrate it here, but next year we hope to celebrate it in the land of Israel. This year we are accounted aliens here, but next year we hope to be children of freedom in the land of Israel.' This blessing is in the Chaldee language and probably dates from the pre-Christian era.

Pentecost (Hebrew: 'Shavuot') follows seven weeks after Passover and the synagogue is decorated with plants and flowers in memory of the pastoral origin of the feast. In rabbinical tradition it was associated with the giving of the Law at Sinai, which converted a company of runaway slaves into a national as well as a religious body of free men and women.

Tabernacles (Hebrew: 'Succoth', i.e. booths) is a typical autumn festival with prayers for rain and for the dead. Its last day (Simchat Torah) is an occasion of rejoicing, especially among the young, and marks the point at which the annual reading of the Torah is commenced anew.

Apart from these festivals there are also two Holy Days, both of which are full of most solemn meaning. Many a Jew who would not come near a synagogue throughout the year would not like to be missed there on those two occasions, one of which is the New Year, the other the Day of Atonement.

Rosh Hashanah (i.e. the head of the year) commences the calendar and is viewed as a day of judgment on which individuals and nations are entered in, or struck off, the divine Book of Life. 'On this day sentence is pronounced upon countries—which of them is destined to the sword and which to peace, which to famine and which to plenty; and each separate creature is visited thereon, and recorded for life or for death' (from the liturgy of the New Year's service). But the day is also one of remembrance, and God is asked to forgive the petitioners on account of the faith of their ancestors who have laid up a store of righteousness upon which the present generation may draw. New Year's Day is also the day of the trumpet, the 'Shofar'. This is a ram's horn which has always been blown as the signal for important occasions of a religious and national character.

A dramatic climax of genuine devotion and emotion is reached on the highest of all holy days, the Day of Atonement (Yom Kippur), described in Lv. xxiii. 32 as a sabbath of solemn rest, with its abstention from food and drink. To put it in the words of the liturgy: 'Thou hast given us in love, O Lord our God, this Day of Atonement for pardon, forgiveness, and atonement, that we may obtain pardon thereon for all our iniquities; an holy convocation, as a memorial of the departure from Egypt.' Four times throughout the day a catalogue of twenty-four definite transgressions is recited, followed by a further enumeration of those sins for which certain sacrifices were offered in the days of the Temple. There is also the narration of the ancient ritual of the scapegoat upon which the nation's sins were symbolically placed, and which was then driven to the wilderness of Azazel where it was cast from a precipice. No one who has attended the services on that day can possibly forget the note of urgency and the passionate yearning for forgiveness that are present throughout the prayers and prostrations, and are perhaps best summed up in these two passages from the liturgy: 'What shall we say before Thee, O Thou who dwellest on high, and what shall we recount unto Thee, Thou who abidest in the heavens? Dost Thou not know all things, both the hidden and the revealed? May it then be Thy will, O Lord our God, and God of our Fathers, to forgive us for all our sins, to pardon us for all our iniquities, and to grant us remission for all our transgressions.' The sevenfold proclamation of God's Oneness, taken from the story of Elijah's triumph over the prophets of Baal on Mount Carmel (1 Ki. xiii. 39), and one blast of the Shofar closes the day whose doctrinal significance has been dealt with elsewhere.

There is, however, an ancient and widespread custom which shows that the lack of a vicarious sacrifice constituted a serious problem to many a Jew who felt that prayer could not altogether take the place of the scapegoat of old. A fowl is taken and waved three times around the head of the penitent. The bird is then slaughtered and given to the poor. Though rabbis inveighed against the rite time and again it has survived to this day.

Reference has already been made to certain practices incumbent upon male members of the community. No prayer meeting, no synagogue service, no marriage ceremony can be held unless there are ten male Jews above the age of thirteen, for that is the quorum required for the divine Presence. No number of women can make up the deficiency as, from the point of the Law, woman does not count. The opening part of the daily morning service contains the following injunction: 'Men say, "Blessed art thou, O Lord our God, King of the Universe, who hast not made me a woman." Women say, "Blessed art thou, O Lord our God, King of the Universe, who hast made me according to thy will".'[1] In the synagogue, men and women are strictly separated and female worshippers do not take any

[1] Prayer Book, p. 6.

official part in the service. But it would be most fallacious to infer from the above that the status of the Jewess in ordinary life was somehow inferior to that held by other women. The truth is that Judaism takes an exceptionally high and lofty view of the true vocation of womanhood, which is seen in the domestic and marital life, in short, in home and family. Judaism does not believe in asceticism and celibacy. On the contrary, its teaching emphasizes that only through married life can sanctity and purity be realized.

There is, finally, another custom in which Judaism differs notably from other religions. It concerns the funeral, which among Jews is a matter of the greatest simplicity. Irrespective of their calling or station in life, the richest and the poorest are given the same plain wooden coffin and the same simple hearse. The anniversary of the death of a near relative is regularly observed by lighting a candle or lamp on the eve of the day and keeping it burning until sunset of the next day.

MODERN TRENDS

Judaism, as has been pointed out before, is not a static but a progressive religion and has been affected by many tendencies which, although they became movements within Judaism, originally arose through its contact with the surrounding world. For example, we speak of Liberal and Orthodox Judaism, but these are not the only trends manifest in the Jewish religion today. Jewish thought has been coloured in distinct and varied ways, as the following paragraphs will show.

1. *Liberal Judaism*

Influenced by the enlightenment of the eighteenth century, a movement in favour of the grammatical and historical exegesis of the Bible started among the Jews on the continent of Europe, in opposition to the dialectic school of Talmudism. Scientific research was made the yardstick of biblical interpretation, the dietary laws were considered obsolete, and only the ethical injunctions came to be regarded as obligatory. This movement came to be called Liberal Judaism. Its protagonist in Britain was Dr. Claude Montefiore, an outstanding scholar who wrote a most interesting commentary on the Synoptic Gospels. In his book, *The Old Testament and After*, he summarizes the programme of Liberal Judaism as follows: 'It modifies or enlarges the doctrines of the past so as to make them consistent with each other and in harmony with the highest conceptions of truth to which it can attain. It deliberately aims at universalism and universalization. It sets out to emphasize the "prophetic" elements in Judaism, and to minimize or negate the "priestly" elements. It gives up all praying for the restoration of the Temple and of animal sacrifices. It sets the Prophets above the Law.'[1] Though bitterly denounced by its opponents, the movement spread and now numbers some twelve synagogues and congregations in Britain. In the United States it has met with even greater success.

2. Traditional Judaism

Orthodox or Traditional Judaism, as it is often called, takes its stand upon the Talmud and consciously remains within the bonds of legalism and particularism. Dr. Hertz, the late Chief Rabbi, has defined it in his book, *Affirmations of Judaism*, as holding the following doctrines: 'The teachings and practices which have come down to the House of Israel through the ages; the positive Jewish beliefs concerning God, the Torah, and Israel; the sacred festivals; the holy resolve to maintain Israel's identity; and the life consecrated by Jewish observances.' At the same time he turned against Liberalism and predicted: 'Liberal Judaism is a moving staircase carrying those who have taken their stand on it, out of Judaism. In the long run there will be no other Judaism but traditional Judaism,' a forecast that has not been proved by the developments of the last ten or twenty years.

3. Chassidism

It was, however, not so much Liberalism which shook the foundations of Orthodoxy, but the secularism and indifference of modern man, who does not believe what he cannot handle. This conflict is still going on and the only group in Judaism that has emerged victoriously from that battle is the mystical movement of Chassidism which began as a reaction against the dry legalism. It started in Poland about two hundred years ago, and after being long connected with the poorer, uneducated mass of Eastern Jewry, gradually won respect and admiration among the learned. Here was a direct approach to God, based on personal experience and prayer rather than on dogma and ritual. Its great textbooks, the *Sefer Yetzirah* and the *Zohar*, are essentially Jewish although they show distinct traces of Hellenistic, Gnostic, and Christian influences. Chassidism is characterized by a

[1] Pp. 557 f.

genuine piety and humility that are the outcome of an intense life of
prayer, combined with cheerfulness and great enthusiasm. It has had
its moments of ecstasy and wild extremes when thousands were carried
away by miracle-working 'holy men' who thrived on superstition;
but it can also claim to have produced some distinguished writers and
scholars. The greatest representative of Jewish mysticism, and doubt-
less the intellectual leader of Judaism today, is Martin Buber who is
at once mystic, theologian, scholar, and philosopher. His book, *I and
Thou*, has been praised by Berdyaev as one of the most eminent manifestations of the religious thought of Europe. It certainly shows an
insight into the mind of God which is unusual in our days.

4. *Zionism*

We turn now to consider a movement which cuts right across all
divisions and groups, and which may eventually supersede most of
them. It is known as Zionism.

We have repeatedly alluded to the drift from the synagogue so
typical of Judaism today, irrespective of the country or social class to
which the individual belongs. It is, of course, perfectly correct to say
that in forsaking his religion the Jew only copies his neighbour, but
we are not here concerned with the question as to how far the religious
poverty of the Jews reflects the low spiritual state of their environment.
In this connection it must be remembered that, after the most ruthless
annihilation of some six million Jews in Europe, about one-third of
Jewry lives in countries that are dominated by Russian Communism.
It is, however, not so much the deified materialism of Marx that
claims most of those Jews who have given up their faith, but the
fashionable pseudo-religious systems of humanitarianism, spiritism,
Christian Science, Freemasonry, etc., or sheer indifference to anything
that savours of human recognition of a power outside oneself.

Some Jewish leaders had cherished the hope that the terrible persecution of European Jewry would result in a great religious revival,
a solemn return to the faith of the fathers. But while a few have
sought refuge in the old traditions, the vast majority have found a
way out of their indifference by throwing themselves into the arms
of nationalism: they have accepted Zionism as the new faith.

Deeply religious and completely secular ideas converge in this movement which is sweeping Judaism in every quarter of the globe like
wildfire, and has gathered further impetus with the setting up of the

State of Israel. On the one hand, it draws upon the age-long yearning of the Jews in the Dispersion to return to their Holy Land and there to serve the God of Abraham, Isaac, and Jacob. On the other hand it provides that haven of safety and liberty which the millions of hunted and pilloried Jews of Europe have been so anxious to find. While the saying quoted from the Passover service echoes the deep spiritual longing of the former motive, the manifestos of the Zionist organizations —with the exception of a small religious group, Misrachi—illustrate the latter. Only occasionally do the two blend.

The father of modern spiritual Zionism was Asher Ginzberg who adopted the pseudonym Ahad Ha-Am (i.e. One of the People). He came of a Chassidic family and saw in Zionism the very essence of Judaism. He never ceased to demand a spiritual revival as the prerequisite of the return to the Holy Land, and to insist upon the Jews becoming heroes of the Spirit, and not of worldly power. His ideas were taken up by Bialik, a poet of unusual spiritual depth whose language resembles that of Jeremiah, and more recently by Martin Buber to whom Eretz Yisrael, the Land of Israel, means the synthesis of Spirit and Reality.

Quite different ideas were prominent in the establishment of political Zionism. It was born of the unspeakable misery and social distress of the Jews in Eastern Europe, who, in the second half of the last century, were made the scapegoat of all discontent and political unrest in Russia, Rumania and Turkey. Every year hundreds of Jewish men, women and children lost their lives in the pogroms connived at, if not inspired by, the authorities of those countries. It was in view of that wretched state that Theodor Herzl demanded a land of refuge for his people, but he did not at first insist on Palestine, nor did he ever link his argument with religious sentiments. His objective was a political and economic solution to what seemed to him a political and economic problem. Only when his plans for such a land of refuge in other parts of the world had come to naught did he fix his gaze upon Palestine, and the First Zionist Congress in Basle in 1897 made no reference to any spiritual tendencies but based its claim to Palestine on political arguments. Helped by the sad events in Europe and the rapid spread of nationalistic ideas, the political group won the upper hand and achieved the establishment of a sovereign country. In the leading American Jewish periodical *Commentary*, Dr. Ernest Munz has written an essay on the reason for the amazing success of Zionism in

which he explains how the Jew first tried emancipation and assimilation, and later on cosmopolitanism and collectivism as a remedy for
his difficult position among the nations of the world, only to come
face to face with the nationalism of his surroundings. Then he turned
and met that monster on its own ideological platform. 'Contrary to
the traditional view, the birth of Zionism actually reflects independent
Jewish thinking less than it does imitation of ideas sweeping the world
at large. Zionism was the true offspring of the combination of
nationalism and neo-romanticism that characterized the nineteenth
century. One can admire in many ways the wisdom and political fore-
sight of the founders of Zionism, yet its rapid spread was not due to
rational political thinking but rather to the enormous appeal that a
new national ideology made to the emotions and irrational, romantic,
even messianic, urges of the Jewish masses.'

It is on the ground of this nationalism that some Jewish leaders have
voiced their misgivings as to the religious and ethical soundness of
the new state. They know that only fifteen per cent of the Israelis
voted for the religious block at the first election. They see the passion
of the Zionist youth who are at times carried away by notions of
totalitarianism and imperialism. They compare all that to Israel's one
and only vocation as a kingdom of priests and as a holy nation. They
argue that God gave the country to their ancestors not unconditionally,
but with the explicit stipulation that Israel must fulfil her divine function and remain unlike any other. They are afraid that once again
Israel may try to be like others and thus commit the sin for which
she was punished times without number, as the Bible records.

While a rousing call for home missions is made in the Holy Land,
there, as elsewhere, a fundamental change is gradually taking place.
Judaism is no longer so much a matter of religious experience as the
expression of a national consciousness. This conception has always
been latent as we have demonstrated before. Where in former days
reference used to be made to the Eternal God and His Holy People,
we now hear and read of the Eternal Nation whose being is from everlasting to everlasting. Arthur Koestler, in his book *Promise and Fulfil-
ment* (1949), considers it imperative for every Jew to make up his
mind whether or not to join actively in the national life of Israel. If
the answer is negative, the Jew should be prepared to renounce his
separateness and give up his faith which, at any rate in the Dispersion,
has become empty traditionalism. It is either Zionism or the Nazarene.

JESUS OF NAZARETH

What, then, is the Jewish attitude to Jesus Christ? Is He still regarded as a sorcerer and impostor as in some Talmudic writings? Not at all. The last forty or fifty years have seen a significant change in so far as the study of the Nazarene has almost become a legitimate branch of Jewish research, whereas it would not have been tolerated in the past. Many non-Jews have been led to believe, at least by implication, that a turning-point had been reached in the Jewish mode of thinking and that it was only a question of time before Judaism would accept the Nazarene as Messiah. This opinion is altogether wrong, because it fails to penetrate to the real cause of the change in the Jewish attitude. The figure of Jesus became attractive to Judaism only to the extent that modernism in Christian theology tended to subordinate traditional orthodox beliefs to modern thought. It is no coincidence that Jewish interest in Jesus occurred at a time when Christian doctrine was toned down and modified. An interpretation of Jesus which stripped Him of His Deity, explained away His miracles, and dissected His words, provided a basis of study quite acceptable to Judaism. It was the time when it became fashionable to question the reliability of the Gospel records, to feel uncertain about the resurrection appearances, and to dismiss everything supernatural as pious myth. Thus we shall understand the more recent interest in Jesus, and also appreciate why the acceptability of the Nazarene cannot go beyond a certain point which is observed by all Jewish writers, no matter how enthusiastic they are in their treatment of Him. There can be little doubt that He has captured the imagination of many who spent years in studying His life and took great care to be as impartial as possible. Nor can the fact be denied that a few individuals, having fallen in love with the object of their literary interest, found themselves unable to withdraw from Him, and discovered, often to their own astonishment, that they had overstepped the bounds of Judaism. But those were exceptions.

It may suffice to quote from some of the more authoritative utterances that have come from prominent Jews in recent years. There is first of all Martin Buber, who said in his *Drei Reden über das Judentum*: 'We must overcome the superstitious terror with which we have regarded the Nazareth movement, a movement which we must place where it properly belongs—in the spiritual history of Israel.' He added later, however: 'Whoever regards Jesus as an historical personality,

D

be he ever so high, may belong to us; but he who acknowledges Jesus to be the Messiah already come, cannot belong to us.' There is Albert Einstein, the outstanding scientist, who said he was 'enthralled by the luminous figure of the Nazarene', and Rabbi Solomon B. Freehof, who in his book, *Stormers of Heaven*, frankly stated: 'The personality of Jesus was such that his sonship to God was magnificently evident. The divine spirit seemed manifest in his words and deeds. He impressed himself upon the world, perhaps more so than other prophets or saints, as a child of the living God.' Then followed Sholem Asch, the distinguished writer, who devoted a whole book of some seven hundred pages to Jesus under the title *The Nazarene*, and said in his more recent publication, *One Destiny*: 'A little less than two thousand years ago, there came into our world among the Jewish people and to it a Personage who gave substance to the illusion perceived by our fathers in their dream. Just as water fills up the hollowness of the ocean, so did he fill the empty world with the spirit of the one living God. No one before him and no one after him has bound our world with the fetters of law, of justice, and of love, and brought it to the feet of the one living Almighty God as effectively as did this Personage who came to an Israelite house in Nazareth in Galilee—and this he did, not by the might of the sword, of fire and steel . . . but by the power of his mighty spirit and of his teachings.'[1]

Finally, here is a quotation from Klausner's *Jesus of Nazareth*: 'In his ethical code there is a sublimity, distinctiveness and originality in form unparalleled in any other Hebrew ethical code; neither is there any parallel to the remarkable art of his parables. . . . The Book of the Ethics of Jesus will be one of the choicest treasures in the literature of Israel for all time.'[2] But that tribute is balanced on the same page by the following: 'To the Jewish nation he can be neither God nor the Son of God. . . . Neither can he be the Messiah. . . . Neither can they regard him as a Prophet.'

When it comes to the question of the resurrection we find that all Jewish writers and preachers are unanimous in denying it, although Klausner makes the concession that it must have been a 'vision' which became the basis of Christianity. 'It is impossible to suppose that there was any conscious deception: the nineteen hundred years' faith of millions is not founded on deception.'[3] And so Judaism cannot go beyond the death of the Nazarene as is emphatically stated in the larger

[1] P. 5.   [2] P. 414.   [3] P. 359.

and more exhaustive *Jewish Encyclopædia*:[1] 'No Messiah that Jews could recognize could suffer such a death; for "he that is hanged is accursed of God" (Dt. xxi. 23), an insult to God.'[2] This complements from the theological point of view those reasons for the rejection of Jesus from the national point of view discussed on page 37.

WHAT OF THE FUTURE?

Of the seventeen million Jews who lived in 1933 hardly eleven million have survived. The focal points of Judaism have shifted from Europe to the United States with her five million Jews, and to the new State of Israel. Many distinct features of Judaism are fast disappearing on account of an ever-increasing loss of faith. Very often the observance of the Biblical rite of circumcision is the only remaining token of allegiance, although we have seen that it is not through any rite or declaration of faith that a Jew is a Jew, but because he is born of a Jewish mother. Is this physical character of Judaism sufficient guarantee for its permanence, or is there something undefinable in Judaism, something that defeats all our efforts to examine and to describe, simply because it touches the very mystery of God?

A most revealing article was recently published in *The Jewish Agency's Digest*[3] in which a member of the Executive, E. Dobkin, writes as follows: 'Surely we must be alarmed by the fact that in the present-day Jewish world eighty per cent of Jewish children are completely ignorant of Jewish traditions and values, and have never seen a letter of the Hebrew alphabet in their lives. Am Haarazut (i.e. people ignorant of Jewish matters) has become widespread and those sources of spiritual substance from which Jewish life in Europe of days gone by drew life and strength and thought, have disappeared. We have grown rich in matter and have become impoverished in spirit.'

Some are tempted to predict the early disappearance of Judaism as a distinct faith. Others expect the Jew to turn to Jesus Christ within a measurable period of time. Others again firmly believe that the Temple will be rebuilt and the practice of sacrifices resumed. We dare not decide a question which is fraught with divine Providence. We know only that Judaism is different from all other non-Christian religions in so far as the salvation of the world depends upon the coming of Israel's Messiah.[5]

[1] 12 volumes, 1901-6. [2] But cf. Gal. iii. 13.
[3] Vol. III, No. 12, December, 1954. [4] Cf. p. 196, para. 2.

CHAPTER III

ISLAM

INTRODUCTION

THE religion of Islam[1] is one of the outstanding phenomena of history. Within a century of the death of its founder, the Muslim Empire stretched from Southern France through Spain, North Africa, the Levant and Central Asia to the confines of China; and, although Islam has since been virtually expelled from Western Europe and has lost much of its political power elsewhere, it has from time to time made notable advances in Eastern Europe, in Africa, in India, and in South-East Asia. Today it extends from the Atlantic to the Philippines and numbers some three hundred and fifty million adherents drawn from races as different as the European from the Bantu, and the Aryan Indian from the primitive Philippine tribesman; yet we can still speak of the 'World of Islam'. As Dr. S. M. Zwemer justly remarks: 'A vertebrate and virile creed counteracts the centrifugal tendencies of nationality, race, climate and environment. The Arab is blood-brother to the Negro convert in Africa. The souls of Indian Muslims and Chinese Ahungs throb with indignation when they read of real or fancied wrongs committed against the Riffs of Morocco or the Arabs of Palestine. The question of Zionism is front-page news in the Muslim Press of India as well as Egypt; it arouses the Muslims of Sa'udi Arabia, but also those of South Africa and Morocco. This unity and solidarity of the Muslim world through its religious creed, the pilgrimage to Mecca, the power of the press and the continued existence and power of the Sufi dervish orders cannot be denied.'[2]

None the less, it is exceedingly difficult to summarize in one short article the history, faith and practice of Islam, since that religion has been, and is, very differently interpreted by a wide variety of sects and schools of thought which would all claim the name of Muslim. In the main, therefore, it will be necessary to confine our attention to

---

[1] 'Islam', the correct name for the religion of Muhammad, is the infinitive of the Arabic verb 'to submit'; while 'Muslim', the correct term for one who follows that religion, is the present participle of the same verb.

[2] *A Factual Survey of the Moslem World*, p. 5.

what may be termed the central current of orthodox Muslim thought, with only brief and inadequate allusions to other and rival interpretations. If one excepts, however, the more extreme sects of the Shi'a—and, of course, those communities such as the Druzes and the 'Alawites which can no longer properly claim the name of Muslim— it is to the person, life and revelations of Muhammad that both the faith and practice of all varieties of Muslims are usually traced. And while the massive body of alleged sayings and doings of the Prophet must be regarded as fictions which mirror the history of the theology, politics and jurisprudence of early Islam, yet there is a real sense in which R. A. Nicholson is correct when he says: 'More than any other man who has ever lived, Muhammad shaped the destinies of his people, and though they left him far behind as they moved along the path of civilization, they still looked back to him for guidance and authority at each step.'[1]

THE ORIGIN OF ISLAM

1. *Muhammad's Early Life*

Born about 570 A.D.[2] at Mecca, Muhammad was the posthumous son of an almost unknown father, and his mother died when he was only six. He was brought up first by his grandfather and then by his uncle Abu Talib, worthy members[3] of the family of Hashim and the tribe of Quraysh. Little is known with any certainty of his early life. The Traditions tell us that his mother gave him to a Bedouin woman to suckle and that he passed his earliest years among nomad tents; that when twelve years old he went with his uncle to Syria, where he met a Christian monk named Bahira; and that he was later employed by a rich widow named Khadija, who put him in charge of her caravans and finally rewarded his fidelity with her hand in marriage. All that can be regarded as certain, however, is that he grew up an orphan[4] and attained economic security only when, at the age of twenty-five,

---

[1] *Literary History of the Arabs*, p. 179.

[2] Some scholars think considerably later, e.g. *c.* 580 A.D.

[3] According to orthodox theory they were outstanding members of the tribe, but this has been seriously questioned by western scholars (cf. Sura xliii. 30, etc.). N.B.—The references to the Qur'an in this chapter adopt the verse numberings used, e.g., in Rodwell's translation, from which the translations are usually, but not invariably, taken.

[4] Cf. Sura xciii. 6 ff.

he married Khadija, then (traditionally) a widow of forty. The marriage seems to have been surprisingly successful, for Muhammad took no second wife until Khadija's death some twenty-five years later. A number of children were born to them, but only one daughter, Fatima, survived.

There is evidence in a Tradition which can scarcely have been fabricated that Muhammad suffered in early life from fits. Be that as it may, the adult Muhammad soon showed signs of a markedly religious disposition. He would retire to caves for seclusion and meditation; he frequently practised fasting; and he was prone to dreams. Profoundly dissatisfied with the polytheism and crude superstitions of his native Mecca, he appears to have become passionately convinced of the existence and transcendance of one true God. How much of this conviction he owed to Christianity or Judaism it seems impossible to determine. Monophysite Christianity was at that time widely spread in the Arab Kingdom of Ghassan; the Byzantine Church was represented by hermits dotted about the Hijaz with whom he may well have come into contact; the Nestorians were established at Hira and in Persia; and the Jews were strongly represented in al Madina, the Yemen and elsewhere. There can be no manner of doubt, moreover, that at some period of his life he absorbed much teaching from Talmudic sources and had contact with some form of Christianity; and it seems overwhelmingly probable that his early adoption of monotheism can be traced to one or both of these influences.[1]

2. *His Revelations*

It was at the age of about forty that the first revelation of the Qur'an (the 'Reading' or 'Recitation') is said to have come to him. It is recorded that a voice three times bade him 'Read (or recite) in the name of thy Lord . . .'[2] Thereafter no more revelations came for some two years: then suddenly, when passing through a period of spiritual depression which made him contemplate suicide, he is said to have seen a vision of the angel Gabriel which sent him home trembling

---

[1] Mecca, too, was a considerable market for foreign merchants, while the number of Ethiopic loan-words in the Qur'an is also significant.

[2] Sura xcvi. 1-5. According to one tradition Muhammad replied, 'I am no reader.' Another tradition, however, makes him reply, 'What am I to recite?' —which sounds like an echo of Is. xl. 6 ('The voice said "Cry". And he said, "What shall I cry?" ')

to Khadija for comfort and covering, only to hear the Voice saying,
'O thou enwrapped in thy mantle, arise and warn...'[1]

There can be little doubt that these passages mark his assumption
of the prophetic office, although many western scholars consider that
certain poetical passages in the Qur'an which breathe the questioning
spirit of the seeker rather than the authoritative pronouncement of the
prophet were composed at an even earlier date.[2] It seems, however,
that Muhammad himself was at first doubtful of the source of these
revelations, fearing that he was possessed by one of the Jinn, or sprites,
as was commonly believed to be the case with Arab poets and soothsayers. But Khadija and others reassured him, and he soon began to
propound divine revelations with increasing frequency.[3]

The earliest Suras[4] of the Qur'an reveal a marked simplicity of concept. They urge the moral response of man created by Allah, foretell
the Day of Judgment, and graphically depict the tortures of the damned
and the seductive delights of a very sensual Paradise. Increasingly,
however, the unity and transcendance of the one true God becomes
the overriding theme. But the response was poor. His wife Khadija,
his cousin 'Ali, his adopted son Zayd, and a few more believed in his
mission, but the leaders of the Quraysh, influenced largely by their
economic interest in the pagan rites and pilgrimage of the Ka'ba (a
Meccan shrine containing a black meteorite) and by their opposition
to his personal pretensions, ridiculed his claims. His preachings and
revelations thereupon changed somewhat in tone. More and more he
began to recount the histories of previous (mostly biblical) Prophets,
and to emphasize how they, too, had been mocked and ignored:
sooner or later, however, judgment always fell on their traducers.

3. The Hijra

But the response in Mecca was still small, and in 622 A.D. Muhammad
took the decisive step of withdrawing with his followers (some two
hundred in all) to al Madina, to which he had been invited by a party

---

[1] Sura lxxiv. 1. This is sometimes regarded as the first revelation of all.

[2] Officially, of course, these, too, are regarded as part of the divine revelation
vouchsafed to him as a Prophet.

[3] Each is regarded as the *ipsissima verba* of God, mediated through the
angel Gabriel (whom Muhammad confused with the Holy Spirit).

[4] Although by no means chronologically arranged (almost the opposite), a
large measure of agreement has been reached regarding the date of the different
Suras or their component parts.

of its inhabitants who had met him during the pilgrimage, had accepted his claims and had prepared their fellow townsmen for his advent. This withdrawal (or Hijra) proved the turning-point in Muhammad's career and has been appropriately chosen as the beginning of the Muslim era.[1] In Mecca he had been the rejected Prophet, pointing his countrymen to the one true God and warning them of judgment to come. In al Madina he at once became the statesman, legislator and judge—the executive as well as the mouthpiece of the new theocracy.[2]

Into the detailed history of the next few years we have no space to enter, but the key to its understanding seems to lie in his attitude to the Jews. There can be little doubt that Muhammad at first believed that he had only to proclaim his message to gain Jewish support, for was not his message the one, true religion preached by Abraham and all the patriarchs and prophets, ever-corrupted only to be proclaimed anew?[3] It was for this reason that his earlier references to the People of the Book (Jews and Christians) were almost uniformly favourable, and that he at first adopted several Jewish practices. At al Madina he found, however, that the Jews repudiated his claims and intrigued against him. More, they ridiculed his inaccurate accounts of Old Testament incidents.[4] This was something he could not endure; for he had recounted these incidents as the direct revelation of God (introduced by such words as: 'This is one of the secret histories which We reveal unto thee. Thou wast not present when . . .'[5]) and had denied that he had learnt them from any human source. When it became apparent, therefore, that certain Suras of the Qur'an did not agree with those Old Testament records of the same incidents which he had previously confirmed as authentic, he was driven to allege that the Jews had cor-

---

[1] For the rest of this chapter it seems best to give dates A.H. rather than A.D. They can be roughly converted into A.D. by adding 622 and deducting 3 for each century (to represent the difference between lunar and solar years).

[2] This is reflected in the new emphasis in his revelations on obedience to the Prophet (cf. Sura iii. 29, 126, iv. 17, 18, etc.) and on how he should be treated (cf. Sura xxiv. 63, 64, xxxiii. 53, xlix. 2-5, lviii. 13, 14, etc.).

[3] Cf. Sura x. 94, xxviii. 52, 53, etc., xlii. 11.

[4] Perhaps the outstanding examples of this inaccuracy are the apparent confusion of Miriam, sister of Moses and Aaron, with the Virgin Mary (Sura lxvi. 12 and xix. 29), and the depicting of Haman as a minister of Pharoah (Sura xl. 38). But several other examples could be quoted.

[5] Sura xii. 103. Cf. also Sura xxxviii. 69, 70, lxix. 43-46.

rupted, or at least misquoted, their own scriptures.[1] From this time, therefore, date his strictures on the Jews, his banishment or massacre of Jewish tribes, and the decisive turn from things Jewish to Arabia and Mecca discernible in his teaching.[2] Henceforth it was to the Ka'ba rather than Jerusalem that the Muslim community must turn in prayer;[3] and the pagan rites of the pilgrimage were to be purified and incorporated into Islam.[4]

This, again, made it necessary for him to impose his will on Mecca and led to his struggle with the Quraysh—although it also paved the way for the latter's ultimate acceptance of Islam. For our present purpose the details are largely irrelevant. Suffice it to say that, after a somewhat chequered career, Muhammad entered Mecca in triumph in 9 A.H., smashed the idols which surrounded the Ka'ba, and had established Islam, nominally at least, throughout the greater part of the Arabian peninsula before his death at al Madina in 11 A.H. It remains, however, to form some estimate of his character and of the source of his revelations: and to this we must now turn.

4. His Character

The idea—once prevalent in Europe—that Muhammed was an imposter from first to last has been virtually abandoned, and of his initial sincerity there seems little doubt. Most scholars explain his earlier revelations in terms of wishful thinking: they depict the misery and frustration of his early life; his deep conviction that the Arabs, like the Jews or Christians, needed a law and a lawgiver; his longing to be favoured with some revelation that would mark him as their Prophet; and his eventual conviction that words, thoughts and stories which various external or internal stimuli summoned from his subconscious mind constituted instalments of this revelation.[5] On such a view he has been regarded as an epileptic, a subject of hysteria[6], a

---

[1] Cf. Sura ii. 70, 73, 169, iii. 72, iv. 48, v. 16, 45, vi. 91, etc. It is not clear whether Muhammad believed that the Jews actually tampered with their MSS. or only falsified their reading or statement of the text.

[2] His religion, he now affirmed, was that of Abraham, who was neither Jew nor Christian. (Sura ii. 129, iii. 60, 89.)

[3] Sura ii. 136-145.   [4] Cf. Sura xxii. 27 ff., etc.

[5] E.g. *Muhammadanism*, by C. Snouck Hurgronje, p. 36.

[6] Cf. *Introduction to the Koran*, by R. Bell, p. 30, where Weil and Sprenger are cited in support of these two views.

'pathological case'[1], or as heir to an 'Ebionitic-Manichaean' doctrine of revelation (which may be thought to have safeguarded his sincerity if not, altogether, his moral character).[2] Others take a less favourable view and suggest that there is reason to believe that his symptoms of revelation were sometimes artificially produced.[3] Alternatively, of course, the phenomena may be explained as symptoms of intermittent spirit-possession, as claimed by modern spiritist mediums. The sharp, staccato style of the earlier Suras of the Qur'an can be explained on any of these hypotheses. But when we turn to the long, rambling accounts of Jewish patriarchs and prophets which occupy so much space in the later Meccan and earlier Madinese Suras, we are confronted by the fact that Muhammad sought (at this stage, at least) to satisfy the natural demand for some miraculous evidence of his Prophetic claims[4] by ascribing exclusively to divine revelation his knowledge of stories which correspond in such detail with the Talmud that of their essentially Jewish origin there can be no doubt.[5] R. Osborn scarcely overstates the case when he writes: 'To work (these stories) up into the form of rhymed Suras . . . must have required time, thought and labour. It is not possible that the man who had done this could have forgotten all about it, and believed that these legends had been brought to him ready prepared by an angelic visitor.'[6] That it must have taken time is admitted by R. Bell, who substitutes 'suggestion' for the angelic messenger as the normal method of inspiration;[7] but this (as

---

[1] *Aspects of Islam*, by D. B. Macdonald, p. 72.

[2] See *Mohammed: the Man and his Faith*, by Tor Andrae (trans. T. Menzel), pp. 260, 264-269.

[3] *Mohammed*, by D. S. Margoliouth, pp. 81, 85 f.; also article by the same author on Muhammad in Hasting's *Encyclopaedia of Religion and Ethics*.

[4] This demand was later met by the assertion that the very style of the Qur'an was inimitable (Sura xvii. 90) and by alleged angelic aid at the battles of Badr (Sura iii. 11, 120, 121, viii. 17) and elsewhere (Sura ix. 25, 26, xxxiii. 9, 10, etc., ix. 25, 26). Later, Tradition added a plethora of apocryphal miracles of every kind, many of which find a place in the most 'canonical' collections.

[5] His opponents alleged that 'tales of the ancients' were dictated to him morning and evening (Sura xxv. 5, 6 cf. xvi. 105, xliv. 13). It is, however, clear that he was quite unable to read the Hebrew O.T. or the Greek N.T. (which is probably the true explanation of the adjective 'ummi'—sometimes rendered 'illiterate'—applied to him in Sura vii. 156) and completely misunderstood the very nature of the latter, which he conceived as a book 'sent down' to 'Isa (Jesus; cf. Sura v. 50, lvii. 27, etc.) and to be 'observed' like the Law (cf. Sura v. 70, 72).

[6] *Islam under the Arabs*, p. 21.   [7] *Introduction to the Koran*, p. 35.

A. Jeffrey points out) does not justify Muhammad's exclusive ascription to revdlation of material obviously obtained for human sources.[1]

The same problem confronts us once more when we turn to the later Madinese Suras, which contain detailed regulations on all sorts of subjects which govern the lives of Muslims to this day. In these Suras, too, Muhammad adopted the same form of rhymed prose, and represented the words as the direct utterance of God. It is difficult, therefore, to avoid the conclusion of D. B. Macdonald: 'You cannot possibly imagine, in the case of long periods dealing with the law of inheritance or with the usages of marriage or with the quarrels of his followers, or emphasizing the position and dignity of the Prophet himself—you cannot possibly imagine that these things rose to him from his subconscious, that he did not know very well what he was saying and had not his own distinct objects in the way in which he expressed himself.'[2] And this conclusion tends to be confirmed when we find that in his later life personal (and other) problems were repeatedly solved by a divine revelation of the most convenient kind: it was thus that he was granted the right, unlike other believers, to have more than four wives[3] and dispensed from the normal obligation to divide his time equally between them;[4] that he escaped criticism when, in defiance of Arab custom, he married the divorced wife of his adopted son;[5] that he was absolved from his oath to have nothing more to do with his concubine Mary and extricated from the trouble caused thereby among some of his wives;[6] and that his wives were bidden to veil themselves,[7] were threatened with a double punishment for unchastity,[8] and were forbidden to remarry after his death.[9]

Some scholars are so profoundly convinced of Muhammad's initial sincerity that they explain all these later enigmas on hypotheses which avoid imputing to him any conscious imposture. Whether he can in fact have been self-deceived to this degree or whether the pressure of circumstances and his own inclinations, coupled with a general sense that the end justified the means, led to a moral declension[10] is primarily a problem for the psychologist to which history can provide no final solution.

[1] In, e.g., Sura xii. 103: see 'The Muslim World', October 1954, p. 256.
[2] Aspects of Islam, p. 80.   [3] Sura xxxiii. 49.   [4] Sura xxxiii. 51.
[5] Sura xxxiii. 36-38.   [6] Sura lxvi. 1-5.   [7] Sura xxxiii. 53 (cf. 32).
[8] Sura xxxiii. 30.   [9] Sura xxxiii. 53.
[10] See A. Jeffery in The Muslim World, October 1954, p. 256.

For the rest, his character seems, like that of many another, to have been a strange mixture. He was a poet rather than a theologian: a master improvisor rather than a systematic thinker. That he was in the main simple in his tastes and kindly in his disposition there can be no doubt; he was generous, resolute, genial and astute: a shrewd judge and a born leader of men. He could, however, be cruel and vindictive to his enemies; he could stoop to assassination; and he was undeniably sensual. It is true that the size of his harim pales to insignificance beside that of Solomon and compares not unfavourably with that of David; that his virtues outshone those of his contemporaries, while his failings can scarcely have provoked comment in his day and generation; and that he introduced a number of genuine reforms. If he had been taken by his followers at his own valuation in the Qur'an (which, while it asserts his prophetic dignity in no uncertain terms, contains some express allusions to his mortality[1] and imperfection[2]), adverse comment on his character would have been largely out of place. But the Traditions of his words and actions which soon assumed an importance second only in theory to the Qur'an itself gave birth to a very different conception, for they present him as something infinitely more than a mere vehicle or mouthpiece for the divine revelation. In words which are either put into his own mouth or regarded as addressed to him by God he is depicted as pre-existent ('I was a prophet when Adam was still between clay and water'); as the purpose of all creation ('Had it not been for thee I had not created the world'); and as the Perfect Man, the impeccable model on which all should mould their lives.[3] Such traditions are, of course, creations of a later date, invented by the Muslim community to put their Prophet on a par with the Christians' Christ. It is his misfortune rather than his fault, therefore, that it is with Him rather than with David or Solomon that he is habitually compared—for in such company he cannot stand.

5. *The Traditions*

It is, moreover, one of the paradoxes of Islam that a religion whose founder expostulated against the veneration given to Christ, and who

[1] Cf. Sura iii. 138, xxxix. 31, etc.
[2] Cf. Sura xviii. 110, xl. 57, xli. 5, xlvii. 21, xlviii. 2, lxxx. 1-10, etc.
[3] Cf. Sura xxxiii. 21. The ethical influence of this doctrine has been lamentable.

unequivocally asserted that he himself was a mere man, should have ended by advocating a slavish imitation of that founder's personal habits such as finds no parallel in Christianity or elsewhere. D. G. Hogarth justly remarks: 'Serious or trivial, his daily behaviour has instituted a Canon which millions observe to this day with conscious mimicry. No one regarded by any section of the human race as Perfect Man has been imitated so minutely.'[1] The well-known traditionalist, Ahmad ibn Hanbal (d. 241 A.H.), is said never to have eaten water melons because, although he knew the Prophet ate them, he could never ascertain whether he ate them with or without the rind, or whether he broke, bit or cut them.

In such circumstances it is no wonder that the collection of Traditions as to what the Prophet had said or done soon became a profession, and that men travelled all over the Muslim world to hear them from those to whom his scattered Companions had allegedly confided them. They were regarded as the uninspired record[2] of inspired words and actions, and were handed down from mouth to mouth by a long chain of narrators whose names were always recorded in the first part of the Tradition (the 'isnad') as a guarantee of the veracity of the subsequent subject matter (the 'matn'). From the first, however, fabricated Traditions flooded the market, one man alone confessing before his death that he had invented some four thousand; and every vagary of political, philosophical or theological thought sought support in some alleged statement of the Prophet. At a later date the Traditions were collected and arranged by the great Traditionalists, some of whom made strenuous efforts to separate the true from the spurious. Unfortunately, however, they confined their criticism to scrutinizing the trustworthiness of the names in the 'isnad' rather than the plausibility of the actual Tradition. Different collections are today accepted as authoritative by the different sects into which Islam has

[1] *A History of Arabia*, p. 52.

[2] Contrast the Qur'an, of which the most extreme form of verbal inspiration is asserted. It was written from eternity on the Preserved Tablet (Sura lxxxv. 22), whence it was sent down to the lowest heaven on the Night of Power (Laylat al Qadr: Sura xcvii. 1), to be revealed to the Prophet piecemeal as need arose (Sura xvii. 107, xxv. 34). Others, however, interpret Sura xcvii. 1 as meaning that the first revelation was vouchsafed to the Prophet on the Night of Power.

divided;[1] but in all cases such Traditions have taken their place beside the Qur'an as the primary source of Muslim theology, law and practice.[2] In addition, cheap collections of stories of the Prophet, some of very questionable propriety, still provide the popular religious literature of thousands.

6. His View of Christianity

Of the tenets of Christianity Muhammad seems to have had a very superficial, and in part wholly erroneous, knowledge. In his early life he was as favourably disposed to Christians as to Jews: and even in his later life they seem to have come under less severe strictures than the latter.[3] 'Isa', the Qur'anic name for Jesus, was the Messiah, was born of a Virgin and is called God's 'word' and 'a spirit from God'.[4] He was a great miracle worker and one of the greatest of the Prophets.[5] But the Qur'an depicts Him as expressly disclaiming deity and emphatically denies that He ever died on the cross:[6] instead, when the Jews sought to crucify Him, God caught Him up to heaven and threw His likeness on someone else who was crucified, by mistake, in His place.

It is interesting to speculate whence Muhammad came to hold such views. Whether he came into contact with an heretical Christian sect called the Collyridians who actually worshipped the Virgin, or merely misinterpreted the excessive veneration given her by some contemporary Christian groups, we shall probably never know. But there is no manner of doubt that he believed the Christian Trinity to consist of the Father, the Virgin and their Child. (Cf. the Ash'arite statement:

[1] The two most famous collections among the 'orthodox' are those of al Bukhari (d. 257 A.H.) and Muslim (d. 261 A.H.). The former, especially, is accorded a reverence almost equal to that of the Qur'an.

[2] A Tradition depicts Muhammad himself as having said 'What I have commanded to believers outside the Qur'an is equal in quality to the Qur'an itself, or even greater'. This is obviously spurious, but illuminating.

[3] The deterioration in his attitude to Christianity at al Madina may be explained as a reflection of his attitude to the Jews, as caused by the change in his own fortunes, or as representing his reaction to Monophysite as opposed to Nestorian theology. For Qur'anic references cf. ii. 59, v. 58, lvii. 27 (favourable); v. 21, ix. 29, 31 (unfavourable).

[4] Cf. Sura iv. 169, etc.

[5] For details, Muhammad's source was chiefly apocryphal works.

[6] Sura iv. 156. Other verses, such as iii. 48 and xix. 34, seem to suggest that He did die, as some (though not most) commentators admit.

'God is One God, Single, One, Eternal. . . . He has taken to Him-self no wife nor child,' and several verses in the Qur'an.[1]) It is not surprising, then, that he not only denounced the doctrine strongly but also repudiated the whole idea of the Sonship of Christ, understanding it as he did in terms of physical generation. Instead, the Qur'an depicts Christ as a Prophet whose followers had deified both Him and His mother against their will. Similarly, in his denial of the crucifixion, he may have been influenced by Gnostic views, by his hatred of the superstitious veneration, largely divorced from true theology or living experience, accorded to the symbol of the cross in seventh-century Arabia, or by his repugnance to believe that God would allow any prophet to come to such an end. He even believed that Christ had foretold the coming of another Prophet, Ahmad (a variant of Mu-hammad); and Muslims frequently maintain that Christians have changed this reference into the predictions of the Paraclete in the later part of St. John's Gospel.[2] The Traditions add that Christ is to come again, to marry and have children, to break the symbol of the cross, and to acknowledge Islam. In Muslim eschatology the second coming of Christ and the advent of the Mahdi[3] (the 'Guided') are inextricably mingled. There is much truth in J. T. Addison's summary: 'If Mu-hammad's knowledge of a decadent form of Christianity had been thorough, or if the Church which he knew so imperfectly had been stronger and sounder, the relations between the two religions might have been very different. As it was, however, what passed for Chris-tianity in his confused mind was a distorted copy of fragments of a notably defective original.'[4]

THE DEVELOPMENT OF ISLAM

The scope of the present chapter allows no space for a summary of the history of Islam after its founder's death. It is impossible, however, to understand the present divisions of Islam—the different Shi'i sects, the four Sunni schools, the Ibadis, etc.—without a passing reference to their origin, and to this we must now turn. It should, however,

---

[1] Cf. Sura v. 116 with iv. 169 and v. 77-79: also Sura xix. 35, xix. 91, cxii. 3.
[2] Some think that Sura lxi. 6 rests on a confusion between 'Paraklytos' and 'Periklutos', a possible Greek equivalent for 'Ahmad'.
[3] An eschatological figure who shall restore Islam in its purity and power.
[4] The Christian Approach to the Muslim, p. 18.

always be remembered that in Islam, as elsewhere, the adoption of sectarian views by ethnical and local groups has often been a mere expression in theological terms of an intense desire for freedom from foreign domination and for the preservation of exclusive traditions.

1. The Caliphate

Muhammad died, according to the best-supported view, without having designated any successor (Khalifa or Caliph). As the last and greatest of the Prophets he could not, of course, be replaced. But the community he had founded was a theocracy with no distinction between Church and State, and someone must clearly succeed, not to give but to enforce the law, to lead in war and to guide in peace. It was common ground, therefore, that a Caliph must be appointed: and in the event 'Umar ibn al Khattab (himself the second Caliph) succeeded in rushing the election of the aged Abu Bakr, one of the very first believers. But the question of the Caliphate was to cause more divisions and bloodshed than any other issue in Islam, and almost from the first three rival parties, in embryo at least, can be discerned. There were the Companions[1] of the Prophet, who believed in the eligibility of any suitable 'Early Believer' of the tribe of Quraysh; there was the aristocracy of Mecca, who wished to capture the Caliphate for the family of Umayya; and there were the 'legitimists', who believed that no election was needed, but that 'Ali, the cousin and son-in-law of the Prophet, had been divinely designated as his successor.

Abu Bakr's short rule of two years was chiefly noted for the 'Wars of Secession' and (traditionally at least) for the first compilation of the Qur'an. On the death of the Prophet many tribes had refused any longer to pay their dues, but Abu Bakr enforced obedience by the sword. It was, indeed, the death in battle of many of those who could recite the Qur'an from memory which is alleged to have convinced the Caliph of the necessity for reducing it to writing. On his death, Arabia had been consolidated for Islam and the principle of 'fighting in the way of God', denounced by the Prophet at Mecca but adopted with such signal success at al Madina, had become the watchword of the young Muslim state.

Before his death Abu Bakr designated 'Umar as his successor, and his election passed off without incident. He has been called the 'second

[1] Themselves at first subdivided into Meccan Emigrants and Madinese Helpers.

founder of Islam', for in his Caliphate Syria, Mesopotamia, Persia, and Egypt fell to the Muslim arms and many vital decisions were taken. He died without appointing a successor, and in the event 'Uthman was elected, himself an aged and pious 'Early Believer', but a scion of the aristocratic house of Umayya which had opposed the Prophet almost to the last. It was under his orders that the present recension of the Qur'an was prepared in 30 A.H. and all variant versions were destroyed. But his family proved his evil genius and he died by the assassin's knife.

2. The Kharijis

The first actual schism, however, occurred during the Caliphate of 'Ali, who succeeded 'Uthman as the fourth and last of the 'Orthodox' (or 'Rightly-Guided') Caliphs. Two leading Companions, Talha and al Zubayr, supported by the Prophet's widow 'A'isha, rose in revolt. They were beaten at the Battle of the Camel, where some ten thousand Muslims lost their lives—to the horror of the pious when they remembered that the Qur'an condemned to eternal damnation those who killed a brother Muslim without just cause. Soon, however, 'Ali had a much sterner foe to meet, for Mu'awiya, the Governor of Syria, marched against him on the plea of avenging the assassination of his kinsman 'Uthman, in whose death 'Ali was accused of complicity. At first 'Ali seemed again to be winning the day, but at the critical juncture of the battle Mu'awiya cunningly succeeded in inducing 'Ali to submit the question of the Caliphate to arbitration.

This deeply offended some of 'Ali's own followers, who held that this question should never be debated on such human terms: by his agreement to such a course 'Ali, they felt, had forfeited their allegiance. Still less, however, could they accord allegiance to Mu'awiya: so they seceded (kharaju) and held themselves apart from the body of apostate Islam (whence their name of Kharijis). Thenceforward they drifted, split into rival sects, and constituted a perpetual thorn in the side of all authority:[1] to them the remainder of the Muslim community was far worse than the Jews or Christians, for the latter were people of a divine Book, while the former were mere apostates who should pro-

---

[1] When beaten they retired, like true Bedouin, into the desert to recuperate. On one view they originated in those Arabs who opposed the predominance of the tribe of Quraysh; on another in the early Qur'an readers. Both theories may be in part correct.

E

perly be killed at sight. They held that the Caliph should be elected
on a basis of personal fitness, regardless of race or tribe; that the community should depose him if he went astray; that 'works' as well as
'faith' were necessary for salvation; and that one guilty of a mortal
sin ceased to be a believer. There were, however, many sub-sects.
Eventually they divided into two main divisions, the one more, the
other less, extreme: and the descendants of the moderate party, the
Ibadis, still survive in 'Uman, in East Africa, and among the Berbers[1]
of Algeria and Tripolitania, today distinguished by little more than
minor points of theology and law from the main body of Sunni (i.e.
'traditional' or orthodox) Islam.

3. The Shi'a

The vexed question of the Caliphate soon led, however, to a far more
important schism—that by which the whole body of the Shi'a (the
'followers' or 'sect' of 'Ali) broke off from Sunni Islam. To the existence of a legitimist party who regarded 'Ali as the divinely appointed
successor of the Prophet we have already referred; and such were
not deterred in their devotion when the ill-starred attempt at arbitration accomplished little, when 'Ali continued to dispute the Caliphate
with Mu'awiya until he died under a Khariji knife, or even when his
elder son al Hasan renounced his claim to succeed him in exchange
for a princely stipend and retired to end his life in dissipation at al
Madina. Instead they maintained that al Hasan had been poisoned by
order of Mu'awiya, accorded him the title of 'Lord of Martyrs', and
transferred their allegiance to his younger brother al Husayn. The latter
seems to have been made of somewhat better stuff: but when he rose
in opposition to Mu'awiya's son Yazid I, he was killed, with most
of his family, at Karbala'—a tragedy still commemorated each year
throughout the Shi'i world by the Passion Play of the 10th of Mu-
harram. The enormity of this butchery of the house of the Prophet,
however, rallied much support to Shi'i doctrines, and increasing numbers came to believe that God would never leave his people to impious
rulers but that there must always be some divinely chosen Imam, or
Leader; that 'Ali, so chosen, had been entrusted by the Prophet with
esoteric teaching as to the real meaning of Islam which he had passed
on to his descendants; and that after the death of al Husayn the office

---

[1] Who probably adopted this 'heresy' largely from racial particularism.

of Imam and infallible teacher had passed, as some held, to Muhammad, son of 'Ali by a wife of the Hanafiya tribe, or, as the majority
maintained, to 'Ali Zayn al 'Abidin, son of al Husayn and great-
grandson of the Prophet.

After the four orthodox Caliphs the Caliphate became hereditary in
the house of Umayya (41-132 A.H.) and Mu'awiya and his successors
ruled for the most part as Arab kings of the old pattern, paying but
scant allegiance to Islam.   In such circumstances Shi'i propaganda
prospered exceedingly, especially among the Persian 'clients'[1] (mawali),
who saw therein a way to escape from Arab arrogance and a doctrine
of the Imamate more compatible with their pre-Islamic attitude to
their kings.   A number of insurrections were put down, but Shi'i
supporters eventually played a considerable part in the downfall of
the Umayyad dynasty—only to find the throne seized, not for a descendant of 'Ali or the Prophet, but for those of the Prophet's uncle
'Abbas. Thus the Shi'a continued under the 'Abbasid dynasty (132-
656 A.H.) as a vast secret community, whose machinations came to the
surface periodically in bloody rebellions, but who were continually
weakened by their tendency to split into innumerable sub-sects. They
split chiefly on the line of succession to the Imamate. Some, like the
Kaysanis and Hashimis, held that it might pass to any child of 'Ali
(e.g. Muhammad ibn al Hanafiya); others, like the Zaydis, held that
any descendant of al Hasan or al Husayn might duly establish himself; but the more general view, shared by the 'Twelvers'[2] and the
Isma'ilis, was that the Imamate passed from father to son in the line
of al Husayn by a special form of transmission of a divine light-
substance. But they differed, also, as to the nature of the Imamate. To
the Zaydis the Imam was not supernatural but could give authoritative
teaching; the 'Twelvers' went further, and believed in the infusion of
a divine light-substance in the person of the Imam which made him
infallible and impeccable; while the Isma'ilis went further still and,
at least in their more extreme sub-sects, believed in a partial incarnation of the Deity either in one individual or, more commonly, in a
succession of Imams.

But this did not exhaust their differences. Another fruitful cause

[1] On conversion to Islam these Persians were attached to Arab tribes in the
subordinate position of the pre-Islamic client (originally either a stranger
attached to the tribe or an ex-slave).

[2] For the origin of this name see below. The Arabic is Ithna 'Ashariya.

of division was their concept of the Mahdi. Periodically, in most of the Shi'i sects, men would become so attached to one Imam that they would refuse to believe that he had died; instead, he had only gone into hiding, whence he would one day re-emerge to bring in the Golden Age: others in the same sect, meanwhile, would transfer their allegiance to his successor. Sometimes the true explanation of this phenomenon seems to have been the intrigues of a series of adventurers who used the house of 'Ali as cats'-paws, and themselves acted in the name of the 'hidden' Imam; at others the prudence of the Holy Family, who frequently refused the danger of leading those insurrections for which their followers seem to have been always ready.

The chief branches of the Shi'a found today are the Zaydis of the Yemen, the 'Twelvers' of Persia and Iraq, and the Isma'ilis (or 'Seveners') of India, Syria, and East Africa. The Zaydis, who are the most moderate of the Shi'a, take their name from al Husayn's grandson Zayd, who rose against the Umayyad Caliph Hisham and was killed in 122 A.H. The Isma'ilis and the 'Twelvers' trace the Imamate not through Zayd, but his brother, Muhammad al Baqir: the former to Isma'il,[1] son of Ja'far al Sadiq, and his son Muhammad; and the latter through Musa'l Kazim, brother of Isma'il, to a certain Muhammad ibn al Hasan,[2] who vanished in about 260 A.H. but is regarded as still alive, as communicating his teaching to his leading divines (who, unlike the Sunnis, still claim the right of ijtihad[3]), and as the Imam-Mahdi of the future. This is the state religion of Persia, where the Shah is regarded officially as his 'locum tenens'. But the strangest story in Muslim history is that of the Isma'ilis, among whom secret ('batini' or 'inner') teaching was carried to fantastic lengths. Emissaries were sent far and wide to make capital out of any anti-Government feeling, out of social and economic unrest, racial anipathies, or any form of scepticism. To the Kharijis their teaching was represented as Khariji, to the Shi'is as Shi'i, and to Persian nationalists as anti-Arab. Their technique seems to have been to excite doubt; to stress the need for an authoritative teacher; and to impose an oath of secrecy and implicit obedience. Initiates were passed, where suitable, through several grades, above the fourth of which, it seems, a mystic

[1] The seventh in their line of Imams, whence the term 'Seveners'.
[2] The twelfth in their line of Imams, whence their name.
[3] See below, p. 71.

philosophy took the place of orthodox Islam. To this movement or conspiracy can ultimately be traced, through varying developments, the Qarmatians, who dominated Iraq at the end of the third century A.H., practised a form of Communism, and scandalized the Muslim world by carrying off the black meteorite from the Ka'ba at Mecca; the Fatimid dynasty, which ruled Egypt for so long; the Druzes of the Lebanon, who still worship as God al Hakim, one of the Fatimids of Egypt; the Assassins, who terrorized Syria and Iraq from their fortresses in the times of the Crusades and to whose last Grand Master of Alamut the Agha Khan traces his descent today; the Nusayris or 'Alawites of Northern Syria, who deify 'Ali; and those rather shadowy figures of history, the Ikhwan al Safa.[1]

Many of these sects are (or were) a law unto themselves, and to their beliefs no further reference can be made. The great majority of the Shi'a, however, fully accept the Qur'an, though they often differ from the Sunnis in its interpretation and even accuse the Caliph 'Uthman of having suppressed a number of verses favourable to 'Ali, and the authority of the Traditions, though they reject the Sunni collections in favour of their own. In matters of faith and practice the differences between the two main divisions of Islam are considerable: but for the remainder of this article it will be necessary to confine our attention, in the main, to the Sunnis, who not only greatly preponderate in numbers, but can also fairly be regarded as the more natural representatives of the central stream of Muslim thought.

4. *The Four Sunni Schools*

It was not only about the Caliphate that controversy raged. The eternal conflict between the disciples of reason and of tradition has also been bitterly waged in Islam, both in law and theology; and it is partly to this conflict that the development of the four orthodox schools of jurisprudence into which Sunni Islam is now divided owe their origin in the early 'Abbasid period. Such are the Hanafi or Iraq school, whose traditional founder was Abu Hanifa (died 150 A.H.), and which is followed today throughout most of the old Ottoman Empire and Northern India[2]; the Maliki or Hijaz school, which derives

---

[1] A group which flourished at Basra in the middle of the fourth century A.H. and endeavoured to construct a universal system of religious philosophy. Their encyclopædic 'Epistles' (fifty in number) exercised a widespread influence.

[2] This is by far the most numerous school.

its name from Malik ibn Anas (died 179 A.H.) and which prevails in North and West Africa, Upper Egypt, and the Sudan; the Shafi'i school, founded by al Shafi'i, the founder of Muslim jurisprudence[1] (died 204 A.H.), which is followed in Lower Egypt, East Africa, Southern Arabia, and South-East Asia; and the Hanbali school, which is named after the great traditionalist Ahmad ibn Hanbal, and whose few modern followers are chiefly limited to the Wahhabis of Central Arabia.

In course of time a bitter conflict developed between the speculative jurists, as their opponents considered the Hanafi school, and the traditionalists, a term claimed by all other schools—although they varied considerably in the degree to which they deserved it.[2] In reality the conflict had not developed in the time of Abu Hanifa and Malik, and the somewhat greater dependence of the latter on tradition and the former on speculation in constructing their systems can be adequately explained by the fact that Malik lived in the very city and milieu of the Prophet, whereas Abu Hanifa in Iraq had to deal with situations for which there was no Prophetic precedent. Even so, however, Malik (in company with all the earlier jurists) felt free to follow his own opinion or appreciation of public welfare when circumstances required. But this was just what the extreme traditionalists sought to exclude, for they held that human reason could not even deduce general rules from specific commands or prohibitions unless the revealed texts themselves indicated the underlying principle ('illa): man must not reason but obey. It was the dominant influence of al Shafi'i which secured the eventual triumph of a middle course which recognized the overriding authority of 'authentic' Traditions from the Prophet but fully accepted the need for extending the divine texts by carefully defined rules of analogy to cover the ever-changing eventualities of daily life. In reality, of course, both customary law, administrative practice, and the early jurists' sense of equity, expediency, and the 'spirit of the law' were major elements in the early development of the Shari'a (as the divinely authoritative law of Islam is called), however much later jurists sought to conceal this fact behind a façade of unhistorical traditions or a convenient doctrine which grew up concerning the inerrancy and binding force of the 'agreement' of the Muslim com-

[1] Article on Usul by J. Schacht in *Encyclopaedia of Islam.*
[2] Strictest of all were the Zahiris, a school of complete literalists which has since disappeared; next the Hanbalis; then the Shafi'is; then the Malikis.

munity.[1] Eventually, however, all four schools came to accept the Qur'an, the Sunna or practice of the Prophet (as preserved in the Traditions), the Ijma' or agreement of the Muslim community, and Qiyas or analogical deduction from these three, as the four main sources of the law—although the Hanafis in particular championed the right to depart on occasions from the conclusion to which a rigid application of analogy would lead in favour of a solution which they 'considered for the better'.[2]

All four surviving schools are now accepted as orthodox by Sunni Islam and in theory any Muslim may adhere to whichever he likes,[3] although in practice his choice will largely depend on where he happens to live. Most authorities now consider, moreover, that he may elect to follow one school in one particular and another in another— which may be a matter of considerable convenience. For centuries, however, this right, if it existed, was seldom exercised, and for the most part a Muslim, having chosen his school, was bound by its tenets in all particulars. In no case, moreover, could he go back to the original sources of the law and re-interpret them: this right, known as 'ijtihad', was regarded as having lapsed for centuries, and its place had been taken by the duty of 'taqlid', or accepting the rulings, down to the utmost minutiae, of a long series of successive jurists. Today, however, Muslim modernists are striving to free themselves from this bondage, and recent legislation in Egypt and several other countries concerning wills, inheritance, endowments, marriage and divorce has been based on an eclectic principle of adopting whatever jurist's views seem, in each particular, most suited to modern needs.[4]

5. The Mu'tazila

The same conflict between reason and tradition was waged even more bitterly in the realm of theology. As early as the beginning of the second century of the Muslim era we find a tolerably definite group of thinkers known as the Mu'tazila, who dissented from the traditional views and applied the solvent of reason to the dogmas of the Qur'an.

---

[1] 'My people will never agree upon an error', the Prophet was ultimately alleged to have said.

[2] Istihsan. Cf. the Maliki istislah, etc.

[3] 'The disagreement of my people is a mercy from God,' is the traditional saying of the Prophet quoted in this context.

[4] Space forbids fuller treatment of this very interesting phenomenon.

They held that there was an intermediate state between belief and infidelity (and thus between bliss and doom). As the spiritual heirs of the still earlier Qadaris they upheld the freedom of the human will and denied that God predestined man's evil and unbelief; and they held that God must of necessity act in accordance with justice and always do what was best for His creatures.[1] The orthodox, on the other hand, denied any intermediate state and held that all man's actions were decreed from eternity on the 'Preserved Tablet': there could be no necessity upon God even to do justice, and whatever He did man must unquestioningly accept. More, they denied the very basis of human speculation, for they taught that man could not perceive or distinguish good and evil by the intellect: good and evil derived their nature solely from God's will and could be known only by His commands and prohibitions. There could be no theology or ethics, therefore, apart from revelation.

Yet another subject of debate concerned the nature of the Godhead. The Qur'an frequently makes use of anthropomorphic expressions: God is visible to some, at least, in the next world; He settles Himself firmly on His throne; He stretches out His arm, etc. Among the Mu'tazila all such expressions were explained away, and God was conceived as the most transcendent of Spirits: but the orthodox replied that the Qur'anic statements must be accepted as they stood ('bila kayfa': 'without asking how') and neither explained away nor carried to their logical conclusion.[2] Again, controversy raged around the question of the relation between the divine Attributes (knowing, willing, speaking, etc.) and the divine Essence—and the kindred dispute as to whether the Qur'an was created or eternal. The Mu'tazila held that the Attributes were not *in* the divine Essence, and thus in a sense separable, but *were* the divine Essence: as for the Qur'an, this was clearly created, for any other conclusion would involve making the Qur'an into a second God. To such arguments the orthodox replied that the Attributes were neither identical with the Essence nor distinct from it ('Not It, nor other than It'—an attitude which bears certain

[1] Partly for this reason they called themselves the 'people of Unity and Justice'. The 'Unity' refers to the controversy, mentioned in the next paragraph, concerning the divine Attributes.

[2] The view here attributed to the 'orthodox' was in fact the *via media* between the Mu'tazila on the one hand and the extreme literalists or 'anthropomorphists', of whom there were many, on the other.

striking resemblances to the Christian doctrine of the Trinity, particularly as developed by John of Damascus and other Greek theologians
whose influence on Muslim thought has never received adequate attention): as for the Qur'an, its inscription and recitation might be created
but its meanings were eternal, being none other than that divine Speech
which was one of God's eternal Attributes. In this the influence of the
Christian doctrine of the Logos is obvious.

But the Mu'tazila were never popular with the masses. For the most
part they were regarded as heretics, sometimes persecuted and sometimes protected by constitutional authority. In the event it was an
evil day for them when the Caliph al Ma'mun tried to enforce their
views by law and penalize all non-conformity. This decision was
reversed by a subsequent Caliph, but the harm was done: the traditionalist Ahmad ibn Hanbal, who had refused either to recant or even
argue but contented himself with repeating Qur'anic texts and 'true'
Traditions, won almost universal support. As time went on, moreover,
the Mu'tazila retired more and more into barren scholasticism, a fate
which Prof. D. B. Macdonald says has fallen on all continued efforts
of the Muslim mind.[1]

6. The Philosophers

Their place as the champions of reason was taken by the philosophers:
al Kindi, al Farabi, Ibn Sina, Ibn Rushd, and their like. These men
seem for the most part to have started from the position of sincere
Muslims, but they also wholeheartedly accepted Greek philosophy,
with all its contradictory theories, as part of the very form of truth.
Their fundamental attitude was simple enough. The Qur'an was truth;
Plato and Aristotle had both expounded the truth: the Qur'an and
philosophy, therefore, whether Platonic or Aristotelian, must all be
reconcilable. So to reconcile them they set out, with unconquerable
spirit: and it was largely through these men that the philosophy and
learning of ancient Greece was preserved and re-introduced into
Europe.

7. The Scholastic Theologians

But parallel with the later development of Mu'tazili views there also
grew up among the orthodox a party who were no longer content

[1] Cf. Development of Muslim Theology, Jurisprudence and Constitutional History,
pp. 158-9, to which my debt will be obvious.

to assert that the statements of the Qur'an must be accepted as they
stood and that any questioning was 'bid'a' (innovation): instead, they
came to use 'kalam' (argument) in order to meet the 'kalam' of the
unorthodox. It was thus that the scholastic theology of Islam was
born. The system must, of course, have been of gradual growth: but
the chief credit has traditionally been given to al Ash'ari (died *c.* 320
A.H.). Brought up as a Mu'tazili and maintaining their views till he
was about forty years old, he then swung over to the other side—and
opposed at once the rationalism of the Mu'tazila and the gross anthro-
pomorphisms of the more extreme Hanbalis. As developed by his
followers, the Ash'ari system was the application to theology of an
extreme atomic metaphysic.[1] Space to them was made up of a multitude of monads each of which has position, not bulk, and is separated
from the next by absolute void; and they conceived of time as being
similarly composed of a multitude of unrelated time monads. Any idea
of causation they utterly rejected. They were compelled, however,
to find some explanation of the harmony and apparent connection
between one thing and another discernible in the world: and this they
found in the will of God, absolutely free and untrammelled by any
laws or necessities, which continually creates and annihilates the atoms
and their qualities and thus produces all motion and all change. A
man sees a beautiful flower; he decides to pick it; he stretches out
his hand, plucks it, and smells it. But this chain of causation is apparent
only. In reality, God at each moment creates and recreates the atoms
of the man's mind, of his hand, of the flower, and of his nose in such
a way as to create the thought, the apparent motion and the result:
there is no mutual connection either of space or time except in the
mind of God and by the continual exercise of His creative power. On
such a basis human free will is neither more nor less than the presence,
in the mind of man, of a choice created there by God; there is no
order in the universe, and the distinction between miracles and what
are normally regarded as the ordinary operations of nature virtually
disappears. The sun does not warm, nor water wet: all that can be
said is that God creates in a substance a being warmed (if He so wills)
when exposed to the sun, and a being wet when submerged in water.

This system seems to have reached tolerably complete form by the
beginning of the fifth century A.H. For long it was bitterly opposed

[1] Cf. D. B. Macdonald, *Development of Muslim Theology*, pp. 202 ff., on
which this section is largely based.

by the Hanbalis, while, as a *via media*, it was unpopular with the liberals also. Persecutions broke out, and the Ash'ari doctors were scattered to the winds. The reaction, however, was not long in coming and the influence of al Ghazzali (died 505 A.H.) firmly established Ash'ari views as the dominant school of Sunni orthodoxy, although the slightly more liberal school of al Maturidi still claims its adherents. Essentially, however, the Ash'ari teaching may be regarded as a vast negative, for it uses reason and logic to demonstrate the barrenness of both. Philosophy cannot even establish a chain of causation, so how can it arrive at any valid conclusion about the nature and attributes of God and the moral duties of man? For any knowledge of such matters man is entirely dependent on divine revelation, whether prophetic, through tradition, or direct, through the mystic's 'inner light'. The profound hold exercised by the former in Islam we have already noticed; and it is to the latter that we must now turn.

8. The Mystics

Mysticism seems to have found some place in Islam from the very first. Muhammad himself, although in most ways one of the least mystical of men, was strongly drawn at times to solitude and fasting: and it was along the line of asceticism, of renunciation of the world and its evils, that mysticism first made itself felt in the religion he founded. There was much to encourage such an attitude in the influence of Christian hermits scattered about Arabia; in the development of that fear of Hell fundamental to primitive Islam; and in the withdrawal of the pious first from the obvious godlessness of some of the Umayyad Caliphs and then from the very limited piety of the Abbasids. From an early date, therefore, it must have been a comparatively common sight to see some wandering ascetic surrounded by his disciples, all dressed in the simple woollen garment from which the mystics or 'Sufis' of Islam ultimately derived their name.

But mysticism soon began to develop along more speculative and philosophical lines. In this development it owed much to the Greek Church; a good deal to Persian and, indeed, Indian influences; but most of all to Plotinus and the neo-Platonists.[1] It was only by refuge in mysticism that the Muslim philosopher could reconcile the crudities of the Qur'an with the abstractions of Greek philosophy; that the scholastic theologian could find any escape (other than that of blind

[1] Probably reaching Islam largely through Christian channels.

obedience to Tradition) from the utter negation of Ash'ari metaphysics; and that the ordinary Sunni Muslim could find any poetry
or warmth in his religion. When the scholastic theologians had
done their work, the orthodox were left with no 'natural laws', no
chain of causation, and no possibility of theology or ethics except
in the revealed will of God. They must either be content to rely
utterly on the prophetic revelation of the Qur'an and the Traditions,
or they must supplement them by that 'minor inspiration' which, the
Sufis asserted, God continuously vouchsafed to those who truly sought
Him. And to this the true Sufi steadfastly gave himself. He believed
that the human soul had in it some spark of the divine, however im-
prisoned in the world of sense; that the human heart was the mirror,
albeit dimmed and blurred, of the Deity. It was the mystic's duty,
then, to wean himself from the world of sense; to cleanse this mirror,
and direct it to God alone: he would then receive divine enlightenment. But chiefly to the Muslim it was in ecstasy that the mystic
received his revelations. A whole science developed as to how a state
of ecstasy could be induced; and a man's piety was judged not by his
holiness of life but by the degree and frequency of his ecstatic states,
for only in ecstasy did he realize his complete oneness with God.

For centuries, however, the mystics were regarded with suspicion
by the orthodox. Nor was this strange, for there was much excess.
Emphasis on the spirit rather than the letter of the law led many to
laxity not only of ritual but of morals: as so often in Islam, there was
one law for the enlightened and another for the vulgar. Others were
not content to claim divine enlightenment: they claimed the very
fusion and union of their beings with God. For them the transcen-
dental God of orthodox Islam was deposed, to be replaced by the Only
Reality of the Pantheist.[1] Perhaps the most famous of these extremists
was al Hallaj, who was put to death with great cruelty in 309 A.H.
for claiming 'I am the Truth'.[2] It needed the immense influence of al
Ghazzali to secure the acceptance of the mystic way within the fold
of orthodox Islam.

Later, there grew up the great Dervish Orders which are such a
feature of Islam today. The Sufi principle of blind obedience of pupil

[1] Even the central dogma of Islam, the divine Unity, was interpreted by
the Sufis as denying any reality outside God.
[2] This is the reason traditionally given for his execution, although the real
reason may well have been political.

to master became increasingly emphasized, and in course of time the group no longer broke up on the master's death but formed a lasting fraternity. Each Order traces its origin back to some famous saint whose miraculous powers are held to descend, in some degree, to his successors, and is made up both of professional dervishes and of non-professional adherents who visit the monasteries with greater or less regularity and take their part in the 'dhikr', or that form of repetition of the name of God adopted by the particular Order to induce a state of ecstasy. Membership of such fraternities is exceedingly common in Muslim countries today, even, to some extent, among the professional classes.

The vast majority of the common people in all Muslim lands, moreover, believe implicitly not only in the miraculous powers of living holy men ('murabits', heads of Sufi orders, etc.), from whose prayers, touch, breath and saliva virtue (or 'baraka') is derived, but also in those of dead saints whose tombs they visit and whose intercession they implore. Under cover of this cult of saints much pre-Islamic animism has been retained in Islam. Stones and trees which were worshipped in pagan days are now commonly connected with some prophet or saint, but the ancient ritual is largely preserved: thus pieces of the clothing of the sick or barren are still attached to the tree in the belief that some of the 'soul-stuff' resident therein will thereby be transferred to the suppliant. Similarly, relics of holy men and charms of all sorts are in constant demand, as protection against the evil-eye, against the jinn, and especially against the genie- (or devil-) mate[1] which is believed to dog the footsteps of every mortal. In popular Islam the pure monotheism of the creed has been diluted with a wealth of animistic survivals, some sanctioned by the Prophet and some plainly contrary to his teaching, which still hold multitudes of simple people in the bondage of fear, taboos, and financial exploitation. To gain protection, healing, fertility, etc., the aid is also regularly invoked of a whole hierarchy of saints, led by the Qutb[2] (or 'Axis', i.e. greatest living saint)

---

[1] The 'qarin' or 'qarina' (see Sura xli. 24, Sura. l. 22, 26, etc.). This mate is regarded as malignant, jealous, the cause of physical and moral ill, of hatred between spouses, barrenness, miscarriage, etc.—except when frustrated by religion or magic.

[2] His two favourite haunts, it seems, are the Ka'ba at Mecca and one of the city gates in Cairo, on which shreds of the clothing of petitioners can always be found. Elsewhere the Ghawth (Succourer) is regarded as the chief, and the term Qutb used for the next grade in the hierarchy.

and his various grades of lieutenants, who periodically hold a sort of mystic parliament, untrammelled by space or time.

THE FAITH AND PRACTICE OF SUNNI ISLAM

The faith and practice of Islam are governed by the two great branches of Muslim learning, theology and jurisprudence, to both of which some reference has already been made. Muslim theology (usually called 'Tawhid' from its central doctrine of the Unity of the Godhead) defines all that a man should believe, while the law (Shari'a) prescribes everything that he should do. There is no priesthood and no sacraments. Except among the Sufis, Islam knows only exhortation and instruction from those who consider themselves, or are considered by others, adequately learned in theology or law.

Unlike any other system in the world today the Shari'a embraces every detail of human life, from the prohibition of crime to the use of the toothpick, and from the organization of the State to the most sacred intimacies—or unsavoury aberrations—of family life. It is 'the science of all things, human and divine', and divides all actions into what is obligatory or enjoined, what is praiseworthy or recommended, what is permitted or legally indifferent, what is disliked or deprecated, and what is forbidden. The Muslim may certainly consult his lawyer[1] as to what he may do without incurring any legal penalty: but he may also consult him as a spiritual adviser as to whether acts of which other systems of law take no cognisance are praiseworthy or blameworthy before God. Until recently the pride and power of the 'Ulama', or doctors of the law, was enormous, and this is still true to some degree today. The whole science of law is known as 'fiqh' and formed for centuries the primary study of the pious Muslim.

1. The Articles of Faith

In Islam no official redaction of the articles of faith ('aqa'id) has ever existed, though much has been written on the subject. For our purpose, however, the summary attributed by tradition to the Prophet himself can conveniently be adopted, that a Muslim must believe 'in God, and His Angels, and His Books, and His Messengers, and in the Last Day, and . . . in the Decree both of good and evil'.

[1] In most Muslim countries there is also an official called the Mufti, whose function it is to give legal opinions (fatwas) to individual applicants, to the government, or to the judges of the Shari'a courts (the Qadis).

The importance attached to the doctrine of God can be easily seen from the space allotted to this subject in any Muslim treatise on theology. The fundamental concept is His Unity; and most of the finest passages in the Qur'an are concerned with this subject. In orthodox Islam, however, this concept has been pressed to logical—but unreal—lengths in the doctrines of 'mukhalafa' (difference) and 'tanzih' (removal). By the former, God is declared to be so different from His creatures that it becomes virtually impossible to postulate anything of Him (He has styled Himself the Merciful, for instance, but this quality need have no connection with the human concept of mercy); while the latter so strips Him of all qualities of impermanence and so emphasizes His self-sufficiency as to deny that He can in any way be affected by the actions or attitude of His creatures. As we have seen, moreover, the God of orthodox Islam maintains the whole creation in being, moment by moment, by a continual miracle: even the impression of choice present to the mind of men is His creation. He is the source of both good and evil; His will is supreme, untrammelled by any laws or principles, whatever they may be; whom He will He forgives, and whom He will He punishes.[1] His nature and qualities are chiefly revealed in His ninety-nine 'most beautiful Names', frequently repeated by the pious as they finger their rosaries:[2] some of these names are constantly on all Muslim lips, whether in prayer, salutation, bargaining or swearing, while others are regularly used as charms and talismans.

A belief in Angels is absolutely enjoined on the Muslim: he who denies them is an infidel. Orthodox Islam acknowledges four Archangels (Jibril or Gabriel, the messenger of revelation—much confused with the Holy Spirit; Mika'il or Michael, the guardian of the Jews; Israfil, the summoner to resurrection; and 'Izra'il, the messenger of death) and an indefinite number of ordinary angels. They are created of light, do not eat or drink or propagate their species, and are characterized by absolute obedience to the will of God. Two Recording Angels attend on every man: the one on his right records his good deeds, and the one on his left his sins. There are also two angels called

[1] The Muslim God can best be understood in the desert. Its vastness, majesty, ruthlessness and mystery—and the resultant sense of the utter insignificance of man—call forth man's worship and submission, but scarcely prompt his love or suggest God's.

[2] In popular Islam the rosary is regularly used (a) as an aid to prayer, (b) as a talisman to indicate whether some proposed action is propitious (istikhara), and (c) as a magical agency for healing.

Munkar and Nakir, who visit every newly buried corpse in the grave. Making the corpse sit up, these angels examine it in the faith: if the replies are satisfactory it is allowed to sleep in peace, but if it does not confess the Apostle they beat it severely, some say until the day of resurrection. Animals are said to hear its cries, although mortals cannot.

Between angels and men there are also a multitude of creatures called jinn. These are created of smokeless flame, eat and drink, propagate their species, and are capable of both belief and unbelief. Muhammad was sent to them as well as to men, and good jinn now perform all the religious duties of Muslims.[1] The disbelieving jinn—who are often called 'afarit, shayatin,[2] etc.—were turned out of the first three heavens when Jesus was born, and out of the last four when Muhammad was born: they still, however, sometimes go eavesdropping to the lowest heaven, whence they occasionally pass on information to human magicians; but they are chased away by the angels with shooting stars if observed.[3] Reference has already been made to the qarina or shaytan[4] which is believed to dog every mortal's footsteps and tempt to evil. The jinn often appear as animals, reptiles, etc., or in human form. Frequently, moreover, a human being will be 'possessed' by one of them—as all poets and soothsayers were held to be; and in such circumstances relief is frequently sought in exorcism, particularly by the incense, dance and sacrifice of the Zar ritual.[5] The Devil (Iblis or al Shaytan) is normally regarded as a fallen angel, or jinn, who disobeyed God's command to the angels to do homage to Adam. He is now the arch-tempter of mankind and the chief of the shaytans, 'ifrits, and all evil jinn.

Orthodox Islam is divided as to how many prophets there have been: some say 124,000, some 248,000, and some an indefinite number. The Qur'an names twenty-eight: most are biblical,[6] while two (Luqman and Dhu'l Qarnayn) have been generally identified with Aesop and

---

[1] See Sura lxxii. 1, 2, 15, 16 and elsewhere, as well as many Traditions.

[2] Sing.: 'ifrit, shaytan.

[3] Sura lxxii. 8, 9, etc.

[4] Devil-mate, see p. 77.

[5] This is purely animistic in origin but is now practised throughout a great part of the Muslim world, particularly among women. Pamphlets have, however, been written against it by the learned.

[6] Including Sulayman (Solomon), who is credited with having attained an extraordinary power over the jinn and animals. He is thus virtually regarded as the patron-saint of 'white' magic of all sorts.

Alexander the Great respectively. Some three hundred and thirteen of these prophets are named Apostles, and the six greatest brought new dispensations: such are Adam, Noah, Abraham, Moses, 'Isa (Jesus), and Muhammad.[1]

Among them these prophets brought some hundred and four divine books. A hundred of these, of minor length, were vouchsafed to Adam, Seth, Enoch, and Abraham, but are now lost; while of the four major Scriptures the Law was 'sent down' to Moses, the Psalms to David, the Gospel to Jesus, and the Qur'an[2] to Muhammad. All originally corresponded to a heavenly prototype and all comprised the same central message.[3] To the allegation that the Jews subsequently corrupted their Scriptures we have already referred, and the same charge is brought against Christians by way of explanation of the New Testament references to the deity and cross of Christ, and other doctrines denied by Islam.[4]

The last day (the resurrection and the judgment) figures prominently in Muslim thought. The day and hour is a secret to all, but there are to be twenty-five signs of its approach. All men will then be raised; the books kept by the recording angels will be opened; and God as judge will weigh each man's deeds in the balances. Some will be admitted to Paradise, where they will recline on soft couches quaffing cups of wine handed them by the Huris, or maidens of Paradise, of whom each man may marry as many as he pleases:[5] others will be consigned to the torments of Hell. Almost all,[6] it would seem, will have to enter the fire temporarily, but no true Muslim will remain there for ever. Other Traditions picture a bridge as sharp as a sword

---

[1] Islam has come to believe in the impeccability ('isma) of all Prophets—but against the plain teaching of the Qur'an.

[2] Not only bibliolatry but bibliomancy flourishes in popular Islam. The Qur'an must only be touched by the ritually pure; certain chapters are of special power against sickness and demons; and extracts are used for every sort of charm.

[3] Cf. Sura xxvi. 195 f., iii. 75, vi. 92, xxxv. 28, xlvi. 11, etc.

[4] Cf. Sura ii. 141, iii. 64. Also cf. v. 116, 117.

[5] These are distinguished from such mortal women as shall attain Paradise (whose position and marital delights are shrouded in obscurity) by most commentators, although some suggest that virtuous wives become Huris hereafter. For the Huris see Sura xliv. 54, lv. 56, 58, 70-74, lvi. 34-36. Cf. also Sura ii. 23, iii. 13, iv. 60.

[6] Except martyrs, and some others.

F

over the pit, from which infidels' feet will slip so that they fall into the Fire, while the feet of Muslims will stand firm.[1]

Finally, a Muslim is required to believe in God's Decrees. As we have already seen, the orthodox belief is that everything—good or evil —proceeds directly from the divine will, being irrevocably recorded on the Preserved Tablet. While the Mu'tazila and others have challenged this view there is much to support it in the Qur'an, although other passages certainly assume the moral responsibility of mankind; and the fatalism to which this cast-iron view of Predestination logically leads plays a large part in the daily lives of millions of Muslims. To this the lethargy and lack of progress which, until recently at least, has for centuries characterized Muslim countries can be partially attributed.

The Shari'a, as we have seen, covers an exceedingly wide field and no systematic division was ever reached. Sunni Muslims sometimes classify it into obligations regarding worship ('ibadat), obligations of a civil and personal nature (mu'amalat), and punishments ('uqubat). Only a very sketchy treatment will be possible here and we shall confine our attention to the main religious observances, to such fundamental social institutions as marriage, divorce, and slavery, and to a few representative crimes.

2. *The Five Pillars*

The religious observances of Islam include the 'Five Pillars' (or foundations) of religion: i.e. the recital of the Creed, Prayer, Fasting, Almsgiving, and the Pilgrimage. The Creed (Kalima) is a simple one: 'There is no God but God, and Muhammad is the Prophet of God'— but disputes have arisen as to what its proper recital involves. The more exacting require that it be recited aloud at least once; that it be understood with the mind and believed in the heart; that it be recited correctly and professed without hesitation; and that it be held until death. To the majority of Muslims, however, a mere recital of the creed is enough to enroll a new convert in the ranks of Islam; and any more stringent requirement is left to divine omniscience.[2]

---

[1] Muslim eschatology is a curious hotch-potch of Jewish, Christian and animistic legends and folklore.
[2] The creed—the shortest in the world—is repeated by Muslims many ti[?] a day in every sort of context.

Ritual prayer plays a big part in the life of a devout Muslim. He is required to pray five times a day at stated hours, and in this many are most faithful. He may pray alone, in company, or in a mosque; but he must pray in Arabic and must follow a set form of words and a strictly prescribed ritual of stances, genuflexions and prostrations which differs slightly as between the four orthodox schools. Particularly important is the congregational prayer at noon on Fridays, attendance at which is incumbent on all adult male Muslims who live in a sufficiently large community. This service includes a weekly sermon; but the Muslim Friday is not prescribed as a day of rest. Prayer is valueless, however, unless offered in a state of ritual purity,[1] so the law books contain detailed rules concerning the different forms of purification (wudu' and ghusl), when each is required and how it must be performed.[2] It may also be remarked that to the Muslim there is little connection between prayer and ethics: a man who rises from prayer to cheat will be rewarded for the prayer and punished for the cheating, but the one is commonly regarded as having little or no bearing on the other.

During the month of Ramadan (the ninth month of the Muslim year) all Muslims except the sick, travellers, pregnant women, nursing mothers and young children are required to fast from first dawn until sunset. This involves complete abstention from all forms of food, drink, smoking or sexual intercourse. As the Muslim year is lunar, the fast sometimes falls at mid-summer, when the long days and the intense heat make complete abstention, especially from water, a severe ordeal. On the whole, however, it is rigidly observed, especially

[1] Muslim prayer—at least in its prescribed form—seems to partake more of the nature of a continual acknowledgement of God's sovereignty than of communion with Him. This is shown (*inter alia*) by the insistence on ritual purity and the use of Arabic, an unknown tongue to three-fourths of the Muslim world.

[2] The basic idea, it seems, is not the virtue of physical cleanliness, but the need for cleansing from demon pollution. This has been brought out by Wensinck and Goldziher. The fact that the passing of the hands over one's sandals may often be substituted for washing the feet supports this view. To a similar preoccupation with demons may be traced the use of some object as a 'Sutra' (that which covers or protects) to mark off the place of prayer ('It protects from the demons': Muslim's *Sahih*, p. 193); certain regulations about the position of the fingers and the covering of the back of the head during prayer and about the exact times of prayer; and parts of the ritual followed in the special prayers for rain, etc. See *The Influence of Animism on Islam*, by S. M. Zwemer, pp. 43-65.

among the lower classes; and even if the more sophisticated often break their fast in secret, the majority observe it outwardly. The fast is much esteemed as inculcating both self-control and sympathy with the poor and destitute; but it may be observed in passing that the average family spends nearly twice as much in Ramadan on the food they consume by night as in any other month on the food they eat by day. It is probably the consequent curtailment of sleep as much as the rigours of fasting which has such a marked effect on the general output of work during Ramadan.

The emphasis Muhammad put on Almsgiving is among the best points in the religion of Islam, although it has inevitably encouraged the indigent in Muslim lands (for whom, it must be added, no other provision is normally made). Himself an orphan, the Prophet felt keenly for the destitute and needy. The legal alms enjoined on the Muslim are, however, less than the Jewish tithe, being limited to one-fortieth of money and merchandise, one-tenth or one-twentieth of agricultural produce (the rate depending on the method of irrigation employed), and different rates for cattle, etc. These legal alms are known as 'zakat' and are to be distinguished from 'sadaqa', or free-will offerings.

To the Pilgrimage we have already referred. The actual ceremonies are direct survivals of the idolatrous superstitions of pre-Islamic Arabia,[1] taken over by the Prophet either because he himself still had some regard for them or, possibly, to conciliate the people of Mecca. At the same time, however, he destroyed the idols which surrounded the Ka'ba and professed to restore the Black Stone to the position it held in the days of Abraham.[2] The performance of the Pilgrimage at least once is enjoined on every adult Muslim, male or female, who

---

[1] Including the sacrifice (Sura xxii. 33-38) which is also offered at the same time by Muslims who are not performing the pilgrimage. This is the Feast of Sacrifice ('Id al Adha), substituted for the Jewish Day of Atonement, but without the same significance.

[2] It is still, however, kissed and rubbed, as in the pagan ritual. Similarly the practice of pilgrims being shaved and cutting their nails at the end of the pilgrimage rites, and the custom of burying the hair and nail clippings in sacred soil (see Burton, *Pilgrimage*, Vol. II, p. 205), are obvious survivals of animism, where hair and nails are regarded as especially charged with 'soul-stuff' and as channels of spiritual communion on the one hand, or deadly means of enemy attack on the other. Such superstitions still survive in Muslim lands quite apart from the pilgrimage ritual.

can afford it, and its value is emphasized in such Traditions as 'Every step in the direction of the Ka'ba blots out a sin', and 'He who dies on the way to Mecca is enrolled in the list of martyrs'. As a consequence, thousands assemble in Mecca each year from all over the Muslim world and return to their homes with a greatly heightened sense not only of the international character of Islam but of its essential solidarity.[1]

It is these Five Pillars, and particularly the profession of the Creed and the performance of prayer and fasting, which chiefly make up the practice of Islam to the average Muslim. He who acknowledges the Unity and Transcendance of God, pays Him His due in prayer and fast, and accepts Muhammad as the last and greatest of the Prophets, may well, indeed, have to taste the Fire, but hopes that he will not, like the infidel, remain in it for ever—through the timely intercession of the Prophet. The most heinous of sins are polytheism, apostasy, scepticism and impiety,[2] beside which social sins and all subtler forms of evil pale into comparative insignificance.

3. The Jihad

One more religious duty (other than the Five Pillars) deserves notice —the duty of Jihad or Holy War. It is incumbent in general on all Muslims who are adult, male and free to answer any legally valid summons to war against the infidels; and he who dies in a Jihad is a martyr and assured of Paradise. The Jihad, with the fanatical courage it evokes, has been by no means limited to the inception of Islam, and its possible relevance for the future must not be ignored. The matter is greatly complicated, however, by the question as to when such a summons can be regarded as legally valid. From the earliest times Muslims have divided the world into Dar al Islam, where Islam reigns supreme, and Dar al Harb (the Abode of War), where Islam must be spread by the sword. Polytheists were given the option of conversion or death, while the People of the Book (Jews or Christians) were given the additional alternative of submission and tribute. Of recent years the question has arisen, however, as to whether a country which has once been Dar al Islam but has subsequently fallen under a non-Muslim government is to be regarded as having lapsed into Dar al Harb. The

[1] But, it has been widely remarked, with no moral uplift.
[2] E.g. a man can be forgiven for breaking the divine law, but scarcely for denying or doubting its validity in the least particular.

majority view seems to be that a Jihad may be proclaimed only by the lawful Caliph—or, presumably, by the Mahdi[1] whom even Sunni Muslims expect; that it is only lawful in Dar al Harb; that a once-Muslim country does not lapse into Dar al Harb as soon as it passes into the hands of infidels, but only 'when all or most of the injunctions of Islam disappear therefrom'; and that it is in all cases essential that there should be 'a possibility of victory for the army of Islam'.[2]

4. Family Law

Under the general heading of mu'amalat, or dealings between man and man, the Shari'a includes provisions corresponding to the modern law of contract and tort (or 'obligations') in addition to those matters of personal status which are almost the only part of the Shari'a applied by the Courts today in the majority of Muslim lands. This law of personal status includes marriage (nikah), divorce (talaq), slavery, concubinage, guardianship, maintenance, wills, and inheritance.

Marriage is enjoined on every Muslim, and even the ascetic orders commonly marry. The Prophet is reputed to have said, 'Marry women who will love their husbands and be very prolific, for I wish you to be more numerous than any other people', and again, 'when a man marries he perfects half his religion'. A Muslim may have as many as, but not more than, four legal wives at any one time; and he may also cohabit with as many slave concubines as he may possess. 'Marry what seems good to you of women, by twos or threes or fours . . . or what your right hand possesses.'[3] Besides Muslim women, he may marry Jewesses or Christians and these may continue to practise their own religion (although, if they do, the spouses will have no mutual rights of inheritance): but a Muslim girl may be given in marriage only to a co-religionist, and there must be no intermarriage of any sort with polytheists. Among some Shi'is temporary marriage (mut'a or enjoyment) is also allowed, based partly on the Qur'anic precept: 'Forbidden to you also are married women, except those who are in your hands as slaves. This is the law of God for you. And it is allowed you, besides this, to seek out wives by means of your wealth, in modest conduct, but not in fornication. And give them their reward for what you have enjoyed of them, as God has commanded. But it shall be no crime in you to make agreement over and above the com-

[1] Their concept, however, differs from that of the Shi'is. Cf. pp. 63, 68.
[2] Cf. Hughes' Dictionary of Islam, 'Dar al Harb'.　　　[3] Sura iv. 3.

mand.'[1] Sunni Muslims deny the Shi'i interpretation of this verse and, although most of them admit that Muhammad at one time countenanced mut'a, maintain that he afterwards forbade it—although it seems in fact to have been first forbidden by the Caliph 'Umar. It is still widely practised among Shi'is, especially on journeys, when it often approximates to licensed prostitution: mut'a marriage, moreover, may be in excess of the four legal wives to which the Shi'a, too, are otherwise limited. In general, however, the Sunnis and Shi'is concur (except in details) in the rules governing the prohibited degrees of relationship and the dower, maintenance and discipline of wives: for a man who fulfils his own obligations may insist on his wife observing the strictest 'purdah' and may enforce marital obedience even by personal chastisement.[2] When a man has more than one wife he is enjoined to divide his time equally between them and to treat them with impartial justice (except, the commentators add, in those matters of the affections which are beyond his control): if he fears he will not be able to do this he should confine himself to one.[3] This verse is much quoted by modern Muslims to prove that the Prophet virtually enjoined monogamy, since few, they maintain, can behave impartially to a plurality of wives. They also emphasize that Islam has always allowed married women to keep their own property.[4]

A Muslim may divorce his wife at any time and for any reason. When the words of divorce are said only once or twice, the divorce is normally revocable at the option of the husband during a short period known as the 'idda, until the expiration of which the marriage is regarded in such cases as still extant and the husband is responsible for his wife's lodging and maintenance: thereafter a new marriage contract is required before the parties can come together again. When the words of repudiation are said three times, the divorce is immediately irrevocable; the parties cannot remarry unless the wife has first been properly married to, and divorced by, another man; and the husband's responsibility for maintaining his divorced wife during the 'idda is disputed between the schools. Should, however, it transpire that the wife—however divorced—is pregnant, the husband is responsible for her lodging and maintenance until she gives birth to his child. The children of divorced women remain with their mothers until they

---

[1] Sura iv. 28.   [2] Sura iv. 38.   [3] Sura iv. 3.
[4] Any other rule would, of course, be farcical in view of the husband's unfettered freedom of divorce.

reach a certain fixed age,[1] and during this period the divorced wife can claim from their father both money for their support and wages for her suckling and care; but after this age the father has an absolute claim on them. It is divorce rather than polygamy—which is decreasingly common—which causes untold suffering to women, and widespread social evil, in Islam today: for it frequently happens that a man will marry a young girl and then, when she has borne him several children and become prematurely aged, divorce her in favour of another adolescent; while the divorced wife can only return to her father or brothers, to be greeted with anything but enthusiasm and married off, if the opportunity occurs, to a second husband, however undesirable. It is not surprising, then, that Muslim women, having no sense of marital security, frequently contrive to put something by against the day of divorce and normally feel more affection for their blood-relatives than their husbands. The better type of Muslim father not infrequently attempts to deter a prospective son-in-law from frivolous divorce by stipulating a large dower for his daughter, the greater part of which is payable only on divorce or at the husband's death (to augment the one-eighth of his estate to which alone his widow will in most cases be entitled). In this connection it must be remembered that the seclusion of women in orthodox Islam means that a large number of men marry women they have never seen; that minor children (and in some schools virgin daughters of mature age) can be compulsorily married by their fathers; and that in most cases such pressure can be brought to bear on an adult girl—whether virgin, widow or divorcee—as to make that consent to a marriage which the law requires more nominal than real. Women, on their part, can in no circumstances divorce their husbands,[2] and it is only in certain schools and particular contingencies that they can appeal to the courts to annul the marriage.

Islam sanctions slavery and the slave trade, and the unlimited right of concubinage which a Muslim enjoys with his female slaves has already been mentioned. This extends even to married women cap-

---

[1] This age varies considerably as between school and school. The Hanafi rule is seven for a boy and nine for a girl (or, according to a variant view, nine and eleven respectively), while the Shi'is (Twelvers) say weaning for a boy and seven for a girl.

[2] Although sometimes husbands expressly delegate to their wives the right to divorce themselves in certain contingencies.

tured in war,[1] and opened the door to terrible abuse during the early wars of expansion, when almost any woman in a conquered land could be considered a slave by capture. Stanley Lane-Poole has some strong words to say on this subject: 'It is not so much in the matter of wives as in that of concubines that Muhammad made an irretrievable mistake. . . . The female white slave is kept solely for the master's sensual gratification and is sold when he is tired of her, and so she passes from master to master, a very wreck of womanhood. Kind as the Prophet was himself towards bondswomen, one cannot forget the unutterable brutalities which he suffered his followers to inflict upon conquered nations in the taking of slaves. The Muslim soldier was allowed to do as he pleased with any infidel woman he might meet with on his victorious march. When one thinks of the thousands of women, mothers and daughters, who must have suffered untold shame and dishonour by this licence, one cannot find words to express one's horror.'[2] In general, however, slaves are well and kindly treated in Muslim lands—including, in many cases, the slave concubine, who is often given no worse treatment than the free wife. Theoretically, of course, the slave has no legal rights: he is a mere chattel, in his master's absolute power. But this is mitigated in practice by the influence of both Qur'anic injunctions and Prophetic maxims extolling kindness to slaves and the virtue of setting them free, and Muhammad himself set a good example in this respect.

4. Other Provisions

It can only be mentioned in passing that in matters of diet the use of the pig, of blood[3] or of alcohol is forbidden to the Muslim; that gambling is taboo; and that the law of contract is largely dominated by the prohibition of usury. As a consequence purists disapprove insurance policies and most forms of investment, whatever the rate of interest. But in this, as in many other respects, the letter of the law has known many evasions almost from the first, and is now largely ignored.

[1] Muhammad quieted the consciences of those who hesitated to violate women captives whose husbands were still alive by the divine Revelation already quoted on p. 86 (Sura iv. 28). In other words, captivity annuls marriage.

[2] *Selections from the Koran*, second edition, Preface.

[3] Animals should be slaughtered by cutting the jugular vein, after pronouncing the name of God.

Circumcision is officially described as 'recommended' rather than 'commanded'[1]: it is, however, regularly practised and is regarded by the average Muslim as one of the essentials of his faith.

The last section of the Shari'a deals with 'Punishments' or criminal sanctions. These provide, *inter alia*, for the murderer to be executed by the family of his victim; for one who causes physical injury to another to be submitted to the like; for the thief to have his right hand cut off; and for the adulterer to be stoned and the fornicator beaten.[2] The severity of these penalties is considerably mitigated, however, by such rigorous rules of evidence that the punishment, in most cases, can seldom be imposed: but much lawlessness and injustice result from the fact that it is commonly regarded as legitimate for a man to kill his wife or close female relative for unchastity. In the vast majority of Muslim countries, however, all these (and many other) provisions of the Shari'a have been superseded by a modern civil and criminal code, and Shari'a courts now confine themselves almost exclusively to questions of personal status, gifts, endowments and pre-emption;[3] for while it would be regarded as infidelity avowedly to change the Shari'a in any particular, those who pay it honour as a divinely authoritative system for the Golden Age often quietly put it on one side in this workaday world in favour of a system more suited to modern requirements. In Arabia, however, the Shari'a is still largely applied.

To many survivals of animistic beliefs and practices in popular and even orthodox Islam references have already been made. The Prophet himself not only firmly believed in the jinn and in the power of the evil-eye, but apparently allowed spells to ward off the latter provided only the names of God and of good angels were used. He is also believed to have said that 'the saliva of some of us cures our sick by the permission of God'. The average Muslim today firmly believes that man can utilize the power of demons and jinn by means of magic, and the practice of 'counter-magic' to protect from evil of all sorts is

[1] Except by the Shafi'is, who regard it as 'commanded' for both boys and girls. Female circumcision is practised in most Muslim lands.
[2] The distinction is whether the guilty party has ever enjoyed a valid married life.
[3] Shuf'a: the right of the co-owner compulsorily to take over a third party's purchase of another co-owner's share in jointly-held land. It is sometimes extended to a neighbour's right over adjacent property.

exceedingly common. Amulets are worn by animals and men, particularly children; magic cups, many of them made in al Madina, are used both for healing and for more sinister purposes; and ceremonies such as the 'Aqiqa[1] sacrifice for new-born children (so called both from the first cutting of the infant's hair and the sacrifice offered on its behalf) are widespread. Some of these survivals can be traced to pre-Islamic Arabia, while others have been adopted from the conquered lands.

ISLAM TODAY AND TOMORROW

1. *The Enigma*

To the detached observer Islam is always somewhat of an enigma. It is not so much its phenomenal expansion in the first century of the Muslim era, which can largely be explained by the decadence and internal divisions of the surrounding kingdoms; by the tough physique and war-like spirit of the Arab armies, intoxicated as they were by the happy alternative of fabulous plunder or Paradisical delights; and by the military genius of Khalid ibn al Walid and others. It is not primarily the splendour of the mediaeval Caliphate, with its enlightened patronage of learning and its absorption of many alien cultures. The essence of the enigma is the power which the religion of Islam has exercised over its adherents all down the ages, so that it is still, in parts, a missionary religion, and is still winning new converts.

The enigma can, of course, be partially explained. The pagan who adopts Islam is normally influenced by three chief attractions: by the manifest superiority of the Muslim's concept of one true God, by the worldwide brotherhood of Islam, and by the unexacting nature of its moral demands. To the Copts who embrace Islam year by year in Egypt the motive is almost always either the pressure of economic inducements or the desire to divorce a Christian wife or marry a Muslim girl. The Muslim himself, moreover, feels a certain superiority, not only to the animist, but even to those Arab representatives of ancient Christian Churches who have tended to develop minority characteristics under centuries of Muslim dominance; whose ritualistic forms of worship seem little short of idolatry compared with the dignified simplicity of that of the mosque; and whose ignorance of the essentials of the Christian gospel is frequently profound. By contrast, the Muslim boasts a doctrine of God which, whatever its ultimate

---

[1] In many respects this should probably be regarded as Jewish rather than animistic in origin, but there has been much accretion.

inadequacy, appears comparatively comprehensible to the human mind; a code of ethics whose ample limits are determined by certain express prescriptions; and a conviction that his Prophet has absorbed and retained all that was best in previous revelations.

Yet there is much on the other side. Orthodox Islam, however lofty some of its theology and simple its ritual, is at best a cold and formal religion, as the widespread devotion to the Dervish Orders goes to prove; and its central doctrine of the Unity of the Godhead has been carried to a length which—even to human logic, itself manifestly inadequate in this context—raises more problems than it solves. Again, the finer soul is repelled by the very laxity of moral standards which attracts others—and especially by the degradation of Muslim woman-hood. That the religion still grips the greater part of its adherents, including women, and can still arouse fanatical devotion is a perpetual enigma, the suggested solution of which can best be reserved for the Epilogue to this book.

2. The Crisis

Today, however, Islam is facing one of the greatest crises of its history. This crisis arises from the very nature of Islam when exposed to the conflicting currents of modern life, and can, perhaps, be summarized under three headings.

Islam is essentially a dominant creed. It is not so much that Islam has sometimes been imposed at the point of the sword[1] as that the whole attitude of Muslims to non-Muslims is conceived as that of victor to vanquished, of ruler to ruled. While polytheists were to be given the alternative of conversion or death, the 'People of the Book' might be treated as 'dhimmis' or protected subjects: as such, their persons and property were guaranteed and they might follow their own religion and personal law; but they had to pay tribute, were excluded from full citizenship, and were frequently compelled to show various marks of deference to their Muslim neighbours. In the event their treatment differed widely from age to age and place to place: some-times they enjoyed much freedom and even attained high office; at other times they suffered persecution to the point of massacre. But all this has raised a difficult problem for the modern Muslim, who may have to live under a Christian (or other non-Muslim) government.

[1] The mass conversion of subject peoples was much more commonly the result of sustained social and economic pressure.

Such a circumstance seems never to have been contemplated by early Islam and has given rise to a number of difficulties, among them (as we have seen) that of knowing where the line should now be drawn between Dar al Islam and Dar al Harb and where a modern Jihad is obligatory or legitimate. There can be little doubt that it is the Muslim's instinctive feeling that the practice of his religion cannot properly be reconciled with living under the sovereignty of a non-Muslim government which, almost as much as the growth of nationalism, has led to the strenuous efforts witnessed during the last few years in many parts of the Muslim world to achieve either nominal or complete independence: and by the success of many of these efforts Islam may be said in this respect partially to have weathered the storm. Even when independence has been won, however, the Muslim state must still face the problem of its relations with non-Muslim countries in a world where almost perpetual war or isolation is no longer practicable. An up-to-date example of this problem is provided by the Declaration of Human Rights recently approved by all Muslim states, except Sa'udi Arabia and the Yemen, which are members of the United Nations Organization: yet the clause which affirms a man's right to change his religion if he so wishes runs directly counter both to the Islamic law of apostasy and to the practice of most of the Muslim states concerned.

Islam is essentially a theocratic creed. In Islam, as we have seen, Church and State are one, and the canon law is the law both of the State and the individual, in every aspect of life. Not only so, but Dar al Islam is in theory one and indivisible, united under a single Caliph. In 1923, however, the Ottoman Caliphate (itself of doubtful legality, since the Caliph was not of Qurayshi descent) was abolished; and the rivalries of Muslim powers will probably prevent any speedy revival. Meanwhile, modern States, strongly nationalistic in character, have grown up in many parts of the Muslim world, in most of which parliamentary institutions and responsible governments have been set up on the western pattern. The subjects of such States, moreover, are granted (nominally, at least) equal citizenship without distinction of religion,[1] and a secular State law has to a great extent been substituted

---

[1] It should, however, be observed that the 'freedom of religion' guaranteed by the Constitution of many modern Muslim States is usually limited in practice to freedom for non-Muslims to worship in their own way. Any attempt to propagate another religion is severely restricted, and no provision whatever is made for a Muslim to change his faith.

for the Shari'a. Much of this seems incompatible with historic Islam.
Yet again, although Islam is usually declared to be the State religion,
the State itself is largely secular in character. Where, in the past,
popular literature, holidays and entertainments were almost exclusively
religious or semi-religious in character, today the press, radio and
cinema are mainly secular. In such circumstances the old cohesion
and theocratic structure of Islam has been greatly weakened. It must,
however, be remembered that Islam represents a complete system of
public and private life as well as a religion, in the narrower sense of
that term: and that many who are influenced by secularist tendencies
still staunchly support the Muslim social order.

Orthodox Islam is essentially a dogmatic creed. The Muslim must
accept the Qur'an as the *ipsissima verba* of God, the Traditions as
equally inspired in content though not in form, and the whole vast
structure of Muslim law and theology developed by generations of
jurists and commentators as binding on his mind and conscience.
There have, of course, been progressive movements in Islam, as we
have seen; but for centuries orthodox thought has been dominated
by Ash'arism. It is no wonder, then, if the modern student, who is
thoroughly up to date in western thought, finds a fundamental conflict
between the teachings of the orthodox and the so-called 'assured
results of modern science'. In so far as the interpretations and developments of mediaeval jurists and theologians are concerned, it would no
doubt be possible (and the attempt is in fact being made) for modern
Muslims to sweep away this superstructure and insist on the right to
go back to the Qur'an and the Traditions and re-interpret them in
terms of modern life. Ultimately, however, the student or reformer
is usually faced with a far deeper problem in some explicit dictum of
God or His Prophet. Thus the would-be reformer of the position of
women finds that polygamy, slave-concubinage, unilateral divorce
and the beating of refractory wives is permitted by divine authority,
while child-marriage and the veiling of women are supported by Prophetic precedent.[1] This, clearly, makes the path of reform a slippery
one. It must be almost equally difficult for the modern critical mind
to accept the whole of the Qur'an as the *ipsissima verba* of God or for
the enlightened moral conscience to regard the life of the Prophet as
a model of right living: but it is just as difficult to compromise on
either of these issues and remain an honest Muslim. Yet it must be

[1] This last point, however, is now disputed.

admitted that the strength of any system of thought or belief and its ability to command men's loyalty is by no means proportionate to its truth or intrinsic spiritual power, and that Islam has many features which still commend it to most of its adherents.

In the more recent past, moreover, other—and in some respects quite contrary—tendencies have become increasingly apparent. There has been a considerable revival of Islam, particularly in the Arab countries, as a political and religious rallying-point against the alleged 'political, economic and cultural imperialism' of the west. This revival is largely the result of purely political factors: in particular of Arab opposition to the 'fragmentation' policy pursued by Britain and France between the wars and to the menace of Zionism.[1] As a consequence there has been an increasing tendency to identify nationalism with Islam and national culture with Islamic culture; and this has led to more severe restrictions on foreign missions and to discrimination against non-Muslim minorities. The revival, however, has been religious rather than spiritual; it has been marked by a larger number of officials going on pilgrimage and a greater emphasis on testing new legislation by the Shari'a, but has not been accompanied by any decrease in official corruption or general rise in moral standards.

3. The Future

How, then, is the Muslim world reacting to these problems and what does the future hold? To this, only the most sketchy answer can be given. Four different tendencies may be observed.

(1) There is a tendency towards secularism. The outstanding example of this is provided by Turkey. There, Islam is no longer taught in the schools; the Dervish Orders have been suppressed; the law has been entirely secularized; the Roman alphabet has been introduced; 'westernism' has been adopted in a wholesale fashion; and monogamy is (officially) enforced by law. True, the mosques are still open and the majority of the population certainly regard themselves as Muslims: but the real religion of many of the educated seems to be Turkish nationalism. Modern Iran is a more moderate example of the same tendency, which seems for the present to be chiefly limited to the non-Arab countries where Islam may be regarded as foreign to their native culture. Alternatively, however, the movement may be described as

[1] The same factors have been the major motives in the formation of the League of Arab States.

an attempt to separate personal religion from social and national life—
and with this many Muslims elsewhere are in sympathy.

2 There is a tendency towards reaction and xenophobia. This directly
opposite tendency can be seen most clearly in the Wahhabi movement
and the early history of the Sanusi Order. Both these movements, in
their different ways, represent a puritanical revival in which an attempt
was made to get back to primitive Islam. Both alike, moreover, tried
to abjure the West and all 'innovation' (bid'a) and find salvation in the
Qur'an and the Traditions of the Prophet. The intrusions of the radio,
the motor car and the aeroplane, however, and the economic pressure
of modern life, have made both these movements, from the religious
point of view, lost causes. But reaction and xenophobia also show
themselves in such organizations as the Muslim Brotherhood and
Fidaiyan Islam.

3   More promising from the Muslim point of view is the tendency
which finds its best example in movements such as that led by the late
Muhammad 'Abduh in Egypt, which attempts a synthesis of piety with
progress, of western science with the Muslim faith. The key to any
such attempt must necessarily lie along the line of the revival of the
right of ijtihad[1] and the abandonment, or metamorphosis, of the doctrine of 'agreement'.[2] Like the Wahhabis and Sanusis, these modernists
would sweep away most of the accretions of the Middle Ages and seek
to re-interpret the original sources of Islam: unlike the reactionaries,
however, they would try to reconcile their re-interpretation with the
realities of modern life. The attempt is a bold one and beset, as we
have seen, with acute problems: but the movement has already exerted
a widespread influence and the issue is still in doubt.[3]

4   Yet another tendency is represented by the Ahmadiya and Babi (or
Baha'i) movements. Founded by Mirza Ghulam Ahmad of Qadian
towards the close of the last century, the Ahmadiya movement has
more recently split into two sects, the smaller comparatively orthodox
and the larger definitely heterodox. The latter teaches that Christ was
in fact crucified but later revived in the tomb, escaped, and made his
way to Kashmir where he died at the age of a hundred and twenty;

---

[1] See above, p. 71.   [2] See above, pp. 70, 71.
[3] The latest tendency in the Middle East, however, is rather more conserva-
tive. Its sponsors carefully distinguish the Christian and Hellenistic elements in
western civilization from its material progress, and want to adopt the latter
but reject the former—particularly the Christian elements.

that Mirza Ghulam was the long-expected Mahdi and Messiah who resembled both Jesus and Muhammad; but that instead of world conquest by battle, his mission was peaceable and his Jihad to be waged by propaganda. The Babi movement was started by Sayyid ʿAli Muhammad of Shiraz when, in 1844, he proclaimed himself the Bab or Gateway of divine truth. In reality it is an extreme modern development of Shiʿi views. The majority of his followers recognized as his successor Baha Allah (Mirza Husayn ʿAli Nuri) who issued a modified form of his master's teaching and whose followers are called Baha'is. This claims to be a universal religion, the wholesale adoption of which would bring universal peace: it teaches the duty of doing harm to no one, of loving one another, of bearing injustice without resistance, of being humble, and of devoting oneself to healing the sick; it has no clergy, no ceremonial and countenances no austerities. It will be noticed that the common element in these very different movements is the propagation of what is really a new religion under the pretext of reforming Islam.

What, then, of the future? Prophecy is notoriously dangerous, but the possibilities seem limited to four:

(1) The advent of a new Mahdi to lead a sweeping movement of reaction. While, however, the possibility of the inception of some such movement can never be discounted, the chances of its ultimate success seem negligible.

(2) The triumph of materialism, whether in the form of secularism among the richer and better educated classes or of Communism among the undernourished masses. This seems a very real danger, signs of which are already apparent in places. If Communism should really spread in Muslim countries, the consequences for Islam cannot be predicted.

(3) The development of a new Islam through an extension of such movements as that of Muhammad ʿAbduh—an Islam which, while it retains the name and professes to carry on the spirit of the past, would be scarcely recognizable to its Founder.

(4) A realization, on a wholly unprecedented scale, of the claims of Christ—never yet adequately presented to the Muslim world.

Since this last subject is frequently misunderstood, a final word must be added concerning past relations between Christianity and Islam and the effect of Christian missions in Muslim lands today. Until the last hundred years, contacts between Christianity and Islam were almost uniformly unfortunate. Allusion has already been made to the distorted impressions of Christian doctrine which clouded the Prophet's mind; to the divisions of Christendom and the decadence of the Church which facilitated the Muslim conquests and swelled the number of Muslim converts; and to the ineffective witness of the remnants of ancient Churches still surviving in Muslim lands—probably still the greatest single obstacle to the evangelization of Islam. To these adverse factors must be added that solitary approach of western Christendom to Islam throughout the Middle Ages, the Crusades—when not only did the followers of the Crucified adopt a method He had expressly condemned, but when they often failed to show to any moral advantage beside their 'Saracen' foes. Apart from a few isolated individuals such as Raymun Lull, the Church did nothing to take the authentic gospel of Christ to the Muslim world until the modern era of Christian missions.

Even in this period the results have been meagre, compared with those from any other faith. This is partly due to the extreme poverty of the effort made, for missions have tended to concentrate on more productive fields; partly to the barriers of antagonism which have had to be broken down; and partly to the law of apostasy in Islam (death for a man and death or perpetual imprisonment for a woman) or its more common modern equivalent of loss of family, inheritance and employment, with considerable danger of death by poison. In the event the effect of missionary work has been threefold: a widespread influence on social conditions and moral outlook, through the medical and educational services which were virtually non-existent before the missionaries came; a more restricted circle of persons genuinely touched by the gospel message who for one reason or another have stopped short of baptism; and a still smaller number of brave souls who have taken their place as open members of the Christian Church. But the world has yet to see what would happen if the gospel of the living Christ was adequately presented to the millions of Islam.

CHAPTER IV

HINDUISM

INTRODUCTION

THERE are some 300,000,000 Hindus in the world today, found almost exclusively in India, the country of their origin. Hinduism has never been a religion imbued with missionary zeal. Indians who have emigrated to Africa, Burma, Malaya, Europe and America have taken their religion with them, but with few exceptions they do not attempt to propagate their faith. Indeed, very little of the ancient characteristics of Hinduism adhere to the religion when it is transplanted to other lands. Generally speaking, therefore, true Hinduism is confined to India.

The study of Hinduism is of great importance. That so large a proportion of the peoples of the world follows this religion should alone be sufficient to make us interested. But more than that, the India of today is fast taking her place among the leading Asiatic nations. What, then, is the traditional belief of her people about the world, about themselves, and about their fellow men, and what do they believe today? This second question is of more practical importance, the first being largely of historic interest. There is a vast gulf between ancient Hinduism as still practised by the majority of illiterate Hindus and Hinduism as understood by the modern intelligentsia. What, then, does it mean to be a Hindu?

To this simple question various answers may be, and are, given. A census officer would reply that a Hindu is any native of India who is not of foreign origin, nor a Christian, nor a Muslim, nor a member of any other defined community. Among Hindus themselves the subject is one of endless controversy, and even of law-suits. Are the outcastes Hindus? Does a man who has been outcasted remain a Hindu? It would require a volume to discuss the various and contradictory answers that have been given. Some time ago an Indian graduate published a book entitled *True Hinduism*, in which his avowed object was to demonstrate that true Hinduism was the religion of humanity. His reviewer, also a Hindu graduate, after quoting some dictionary definitions of the word Hindu, proceeds to say 'we venture to predicate that Hinduism is not a religion at all, but a series of loosely strung and infinitely varied sacerdotal and sociological artificial conventions to which a religious verisimilitude has been imparted by the ancient law-givers, but which is nevertheless daily undergoing endless fluctuations, not only in any given locality, but throughout the Hindu world'.[1] This goes to show the difficulty which faces anyone who tries to describe the 'religion' of Hinduism.

Hinduism is not a credal religion, like Islam. Anyone can become a Muslim by saying the Kalima, 'There is no God but God, and Muhammad is the Prophet of God'; but a Hindu is born, not made. An Englishman may hold exactly the same beliefs as his Brahman friend, but he remains an outcaste. There is only one path by which, according to orthodox ideas, he may attain entrance into the Hindu fold. Let him live a pious life and then, after many transmigrations, his soul may be at last reborn into a Hindu family.[2]

Hinduism may be positively defined as an 'ethnic' or racial religion, like that of ancient Greece, with which in its origin it had a real kinship. Today in India age-long customs, rival philosophical systems, animistic beliefs, a luxuriant mythology derived from many sources, epic legends of ancient heroes and sages, and, during the last two hundred years, waves of influence from the West, have gone to make up that welter of beliefs and practices which we recognize as Hinduism.

A brief outline of its origin and development will help to make this clearer.

ORIGIN AND DEVELOPMENT OF HINDUISM

1. *The Vedic Period, c.* 1500–500 B.C.

The ethnological survey of India derives the present population mainly from the Aryan and Dravidian stocks, with an infusion of Mongol blood in Bengal and the North-East, and with several aboriginal tribes like the Gonds and Santals, to mention only two, still forming island groups. It is estimated that the Dravidian element predominates, and that the percentage of Aryan origin is roughly 20 per cent in the North and 10 per cent in the South. This represents approximately the membership of the higher castes, although there are many Dravidian Brahmans in South India.

It was at some period in the second millenium B.C., at a time when the indigenous population of India was mainly Dravidian, that a

---

[1] V. N. Narasimmiyengar, *True Hinduism*, p. 5.

[2] A few foreigners, after certain ceremonies and change of name, have been received by the less orthodox.

branch of the great fair-skinned Indo-European family, speaking Sanskrit, descended from the North-West and conquered that part of the country now known as the Punjab. They were the authors of a collection of hymns, composed at different times, amongst which the best known is the Rig-Veda (lit. knowledge enshrined in verses). Like the Greeks they practised ancestor worship and observed a patriarchal family system; they worshipped nature gods or *devas* (cf. Lat. *deus*), such as Agni (cf. Lat. *ignis*), the god of fire. These they invested with personal attributes, and conceived of as bright beings, possessed of superhuman powers and dwelling in celestial regions. To them they offered sacrifices, and to them the majority of the hymns of the Rig-Veda were addressed.

In process of time the sacrificial system was elaborated, and its importance exaggerated, until it was thought that by means of it the gods could be compelled to grant appropriate rewards. To the Rig-Veda were added the hymns and ritual directions contained in the Sama-Veda and the Yajur-Veda; and as the priests or Brahmans alone knew how to offer sacrifice aright and extract favours from the gods, they gained in power and influence, until they came to be regarded as nearly gods themselves.

The Aryan invaders kept themselves distinct from the older Dravidian population, whom they designated Sudras, or serfs; they described themselves as Dvija or twice-born, and the distinction between the two races as *Varna* or colour; and here we have the fountain head of the caste system.

Among themselves the Aryans were divided by occupation into three caste divisions: the Kshatriyas, who were the warriors and princes, amongst whom the mediaeval Rajputs ('princes') were later supposed to be outstanding examples; the Brahmans, who were the priests and instructors; and the Vaisyas, who were the agriculturalists and merchants. These members of the Aryan community emphasized their 'twice-born' character by a ceremony wherein every adolescent boy was invested by the Brahman priest with the sacred thread[1] and taught to repeat one of the sacred texts (the *gayatri*). After this thread-ceremony the twice-born youths were entitled and expected to receive regular training in Vedic studies and the *shastras*; and since until recently the Brahman caste was the sole custodian of the arts and

---

[1] The sacred thread was not worn by boys outside these three groups, nor by any girls. For girls, marriage took the place of initiation.

sciences, its ascendancy and extraordinary influence may be attributed to the awareness on the part of the other castes of the privilege and responsibility involved.

During this time wars were constantly being waged with the indigenous people, until eventually the whole of India was brought under Aryan rule. This warfare is reflected in the stories of battles between the *daitas*, their bright gods, and the *dasyus*, dark spirits or demons. The Sudras were allowed to retain their own gods and worship, but were compelled to acknowledge the Brahman rule. It was only natural that many of their ideas and stories should be assimilated by their masters, and it seems probable that among these was the belief in transmigration which was destined to exert so great an influence. At the same time there was growing up an exaggerated view of the value of ascetic practices. It began to be said that the gods had gained immortality by means of mighty sacrifices or through the exercise of great austerities; and a regular order of ascetics arose which aimed at obtaining miraculous powers by enduring extremes of heat or cold, by maintaining unnatural postures or by long abstention from food. They were mainly worshippers of Siva, a god much feared in one of his aspects for his cruelty.

Before the end of the period a fourth group of writings was collected, called the Atharva-Veda, which consisted largely of spells and incantations addressed to gods or demons, with marked animistic features. It did not secure immediate or universal acceptance.

2. *The Philosophic Period*, c. 500 B.C. – A.D. 500

The period which saw the spread of Aryan rule over India and the increasing supremacy of the Brahmans was also the golden age of Sanskrit literature.

The philosophers' search after the ultimate secret of all existence and the way of release from endless transmigrations is embodied in the writings known as Upanishads, which often take the form of dialogue. Other books, called Brahmanas and Shastras, are composed of ritual directions, interpretations of older texts and philosophical discussions. In addition there has come down to us from these early days a great epic literature, dealing with legends of gods and heroes, of which the best known are the Mahabharata and the Ramayana.

This age also saw the rise of Buddhism,[1] based originally, it has been

[1] See pp. 118-135.

suggested, on the atheistic Samkhya philosophy. It spread over India, but ultimately disappeared as a separate sect, leaving behind, however, a marked influence on Hindu thought, especially by enhancing admiration for the quietist qualities of gentleness and non-resistance.

Two examples may be given to illustrate the gradual evolution of Hindu thought which was taking place. The first was the rise to the highest importance in the pantheon of the two great gods of modern Hinduism—Vishnu and Siva, the one gracious and the other as often arousing terror. These two were associated with Brahma to form a triad, sometimes depicted as Trimurti represented by one body with three heads, which ruled over the whole universe. Under this presentation Brahma is said to be the Originator or Creator of all visible things, who, since his work has been accomplished, no longer needs worship. Vishnu became the Preserver, who came down in ten (some say twenty-two) *avatars* or 'descents', for the preservation of humanity from threatened calamities, and Siva is regarded as the Destroyer.

These *avatars*, often called incarnations, of Vishnu are assumptions of a form, sometimes animal, sometimes human, which veiled rather than revealed the god within. The first of these incarnations was as a fish, two later ones were as Rama and Krishna,[1] and the ninth was Buddha. The tenth *avatar*, the *Kalki*, is still future.

The second example reveals the conception of the four great castes as a divine institution. The evolution of religious thought led to the conception of a creator or originator of the universe, distinct from, and inferior to, the Vedic gods. In the cosmogonic hymns he appears sometimes as Prajapati (lord of creation), sometimes as Hiranyagarbha (golden egg) and sometimes as Purusha (man, cf. the conception of Adam). Under the latter name the Purusha-Sukta pictures him as a giant with a thousand heads and a thousand arms, whose body included the earth but extends beyond it, from whom sprang the gods as well as men. Of him it is said, 'Purusha is all this world, what has been and shall be.' As regards the creation of mankind, in the Rig-Veda it is said that 'His mouth became the Brahman, his arms the Rajanya (Kshatriya), his thighs the Vaisya, and his feet the Sudra.'

CASTE

The origin of caste, we have seen, lay largely in the primitive colour bar. It was developed as years went by through confining to each

[1] See p. 114.

separate caste sub-division as it arose, the occupation of the group which originally constituted it. In this way today a man's caste will tell you what his work is, even to the extent of the professional burglar and robber caste. In the post-Vedic period and afterwards new classifications were introduced and caste divisions multiplied until the number of separate castes ran into many hundreds. As the Sudras became absorbed in the Hindu system, the majority were acceptable to the twice-born as members of the Fourth Caste, but there were some whose occupation or racial origin were thought to be too degraded for this. The Brahmans also split up into many castes according to differences of religious views, social practice and place of origin. Outside the castes are the outcastes, or scheduled castes, who number some 60,000,000. The limits assigned to each caste, beyond which marriage was prohibited, were settled by custom, and breaches of caste were judged by the panchayat, or community council.

Caste is sometimes compared to social distinctions in the West, but it really belongs to a quite different realm of thought, and can be best understood by a study of the Indian words used in connection with it. The ordinary Hindustani word for caste is *zat* or *jat*,[1] which also denotes a 'kind' of thing, or a 'species' of animal. Thus a hammer is one sort of thing, a pudding is another; they are essentially different in their nature and in the purpose they serve. In a similar way a Brahman is thought of as serving one purpose, a tradesman another; they cannot mix or interchange. Similarly, and this analogy is even more to the point, the dog belongs to one species, the cat to another, whilst man, though also an animal, is distinct from and superior to both. Now no one would expect a dog to mate with a cat, for it would be contrary to nature. Why, therefore, should a Lohar seek a wife among the Dhobis? Nor would you like to feed from the same plate as your dog: so how can you expect a Brahman to sit down at table with one of a lower caste, or of no caste at all?

Another important Hindustani word is *baradari*, a 'brotherhood' or 'joint family'. This aspect of caste has been fostered by the joint family system which has been one of the sources of strength in Hinduism. Marriage takes place soon after puberty, though there have been

[1] The word *jat* comes from the Sanskrit *jati* (caste), which is derived from the root meaning 'birth', 'to be born'; thus a person is a member of a caste because he is born in it. The use of the word with regard to chattels is metaphorical.

several attempts to raise the age at which a child may be legally married.[1] Sooner or later after marriage the bride moves to her husband's home, and as one bride after another, of sons and grandsons, is introduced, so the joint family grows. The power of the father or grandfather is paramount, as is that of the older women over the younger. Little can be done apart from their advice and permission. So the Indian grows up to think and act in terms of the joint family more than of the individual.

When, for instance, it is a question of sending a promising boy to an English university, it is the joint family which decides and which raises the funds, and if he succeeds it is expected that he will use his money and influence on behalf of his relatives and fellow-caste members in return. If he disgraces himself, on the other hand, by becoming a Christian for example, or by flagrantly breaking the rules of caste in some other way, the whole family comes under a cloud, and his father may have to offer a higher dowry to secure husbands for his daughters.

Caste is connected with religion through all that is connoted by the word *dharma*, which may be translated by 'religion' or 'duty'. The Dharma-shastras are the books which lay down laws of conduct. It is the *dharma* of a Brahman to study, sacrifice and teach, the *dharma* of a Kshatriya to fight, of a householder to rear his family and offer the accustomed sacrifices to departed ancestors. Each must perform his destined duty. Religious *dharma* is performed by reciting sacred formulas, repeating the name of a god, visiting temples or by Yoga exercises.[2] In these ways merit is increased and the soul's release brought nearer.

In the famous poem of the Bhagavad-gita the scene is cast in the battlefield where the warrior, Arjuna, finds himself at war with another branch of his family and shrinks from shedding their blood. Then Vishnu, in the form of Krishna, appears as his charioteer and urges him to do his duty (dharma) as a Kshatriya (warrior) and fight. The performance of dharma, he exhorts him, is the only right course to

[1] The Sharda Act provides punishments for the bridegroom, the guardians and the priest who officiates at the marriage if the bridegroom is under 18, or the bride under 15, while the draft Hindu code proposes to make such a marriage voidable. But in a country where illiteracy is very high and where vital statistics are not kept, except in certain small communities, the enforcement of these provisions will be difficult.

[2] See p. 110.

follow. Various philosophical arguments are then used to prove that the world around, the world of sense, is *maya* (illusion), and to think in terms of it is *avidya* (ignorance): the *atman* (ultimate reality) is no more affected by it than are the ocean depths by the ripples on the surface. Let Arjuna lift his thoughts above it, from the unreal to the real, from the visible universe to the invisible self; let him then disregard his feelings, fulfil his *dharma* and fight.

This view of religious duty and its connection with caste helps to explain the Hindu view that every community should have its own religion and every man do his duty therein. For a man to wish to change his religion is contrary to nature and to the destiny indicated by his birth.

Finally, the keeping of caste is thought of as the preservation of social and ceremonial purity. Many ancient books call it a sin to cross the ocean, because India alone was held to be sacred ground. In a certain caste dispute the judgment of the caste tribunal occupied eighty-four typed pages, discussing and citing authorities upon what constituted breaches of caste, such as travelling to Europe or eating defiled food. Many a graduate of our British universities has been forced on his return to India to call in a Brahman priest and submit to a purification ceremony before he could be received back into caste.

For centuries caste has had a firm grip on India, and there is undoubtedly some good to set over against the immeasurable evil for which it has been responsible. It has preserved learning, for example, by isolating the priestly caste and giving them the responsibility of teaching. But although its grip is still strong and real, very slowly it is beginning to weaken. The average villager still tells you his caste when you ask him who he is, but no longer does he fear the higher castes as he did. Mahatma Gandhi made repeated efforts to have temples opened for worship by Harijans ('people of Hari'[1]). It is one of the Fundamental Rights, as expressed in the Indian Constitution, that no citizen may be discriminated against on account of caste, but such deep-rooted practices and customs cannot be made to disappear with the stroke of the pen. Education, the impact of the second world war, and greatly increased travel both outside and inside India have all helped to storm the citadel, but only here and there are its walls beginning to crumble. The final stronghold will be the family and there the women will be the last to free themselves from its grip.

[1] Gandhi's euphemistic title for outcaste peoples. Hari is another name for 'the deity'.

HINDU PHILOSOPHY

I. *The Ultimate Reality*

As the caste system forms a background to the social life of India, so the philosophy of the abstract underlies and penetrates its religious thought.

Towards the close of the Vedic period, Indian seekers after truth set themselves to discover, if they might, the Ultimate Reality, that which lies beyond the changing phenomena of the world of sense, and that which constitutes the inmost being of man. The answer to this twofold search and its unification can be summed up in two words, *brahma* and *atman*.

In the Rig-Veda the word *brahma* means 'prayer' or 'devotion': hence the priest who leads the devotion of the people is the Brahman, and the writings which describe his duties are called Brahmanas. With the development of the philosophy the word *brahma* (still neuter) came to be used for the unchanging *something*, the substance which endures and forms the substratum of the outward form which changes and passes. The potter fashions the clay into a bowl, and breaks it again; the form and appearance change, but the clay persists. What is it, then, in the sum total of things, that corresponds to the clay? The answer is, *brahma*. *Brahma* is all pervading, but one does not see it any more than one sees a razor in its case. It is known in the mystic formula, *Tat Sat*, i.e. it is (reality).

> 'Since not by speech and not by thought,
> Not by the eye can it be reached,
> How else may it be understood,
> But only when one says, "it is"?'[1]

Approached from the standpoint of the individual, *atman*, or self, is not the body, nor the senses, which convey impressions to the mind, nor the mind which receives them, nor even the intelligence which dominates the mind, but the very self behind and within all these. Like the Latin *spiritus*, the word *atman* originally meant 'breath' in the physical sense; but to the philosopher it is that innermost enduring self which changes not and which is unqualified even by thought or desire. It is only one step from this to identify it with *brahma*, the

---

[1] Katha Upanishad.

soul of the universe. As the air within a jar, though enclosed, is one with the air outside, so the atman within the man is one with the *atman* everywhere. 'Whoever knows this, "I am *brahma*" becomes the All. Even the gods are not able to prevent his becoming "it", for he becomes their self (*atman*).'[1]

Hindu philosophy developed along two lines, known as the Samkhya and the Vedanta. The Sankhya[2] is dualistic and in reality atheistic. It denies the existence of any beginning, or of a creator, but postulates two eternal realities, *praakriti* and *purushas*, or finite selves. These are both considered real and correspond more or less to the western division into matter and spirit, but with characteristic differences.

The Vedanta, on the other hand, is, according to some schools, *a-dvaita* (non-dualistic) and admits only the one existence, the *atman*. All else is *maya* (illusion) and the fruit of *avidya* (ignorance). It is like the desert mirage, appearance and not reality, which vanishes with a nearer approach. So when the seeker knows 'I am *brahma*', ignorance is banished, desire ceases, and the soul is released from the circle of births and deaths.

Amongst Hindu reformers whose influence on Hinduism was permanent we may remember Sankara of the eighth century, and Ramanuja of the twelfth. Sankara was a revivalist who died young, but not before leaving behind him four monasteries, wherein was preserved his teaching, a purified form of Vedantism. To him the world was totally illusion (*maya*), and the only reality was the Absolute *brahma*. The only real religion to Sankara was the pursuit of this knowledge, deliverance from the deception that there could be anything else but *brahma*.

Ramanuja also founded religious orders, but in opposition to the teaching of Sankara. He affirmed the absolute reality of this world as the *lela* of the Almighty, the theatre of his play. The world he did not regard as destined to be permanent. The human soul was distinct from the godhead, and could relate itself to God not by absorption but by devotion. Followers of both schools are to be found amongst Hindus today, and it is characteristic of that religion that you can disagree upon such fundamentals and yet remain perfectly good Hindus.

[1] Brihadaranyaka Upanishad.
[2] Gautama, the Buddha, and his contemporary, Jina (the founder of Jainism), both followed this system.

2. *Transmigration and Karma*

The Vedic idea of the future life, like the Greek, pictured the soul which had left the body as dwelling in an underworld of bliss or sorrow, or ascending to the realm of the gods. The theory of transmigration gained its hold on India in the post-Vedic period and was firmly fixed before the rise of Buddhism. This is, perhaps, the most typical feature of Hindu thought even today. There is a basic desire to be rid of existence which is essentially evil, and to cast off the toils of *samsara*, the chain of finite existence, which holds the soul to this world. A chain, that is, which also holds it from one existence to another, for an individual, according to his behaviour in one life, attains a position in the next, when reborn, which is suited to his merit or lack of merit. Every activity, whether of thought or deed, sets in motion a series of consequences, just as a stone thrown into water creates an expanding series of ripples. The Mahabharata puts it thus: 'Among a thousand cows the calf finds its mother, so the deed once done follows after the doer.'

A man's life consists of actions, good and bad, each bearing fruit, and when he dies there is an accumulation of *karma*, merit and demerit, remaining to be worked off. This determines his status in the next life which may be that of a god, a Brahman, an outcaste, a woman, a dog, a plant, and so on. Once again he is caught up in the round of desire, action and consequences, as the water in the water-wheel is passed from one plate to the next, and finds no release.

This doctrine gives an easy explanation for all the differences in human life. Bad and good fortune, health or sickness, poverty or riches, are all ascribed to *karma*. Not only every calamity of the world, but the caste system itself is explained by this doctrine. It also accounts to a great extent for the pessimism found in Hindus today, and largely explains the apparent callousness towards suffering. A man's moral and spiritual state are not really under his control, since it is the result of a former life.

In accord with this conception, conduct depends on *karma* and *karma* again upon conduct. The present is but a small part of a great whole. This life depends on the past. It is the harvest of a former sowing, and the seed which will bring forth fruit for a future harvest.

The Indian mind never gave up the hope of finding a 'way' (*marga*) to release (*moksha*) from this ceaseless round of action and rebirth, and looked for it in *nirvana*, when by knowledge (*gyan*) of the Supreme

Truth of the *brahma-atman* the soul is released from its ceaseless pilgrimage by absorption into the nothingness of the heart of the universe. This is a destiny worked for by millions, but attained, they say, by the very few.

> 'As rivers flow and disappear at last
> In ocean's waters, name and form renouncing,
> So too the sage, released from name and form,
> Is merged in the divine and ultimate existence.'[1]

Among adherents of the Sankhya system another way arose, that of *Yoga*, or perfect poise, whereby every desire should be subdued, every activity stilled, no fresh round of *karma* set in motion, and so release might come. So Gautama attained it: and hence the familiar postures in which the Buddha is commonly depicted.

Yet another way as the centuries passed was found in *bhakti*, or 'devotion', rendered to some god, and in particular to Vishnu in one of his incarnations. Marks on the forehead made with lime and vermilion paint, and rosaries round the neck, are marks of devotion to the god, a trident for followers of Vishnu, and horizontal lines for the devotee of Siva.

There are said to be sixty-four ways of showing ecstatic devotion to a deity, and of these the most commonly observed are pilgrimages to holy places, reciting the *shastras* extolling the deity, repetition of his name, making a round of holy places on appointed days, and observing fasts and austerities. In these ways the favour of the deity may be gained, and the way opened to *Vaikuntha* and to becoming merged in the existence of the Supreme Being.

EFFECT OF PHILOSOPHY ON INDIAN THOUGHT

The effect of Indian philosophy shows itself in various ways, particularly in the difference between their modes of thought and those of the West. The appeal to facts which the European or American regards as conclusive makes little or no impression on the Hindu, who thinks of facts as belonging only to the surface of things: it is ideas that count. So the marvels of science may excite his interest, and he may study history under compulsion; but he idealizes metaphysics and revels in mystery and mythology. This latter tendency explains how it is that a pious and intelligent Hindu can justify idolatry in its extreme forms.

[1] Mundaka Upanishad.

By nature the Hindu is more impressed by the Sadhu who despises the material world and spends his time in meditation or repeating the name of his god, than he is by the busy evangelist with his ceaseless activity. Service and duty are all on the plane of action: the superior plane is inaction. He is fascinated by the mystery that hangs round the genuine Sadhu and is prone to believe the stories of the miracles attributed to him. As the image of the god dwells in the dark recesses of the temple, so the deepest knowledge of the infinite can be attained only by the initiated few.

Such modes of thought may not be explicit, but they are widespread and underlie many aspects of Hinduism that present an enigma to those unacquainted with Indian philosophy.

POPULAR HINDUISM

1. *Primitive Customs*

Custom is perhaps stronger in India than anywhere on earth, and the remark '*Dastur hai*' (it is the custom) is considered to put an end to argument. Many of the day-by-day acts of the orthodox Hindu family, especially among the twice-born castes, date back to Vedic times. The *gayatri*, a Vedic prayer to the sun for enlightenment, is still repeated morning by morning by the Brahman caste; and *pindas*, small balls of rice, are placed on the ancestral shrine. The horoscope is regularly cast when a child is born, and the wedding ceremonies, including the circling of the sacred fire, may go back even to pre-Vedic times. The same is true of the funeral rites and offerings which few would dare to neglect.

The veneration of the cow is also primitive and an ancient law decreed the death penalty if one were killed. Gandhi calls this the distinguishing mark of the Hindu. 'Cow protection is the dearest possession of the Hindu heart. It is the one concrete belief common to all Hindus. He who does not believe in cow protection cannot possibly be a Hindu.'[1] It goes further than protection, however, and to eat the five products of the cow is still resorted to as the most powerful means of purification.

The sacredness of certain plants and rivers, and the worship of tools, all go far back, as well as serpent worship which, though primitive, is post-Vedic. The Mahabharata relates how the River Ganges was brought down from heaven in order to purify the earth from the

[1] *Young India*, pp. 411-12.

remains of the 60,000 sons of Sagara, who had been reduced to ashes by the sage Kapila, when they had disturbed his devotions. Today the source of the Ganges is a famous place of pilgrimage, and to visit it confers untold merit. To die upon the banks of the river is the yearning desire of thousands, and the devout feel a thrill of devotion as they bathe in its waters.

2. The Position of Women

In Vedic times women occupied a position of respect: though not counted among the 'twice-born', they shared in the sacrifices and joined in religious discussions. Yet already in the Atharva-Veda the birth of daughters is deprecated, and the Atareya Brahmana says that 'to have a daughter is a misery'. With the growth of the belief in transmigration it came to be thought that to be born a woman was a sign of sin in a former life. Similarly, when a woman is left a widow, her husband's death may be attributed to her former misdeeds.

Marriage is arranged by relatives and friends, the persons concerned having no choice in the matter. Betrothal frequently takes place at the age of five or six and is regarded as binding.[1] A man may remarry after being widowed, but custom forbids the woman to do so. Because betrothal takes place so early, and because when a man remarries there is often a great disparity in age between him and his bride, there are many thousands of child widows in India. Although occasionally treated with pity and sympathy, they are regarded as persons of ill-omen, and are often abused until life is made well-nigh intolerable.

A woman's duty to her husband is to bear him sons, who may be profitable in life, and can offer *pinda* to him after his death. The Law of Manu says 'women were created to be mothers' (ix. 26); and the mother is still looked up to by all right-thinking sons. But the lot of a wife may be pitiable if her children are only girls, or if she has none at all. The fact that a dowry must usually be provided when a daughter is married[2] is one very practical reason why parents prefer boys to girls.

One of the most ancient customs in Hindu worship is the provision at all the large temples[3] of groups of *deva-dasis*, or dancing girls, whose

[1] Marriage follows later. See pp. 104 f.
[2] The dowry is not, as some think, universal. Large communities expect the bridegroom to pay a bride-price.
[3] This practice obtains chiefly in South India, there being very few large temples in the North.

duties are those of performing on festival occasions, and of acting as religious prostitutes at other times. Although the giving of small children to be brought up in this way is now illegal, the practice dies hard, and this association of licence with worship is one of the worst features of Hinduism.

Sati, or the act whereby a widow offered herself to be burned alive upon her husband's funeral pyre in order that she might accompany him to the nether world, can be traced back to the earliest times. *Sati* means 'true', and this was once considered the supreme proof of wifely devotion. It was sternly suppressed by the British Government, which, however, never interfered with Hindu temple practice.

3. *Mythology*

Hindu mythology is like a tangled forest where beautiful, interesting and fantastic things grow, but where it is difficult to find one's way. Many and wonderful are the stories of gods and heroes that fill the pages of the Mahabharata and other epics, although, by Western standards, they are marred by much obscenity. The Vedic pantheon consisted of thirty-three gods representing the sky, earth, storm, fire and other natural objects, which were little removed from nature myths. But new gods were introduced from Dravidian and other sources until it was said, with characteristic exaggeration, that the gods numbered thirty-three crores, that is, 330 millions!

One popular deity is Ganesh, the god of wisdom and of worldly success, whose image with a human body and elephant's head can be seen in shops, and indeed in Hindu colleges and schools. Another deity often seen in pictures or marble images is Hanuman, the monkey god, the friend of Rama. He is usually represented as casting rocks into the sea between India and Ceylon, which brought into existence the chain of islands which still form, as it were, a bridge between the two lands.

Is such a story believed? Just enough to secure the worship of the god to whom it relates, and give rise to attempts to secure his favour; but not enough to be of any religious value. A monkey dropping from a tree down among a shopkeeper's goods may be reverently saluted as 'Hanuman, ji' and then driven off with a stone; or the same shopkeeper will regularly place a little rice before the image of Ganesh at the back of his shop, and yet be sceptical of the value of his action. The fact is that to the Hindu it does not matter whether a tale is

H

historical or mythical, nor does he think in terms of what the Western world calls sin or immorality. The behaviour of almost all his deities would be condemned by Christian standards, but not by Hindu ones, for to the Hindu sin consists of ritual disobedience or infringement of caste custom, rather than indecency, untruth, cruelty, and so on.

Strangest of all to western minds is the worship of Krishna in its combination of mythology, philosophy and modern re-interpretation. The stories of his licentious doings as a man do not bear repetition, but in the Bhagavad-gita Krishna becomes the exponent of the Vedantic philosophy.[1] The modern Hindu student of the Gita, however, is very apt to read into it ideas which are really derived from his western education and, indeed, from the Christian religion. To the educated Hindu the Gita is his most treasured sacred book, and the main contribution which it makes to Indian religious thinking is threefold. Firstly, the idea of a personal Lord to whom *bhakti* can be rendered; secondly, the importance of *yoga* and the technique of religious control of the mind; and thirdly, that ordinary daily life can be just as religiously observed as retreat into the life of an ascetic. These were largely new emphases, and have left a permanent mark on the more educated Indian's outlook on life.

The life-story of Rama, another *avatar* of Vishnu, as told in the Ramayana, is in marked contrast to that of Krishna. It describes the constancy to each other of Rama and Sita, his wife, when put to many a test, the faithful affection of Rama's brother Lakshman, and the wonderful assistance rendered to them by Hanuman which secured the release of Sita from the demon Ravana and brought about a happy ending to the story. It is deservedly popular and exerts a healthy influence on Hindu family life.

4. Temples, Priests, and Images

India is covered with countless temples and shrines inhabited by different members of the Hindu pantheon. Large ornate temples are found in the cities, particularly in South India, for the Muslim invaders destroyed many of those in the North; and every village has its shrine where can be seen an image of some primitive deity.

The temple is not the equivalent of a church as a place for congregational worship, which is unknown to orthodox Hinduism, although upon special occasions worshippers may gather to listen to the recita-

[1] See p. 108.

tion of *shastras* and join in the singing of *bhajans*. It is rather the dwelling-place of the god and as such is an earthly replica of his heavenly home. Its tremendous sculpturing is intended to represent the architecture of the celestial abodes. The image of the particular god is placed upon the mount specially sacred to him, Ganesh upon his rat, Durga upon her tiger, and so on. At some temples the *deva-dasis* ('slaves of the god', i.e. temple girls) dance before him and the Brahman priests are his servants.

When an idol is first erected, a ceremony with Sanskrit incantations is performed, to induce the god to come and dwell there. Thence-forward he is served faithfully by the priests. In the morning he is wakened by the ringing of bells, and may be given a bath. Incense is burned before him, and offerings made of flowers, food and drink. At night the temple is closed and he is left to sleep. The ritual is all per-formed by the priests,[1] but the worshipper is not left out. He is the guest of the god and receives the honour of the temple. He shares the food of the god and makes his prayer before him. Actually, of course, it is his own food which has been offered to the god and is then returned to him by the priest who may or may not keep some for the use of the temple servants and himself. If the worshipper visits the *deva-dasis*, he is doing only what is customary and taking advan-tage of what is provided for him by his gracious god. Each separate idol is a god, and has its own special power. So the devotee will go to one to pray for the gift of a son, to another for success in some enterprise, and to a third for protection during an epidemic of cholera.

All temple priests are Brahmans, but the converse is not true. Brahmans may be politicians like Pandit Nehru, or members of the legal and other professions, whilst many in the villages are landowners exerting their power for beneficence or the reverse over their peasant tenantry. They are regarded with great reverence by the simple, but treated as equals by the better educated.

Famous shrines such as those at Mathura, Krishna's birthplace, or Vrindavana, where he spent his youth, are centres of pilgrimage, where at certain seasons worshippers gather in their thousands. It is on the religious festivals, when the god is given a day out with all due cere-

---

[1] A similar ritual will often be carried out by the women in the home. The god will be washed and dressed and offerings of food placed before it. In the lives of many of the more secluded women in particular, these ceremonies count for much.

mony, that the popularity of primitive Hinduism amongst the illiterate masses shows itself most forcibly.

MODERN INFLUENCES

Since gaining independence the government of India has been able to exercise control over the whole of that part of the sub-continent now known as India. Great industrial developments and undertakings are changing the face of the land. Many legislative reforms have been introduced and there has been great economic advance.

Rapid means of communication both inside and outside India, industrialization and the spread of education have affected Hinduism in a twofold manner. They have set in motion certain reforming sects and movements, and they have at the same time produced a defensive and apologetic attitude among its professed adherents.

In the year 1820 there appeared a book, *The Precepts of Jesus, a Guide to Truth and Happiness*, written by a Brahman named Ram Mohan Roy, and this was soon followed by the formation of a society called the Brahmo Samaj, which aimed at abolishing caste and combining all that was best in Christianity and Hinduism. In 1841 this society was joined by Rabindranath Tagore, whose religious poetry is still widely read and valued. Under the leadership of Keshub Chandra Sen and others the Samaj has spread and developed, some of its members holding almost every Christian doctrine, and some, at the other extreme, differing little in thought from other reforming Hindus. In 1875 the Arya Samaj, a movement of a different character and strongly opposed to Christianity, was founded by Dayananda Sarasvati, who denounced both idolatry and caste (though his followers have not broken with either), and allowed the remarriage of widows. The work of Christian missions was copied by founding schools and orphanages, and certain reforms such as the raising of the age of marriage for girls were advocated. Efforts were made to raise the outcastes, some of whom were invested with the sacred thread and initiated with sacred ceremonies, but their lives remained unchanged and they were not recognized as converts by orthodox Hindus.

Apart from such movements western education and culture is speedily affecting Hindu ideas. The old customs still have a firm hold upon the women, but the education of girls is on the increase, and young men of education are making their own marriage arrangements. More freedom is being claimed among the educated classes in the matter of eating with members of other castes, but it is only in a few exceptional cases that the caste rules concerning marriage are broken.

The religiously orthodox justify idol worship on the ground that God is everywhere, and it is God in the idol and not the idol itself that is reverenced. They defend the popular mythology as being necessary for the masses in order to give them something within their grasp, and they read into the old Hindu writings modern and Christian ideas. Gandhi, who in early life was much in contact with Christian teachers, and at one time contemplated baptism, exemplified this syncretistic tendency of Hinduism by his endeavours to combine Christian ideals with Hindu practice.

This genius for syncretism has been the secret of the strength of Hinduism over the centuries. It is above all an eclectic religion with amazing powers of absorbing ideas and theories from outside whilst remaining Hindu. Buddhism, Jainism, Muhammadanism and Christianity have all influenced it, and no doubt will continue to do so; and now the teaching of Marxist Communism has begun to percolate through India, and what the Hinduism of a new generation may be if these new ideas are absorbed on a large scale no one can say. What does seem probable is that the power of the priest will decrease as life becomes more and more secularized, and this will inevitably result in the abandonment, by large sections of the people, of many of the present-day religious customs and ceremonies.

CHAPTER V

BUDDHISM

INTRODUCTION

BUDDHISM is the offspring of Hinduism and of India. While Muhammadanism arose to claim the allegiance of mankind about six hundred years after the appearance of Jesus Christ, Buddhism came into existence almost six hundred years before Christ. Of these three religions which share a worldwide appeal, Buddhism was by several centuries the first to become international.

The successes of Buddhism have been almost entirely confined to the continent of Asia. While Christianity spread primarily westwards into Europe, Buddhism moved in the opposite direction, and it claims attention today as the predominant faith of the Far East, that immense region which stretches from Manchuria to Java and from Central Asia to the islands of Japan.

We are apt to think of an unfamiliar faith as a homogeneous whole, but Buddhism presents in reality a vast variety of doctrine and practice. It knows the rival trends of conservatism and liberalism, of orthodoxy and revolt, the tensions of sects and parties, the corrupting influence of other systems and cultures, and the recurrent return to the original fountain of the faith. The differences to be found within Buddhism are probably comparable to those existing between Protestantism, Roman Catholicism, and the Greek Orthodox Church, including the numerous movements and groupings which each of these itself contains. It should be clearly grasped at the outset that there are two types of Buddhism current today, two expressions of the one faith. These are known as Theravada or Southern Buddhism and Mahayana or Northern Buddhism. Theravada means 'The Teaching of the Elders, and looks back to the body of doctrine approved at an important conference held in India not long after the founder's death. It is common to see it referred to as Hinayana, 'The Little Vehicle', a disparaging title given by those who feel that it is too difficult a way for the mass of mankind. It survives today principally in Ceylon, Burma, Siam, and Cambodia. Mahayana, 'The Great Vehicle', the way made broad and comprehensive enough for all peoples, was not developed for several centuries, but is today the religion of vast populations in China and Japan as well as of Tibet, Mongolia, Korea, Vietnam and Nepal.

The canon of Theravada Buddhism, called the Three Pitakas, written in the Pali language, and held to contain the words of the Buddha (although not committed to writing until he had been dead for several centuries), is approximately eleven times the size of the Christian Bible, and thus gives abundant scope for variety of inter- pretation. Yet it would be quite wrong to imagine that so much diversity means that the characteristic features of this influential teach- ing cannot be distinctly perceived. They were laid down in no un- certain terms by the master mind of the founder and it is to him we must turn if we would understand the development and long-standing influence of The Light of Asia. In tracing the course of his ideas we shall in effect be laying down the fundamental teachings of Buddhism, especially as seen in the Theravada school, leaving the innovations of Mahayana for later consideration.

THE EARLY LIFE AND ILLUMINATION OF GAUTAMA

The word Buddha is not a name but a title signifying The Enlightened One, or The Awakened One. It is especially given to Siddhartha Gautama, who was born about 563 B.C. near Kapilavastu on the borders of Nepal, 130 miles to the north of Benares. It is held that this was the last of five hundred (though some say myriads of) reincarnations during the course of which he suffered, sacrificed, fulfilled every per- fection, and drew gradually nearer to his goal of winning Enlighten- ment for himself and all mankind. His father, Suddhodana, belonged to the proud Sakya clan, so that Gautama[1] is sometimes called Sakya- muni, the sage of the Sakyas. He is also known by the word Tathagata, meaning probably 'He who follows in the footsteps of his predecessors', which he often used in reference to himself.

It is not easy to feel sure about the details of his career since no biography was written until hundreds of years later. It appears, how- ever, that his early life was spent in ease and luxury, and his father made every effort to see that the boy experienced only beautiful and pleasant things. At the age of sixteen he married his cousin, Yasodhara, by whom, more than ten years later, he had a son whom he symbolically named Rahula, 'the fetter'. They lived together in a palace which his father had built for him. One day, however, in spite of every precau- tion, he saw on his way to the royal park an old man, a sick man, a dead man, and a begging monk. Thus the hard realities of the world were

[1] The name may also be spelt 'Gotama'.

brought home to his mind. So deeply affected was he by the problem of human suffering that when Rahula was born, he felt it imperative to break forthwith the chains of home life which might prevent him from ever finding the answer to the questions which tormented him. His decision once made, he stole in during the night to look again at his sleeping wife and child and then abandoned home and family, wealth and prospects, in order to seek the answer to the riddle of life.

He was then twenty-nine years old, but it was not until six years had passed that his quest was rewarded. To begin with he put himself under the instruction of two famous Brahman hermits, Alara and Uddaka, but he was unable to find satisfaction in their teaching, for they could not tell him how to put an end to rebirth. As a next step he devoted himself with five companions to a life of extreme asceticism in the jungle, existing, it is said, on a mere grain of rice each day, until his delicate body was reduced almost to a skeleton. This led him to another decisive experience, for he perceived that asceticism and extreme self-mortification were delusions; they did not lead to self-realization, but rather enfeebled both body and mind. Accordingly he turned away from such excesses and devoted himself to a simple life of intense mental activity.

Eventually, as the culmination òf prolonged meditation, he sat beneath a fig tree at Uruvela (known henceforth as the Bo, or Wisdom, Tree) and there received the thoughts which constitute the essential message of Buddhism. This was the turning point in his life; the seeker had at last found what he sought and had thereby not only solved his own burning problem, but possessed a message which the world must hear. Buddhists would probably claim that words are inadequate to describe Prince Gautama's Enlightenment, but so far as they can do so it consisted in the following four truths.

1. The Four Truths

The first is the truth of suffering. The original Pali word has been variously interpreted. It is a complex state of suffering, both mental and physical. This truth simply asserts that suffering is omnipresent and involved in the very nature of life. All forms of existence are subject to it. It is inextricably bound up with individual existence.

The second truth deals with the cause of suffering. This Gautama felt to be desire, desire for possession and selfish enjoyment of every kind, but particularly the desire for separate, individual, existence.

The third truth states that suffering ceases when desire ceases, when this selfish craving, this lust for life, has been renounced and destroyed.

Lastly comes the truth of the path which leads to the cessation of suffering. This path is eightfold and much more difficult to comprehend than the preceding three truths. Gautama took over from Hinduism the doctrine of rebirth, teaching that people pass away and are reborn according to their behaviour in a previous lifetime. He believed that only by complete detachment could a man's thoughts, words, and actions be deprived of their power to bind him to the inexorable wheel of life and death, life and death, following one another hundreds of times throughout the ages. The path to this perfect detachment is also known as the Middle Way, avoiding the two extremes of self-indulgence and self-mortification, both of which Gautama had tested and found wanting.

2. The Eightfold Path

The eight steps in this path are as follows:

1. *Right Views.* This involves acceptance of the four truths and a resolute rejection of unworthy attitudes and acts, such as covetousness, lying and gossip.

2. *Right Desires.* The thoughts are to be free from lust, from ill-will, and from cruelty. In this case the desire for selfish possession is to be distinguished from a wholesome zeal to achieve the highest ends.

3. *Right Speech*, plain and truthful, abhorring lying, tale-bearing, and harsh or vain talk. Words must be gentle, soothing to the ear, penetrating to the heart, useful, rightly timed, and according to the facts.

4. *Right Conduct.* This includes charity and abstention from killing any living being (even the breaking of an egg, a potential life, is condemned), from stealing, and from unlawful sexual intercourse. In Buddhism, morality and intellectual enlightenment are inseparable, in accordance with the saying, 'While morality forms the basis of the higher life, wisdom completes it.'

5. *Right Mode of Livelihood*, harming no one and free from luxury. Each must take up work which will give scope to his abilities and make him useful to his fellow men.

6. *Right Effort*, always pressing on and particularly in four directions. First, the effort to avoid the uprising of evil; secondly, the effort to overcome evil; thirdly, the effort to develop meritorious conditions such as detachment, investigation of the law, concentration, and rap-

ture; and lastly, the effort to maintain the meritorious conditions which have already arisen and to bring them to maturity and perfection. The climax of this achievement is universal love.

7. *Right Awareness*, the four fundamentals of which are the contemplation of the transitoriness and loathsomeness of the body, the contemplation of the feelings of oneself and of others, the contemplation of the mind, and the contemplation of phenomena.

8. *Right Meditation.* This amounts to complete one-pointedness of thought, concentrating the mind on a single object, all hindrances having been overcome. Such arduous mind-development is the principal occupation of the more enlightened Buddhist and an integral part of the daily life of the humblest follower of Gautama. It leads on into trances where the devotee is purified from all distractions and evils and filled with rapture, happiness and equanimity. Finally he passes beyond sensation of either pleasure or pain into a state transcending consciousness, ultimately attaining full Enlightenment, which is the highest possible state of perfection.

Such is the Way according to Gautama, a combination of morality, concentration, and that wisdom which consists in the long spiritual processes leading at last to Buddhahood. The place given to morality should not be overlooked; failure there spells total failure, for it is only as the mind is pure and the heart is soft that the divine seed of wisdom grows. Such wisdom means the power of seeing things as they really are and perceiving the right way to peace; it is an ideal state of intellectual and ethical perfection which can be attained by man through purely human means.

Buddhism has been well called the most radical system of self-deliverance ever conceived in the world. It is in fact infinitely more complicated, rigorous and intellectual than the outline just given might lead one to expect, for to walk the eightfold path involves passing through Four Stages in which the Ten Fetters are successively broken. In the first stage a start towards the goal is made, and three fetters, the delusive belief that the individual self is real, doubt regarding the truth of the teaching, and confidence in the efficacy of religious rites and ceremonies, are shattered. During the second and third stages substantial progress is made and the fetters of sensuality and unkindness are done away with. Five hindrances remain to be overcome during the final stage, the desire for separate life in this world and in realms beyond the grave, spiritual pride, self-righteousness, and ignorance. It must not for a moment be imagined that a normal lifetime will suffice to complete these stages. Even the first one may be but the culmination of many lives of preparation and the whole process covers great periods of time, for which reincarnation after reincarnation is required, while to undertake fully so drastic a course of self-discipline ultimately necessitates the abandonment of family life in accordance with Gautama's example.

SOME IMPORTANT DEFINITIONS

For a right understanding of the Middle Way it is essential to grasp what is meant by Karma, Impermanence, and Nirvana, conceptions of frequent occurrence in Buddhism.

1. *Karma*

Karma signifies action-reaction and denotes the law of cause and effect. What you sow you reap, and neither man, priest, nor deity can suspend the operation of that law or withhold the consequences of a deed. But Karma has a twin, Rebirth, which is necessary for its comprehension. The law of cause and effect is an unbroken chain through the ages. You are and do what you are and do as a result of what you were and did in a previous incarnation, which in its turn was the inevitable outcome of what you were and did in still earlier incarnations. Similarly your future rebirths will be conditioned precisely by what happens in your present life. 'Karma is father and mother.' 'Each is heir to his own action, each is the fruit of his own action's womb. Each is kinsman of his own action and each has his own action as overlord and protector.' Furthermore, it is not possible to cancel the influence of evil deeds by performing good deeds. Good will bring its reward; evil will brings its reward; the two operate independently. Directly an individual's present existence terminates, a new being appears by the sheer force of his Karma. This new being is really identical with the one just passed away, because the Karma link preserves individuality through all the countless changes that take place.

The doctrine of rebirth attempts to account for differences at birth which Buddhists attribute neither to chance, environment, nor Creator. The law of cause and effect is held to operate in the mental and moral domain no less than in the physical world. By its aid circumstances such as love at first sight are readily explicable; the individuals were associated in a former existence. Indeed there is no calamity met with or inherited, no event of life, whether favourable or otherwise, which this theory cannot readily explain. The period which elapses between one life and another is commonly thought of as longer than a normal life-span. While it is sometimes held that acts of a bestial nature may occasion the birth of a beast after the dissolution of the human form at death, others maintain that it is not possible for this to take place. Buddhism does not accept the theory of transmigration, for it rejects the idea of a soul existing in a body and thus forming the connecting link between successive incarnations. What lives on after death is simply Karma, the result of what has happened before, not some inward and invisible part of the individual. The true Buddhist doctrine is therefore rebirth without transmigration.

'The King said: "Where there is no transmigration, Nagasena, can there be rebirth?"

"Yes, there can."

"But how can that be? Give me an illustration."

"Suppose a man, O king, were to light a lamp from another lamp, can it be said that one transmigrates from, or to, the other?"

"Certainly not."

"Just so, great king, is rebirth without transmigration." '[1]

But in spite of this it is probable that many Buddhists in practice hold to the view of transmigration.

2. *Impermanence*

This brings us to the doctrine of Impermanence and its influence upon the conception of the self. Buddhism teaches that all that exists passes through the cycle of birth, growth, decay, and death. Life is one and indivisible; its ever-changing forms are innumerable and perishable, for though there is really no such thing as death, every form must die and give place to a different one. The world of phenomena, the very universe itself, has a purely relative existence, and this impermanence, this lack of absolute objective reality, applies to the individual's 'self'. There is nothing eternal or immortal inside a man's body. Separate individual existence is really an illusion, for the self has neither beginning nor ending, is eternally changing, and possesses only a phenomenal existence. So long as the phrase is rightly understood, this doctrine can be represented by saying that Gautama denied the exist-

[1] Extract from *The Questions of King Milinda*, quoted in C. H. S. Ward's *Buddhism*, p. 87.

ence of the self as a separate entity. 'There is no permanent ego.'

'Misery only doth exist; none miserable.
No doer is there; naught but the deed is found.
Nirvana is, but not the man who seeks it.
The path exists, but not the traveller on it.'[1]

'From time immemorial the ignorant unconverted man has held, cherished, and affected the notion, This is mine; this am I; this is my ego!'[2]

3. Nirvana

We move on to slightly more familiar ground in seeking to explain Nirvana, although it is not easy to do so adequately. A collection of definitions may perhaps give an impression of its significance. Nirvana is an ethical state, a condition which eliminates any future rebirth, the extinction of all craving, the final release from suffering. It may be defined as deliverance from the trammels of the body, a supreme consciousness of peace and rest, a perfect, passionless happiness. It is a state of mind in which Karma comes to an end. It is the cessation of becoming, for when a process is not continued it simply ceases. It is remainderlessness. It is the peace of the man for whom there will be no rebirth; separateness is ended, the flame of desire has gone out, the limitations of selfhood are extinguished. However nearly this may seem to approximate to total annihilation, orthodox Buddhism frowns on the suggestion as much as it does on the notion that it means continued existence. With our totally different mental attitude the best we can do is to say that it falls somewhere between the two. The wick is finished and the oil is dry. 'The dew-drop slips into the shining sea.' If this goal seems unattractive, it should be remembered that to the Buddhist the curse from which he longs to escape is life itself. Believing that he has been for milleniums upon his journey, he sees the highest bliss in the knowledge that he has at last stopped. Gautama persistently refused to give a plain answer to the enquiries of his disciples whether he would, or would not, enjoy any kind of existence after death. Probably the fullest reply he ever provided is this:

'There is, disciples, a condition, where there is neither earth nor

[1] *Visuddhimagga*, xvi.   [2] *Samyutta-Nikaya*, xii. 62.

water, neither air nor light, neither limitless space, nor limitless time, neither any kind of being, neither ideation nor non-ideation, neither this world nor that world. There is neither arising nor passing-away, nor dying, neither cause nor effect, neither change nor standing-still.'[1]

It can hardly have escaped the reader that in defining original Buddhist doctrine no mention has been made of God. Nothing could be clearer than that Gautama himself eschewed all claims to divinity. He professes to point out the way and give guidance to those who seek to walk in it, but it is for every man to do the walking on his own. Gautama is just the Teacher and the commonly used phrase, 'I take refuge in the Buddha', denotes an undertaking to follow his instructions: not an attitude of faith that he has saved or can save anyone by his own virtue or self-sacrifice. God in the objective, personal, sense does not fit into the system. The Middle Way has been described by Prof. Kraemar as 'a non-theistic ethical discipline', a system of self-training, anthropocentric, stressing ethics and mind-culture to the exclusion of theology. Buddhism as taught by its founder is in no sense a system of faith and worship. He inculcated neither prayer nor praise; he offered neither redemption, nor forgiveness, nor heaven; he warned of no judgment and no hell. He refused to speculate on ultimate reality or the First Cause which originated the long chain of cause and effect, for that of which the universe is the outward form is far beyond human understanding. He was silent regarding any future life, putting a minimum of positive content into his conception of Nirvana. Faced with the problem of suffering, he taught the way of deliverance from Karma and the cycle of existence by the elimination of desire. It is an evolutionary process to be achieved by one's own effort, for Buddhism does not accept the view that man is by nature evil, nor does it seek any external agency for the carrying out of its moral precepts. It addresses itself primarily to the problem of pain and suffering rather than to that of moral evil. The inequality of suffering and its frequently inexplicable character often seems to its adherents to clinch the argument against the existence of a personal God. Thus Buddhism is hardly a religion in the generally accepted sense of the word as connoting some contact between man and his Maker. It is rather a moral philosophy and a Way.

[1] *Sacred Books of the Buddhists*, Vol. II, p. 54.

THE LATER CAREER OF GAUTAMA

After attaining Enlightenment, Gautama was tempted to keep his discovery to himself, fearing that men's minds were so benighted that any attempt to convince them would be in vain. Having overcome this reluctance he sought out the five men with whom he had formerly experimented in the way of austerity. He found them in the Deer Park at Benares and preached to them his first sermon with such success that they became the original members of the Order which did so much to propagate his doctrine throughout the East. And so 'there were six holy persons in the world', but within three months their number had grown to sixty, most of them being wealthy young noblemen satiated with luxury and pleasure, as Gautama himself had been. These sixty he then sent forth in all directions as missionaries, while he himself shared their success and gained adherents even from among his own family. For upwards of forty years Gautama lived as a mendicant preacher in Bihar, Oudh, and Nepal. It was his custom to spend the three wet months of the year in retreat and the nine dry ones itinerating. His usual routine is said to have been as follows:

'Rising very early in the morning it was his daily habit, first of all, to accept water from his body-servant to rinse out his mouth, and afterwards to sit down and meditate until it was time for him to go begging. Then, taking his alms-bowl in hand, he went out into the town or village, with eyes fixed on the ground, and passed silently from door to door, accepting whatever food was put into his bowl.

'If he were invited to take his meal in a house, he usually accepted the invitation and ate whatever was put before him. The meal being over, he washed his hands, discoursed to those present on his doctrine, and then returned to the place where he was staying at the time. After sitting quietly on one side while his disciples finished their meal, he retired to his chamber and allowed his body-servant to bring him water to wash his feet. This being done, he returned again to the assembly of the disciples, and addressed them on some point of doctrine or discipline.

'The discourse ended, he retired again to his "fragrance" chamber and rested through the heat of the day, and then, rising refreshed, he went out to receive visitors, and, after accepting their gifts, he taught them such doctrine as he considered suitable for them. When the visitors had gone away, he would go to bathe at the bath-house, or at some bathing-tank or pond, and would afterwards retire to his chamber for further meditation.

'When the evening was come, it was his custom to receive any of his disciples who had come to see him from a distance, giving them counsel and advice, and clearing up any difficulties they might have, so that he sent them away cheered and strengthened. The evening being now far advanced, and feeling cramped with so much sitting, the Buddha would spend some time in just pacing up and down to relieve his legs until it was time for him to retire to his rooms for the night.'[1]

His popularity with both high and low was remarkable, while his self-sacrificing life, his gentle and calm spirit, his love for mankind, and the lofty character of much of his moral teaching, have been largely responsible for his influence in history. He was eighty when he died at Kusinara, travelling northward towards the Himalayas.

THE SPREAD OF HINAYANA BUDDHISM

From the beginning, Buddhism was a religion of monks. Gautama himself established the Sangha, the Buddhist Order. On entering it, new recruits are required to pronounce the formula of the Three Refuges: 'I take refuge in the Buddha: I take refuge in the Doctrine: I take refuge in the Order.' Criminals, soldiers, debtors, slaves, or those afflicted with such diseases as consumption, leprosy and epilepsy are disqualified. Applicants must also be over twenty years of age and have their parents' consent.

Members vow to observe the ten precepts, to the first five of which most practising Buddhists are committed. These forbid murder, theft, sensuality, deceit, and the use of intoxicants. The remaining five exclude food taken after midday and any form of self-adornment, involve sleeping on a mat on the ground, and prohibit dancing, theatricals, and the use of gold or silver. In Buddhist monasticism physical labour has been discouraged and there are few celebrations to divert them from seeking their own salvation, apart from two 'abstinence days' every month and an annual 'ceremony of invitation' when mutual criticisms are invited.

Tonsured, celibate, and clad in long yellow robes, the monks begged from house to house and spent their lives in meditation and study. Monasteries were built in Gautama's lifetime, and with the greatest

[1] C. H. S. Ward, *Buddhism*, pp. 44-45.

reluctance he yielded to the request of his foster-mother to admit women to the Order. The Order of Nuns, which has in some countries ceased to exist, was made subject to the Order of Monks. Outside these stand the Buddhist laymen, who often have a truer conception of the real nature of their religion than the mendicants. These keep some of the ten precepts for longer or shorter periods; they do not seek for Nirvana now, but aim by good living and almsgiving to improve their chances of attaining it in a subsequent rebirth.

For hundreds of years after Gautama's death the influence of Buddhism continued to expand. By the seventh century of our present era, however, it was declining in India, due largely to its corruption by local superstitions and magic. The deathblow was delivered by the Muslim invasions of the eleventh century and since that time there have been few Buddhists to be found in the land of its origin. Yet it was there that its most famous protagonist arose, the monk-king Asoka, the Constantine of Buddhism and its greatest missionary, who sought to establish a realm of righteousness in Northern India during the third century before Christ. Magnificent rock inscriptions still remain to testify to what so nearly become the faith of India, but a more enduring memorial of Asoka's work is contained in the lands of southeast Asia to which he sent the teaching of Gautama to mould the lives of men and women until this day. It was due to his influence that Ceylon and Burma entered the Buddhist fold, and it is these two countries along with Siam, which was not won over until the seventh century after Christ, which are now the stronghold of Theravada Buddhism. Among the more famous relics in Ceylon are a reputed cutting from the original Bo tree, a collar bone of Gautama, the imprint of his foot on a lonely mountain peak, and one of his teeth, to which immense reverence is paid in the Temple of the Tooth at Kandy.

In May 1954 the Sixth Great Council of Theravadin Buddhist countries opened in Rangoon, attended by representatives of Buddhist lands throughout the world. This synod is planned to last two years and will terminate in celebrations to mark the 2,500th anniversary of the Buddha's birth. The object of the Council is described in *The Middle Way* as being the rediscovery of Buddhism and the Buddhist way of life, and the influencing of all adherents throughout the world to a correct appreciation of the teachings of the Buddha. Buddhist scholars will re-examine the sacred texts with the object of revising and purifying them.

MAHAYANA BUDDHISM

Although the successes of Southern Buddhism have thus been considerable, the most striking advance of this complex system of thought has been gained under the banner of Mahayana, 'The Great Vehicle'. The origin of this principal division of the Buddhist forces is obscure, but it seems to date back almost to the days of Asoka, when India was the one stronghold of the faith. Mahayana Buddhism has a different canon, which has never yet been codified. Its sacred books are written in Sanskrit and it has carried a revised version of the tenets of Gautama far and wide across Central Asia, Tibet, Mongolia, Korea, China, Japan, Vietnam, Nepal, Java, and Sumatra. While some of these lands are wild and sparsely peopled, most of them teem with vast populations, and to the student of the Far East Mahayana Buddhism cannot be overlooked as an historical force and a dominant influence to this day. It is the faith of the majority of living Buddhists.

This great missionary movement took place very gradually. Speaking rather generally, China was reached soon after the time of Christ, Korea in the fourth century of our era, Japan in the sixth, and Tibet in the seventh. Buddhism was also flourishing in Java and Sumatra in the seventh century, only to be largely obliterated by the Muslim invasion of the fifteenth. One very potent factor in the spread of Buddhism has been the tolerance with which it has incorporated ideas and practices really alien to its spirit. While this has given it popular appeal, it has also gravely contaminated its original character.

It is an almost irresistible temptation to compare Mahayana Buddhism broadly to Roman Catholicism and Hinayana to Protestantism. The relative purity and simplicity of Gautama's message is in Northern Buddhism transformed beyond recognition, although its adherents claim originality and the sanction of the founder for their views and practices.

1. *Innovations*

It is not easy to epitomize fairly doctrines which are claimed to be the most comprehensive known to mankind, and in which it is maintained that every seeker can find what is suited to him. Among the more striking innovations of Mahayana Buddhism are the following:

1. The introduction of a supreme Reality from which the universe emanated.

2. The deification of Gautama himself, regarded as a transitory manifestation of that Reality. Some would go to the length of denying that he was really human at all.

3. The ideal of actually attaining full Enlightenment gave way to another in which the element of Compassion for humanity predominated. Those who might have attained Buddhahood, but voluntarily abstained from Nirvana in order to help in the deliverance of erring men, are known as Bodhisattvas. A vast number of such Wisdom Beings constitutes the pantheon of Mahayana Buddhism.

4. The way of salvation became faith in Gautama and the Bodhisattvas. The repetition of their names was inculcated to an extreme degree. Of this salvation the lotus flower, rising pure and white from the muddy pool, became the emblem.

5. Vivid portrayals of heaven and hell were given and individual immortality was the hope set before the devotee.

6. Images were introduced to aid the illiterate and idolatrous polytheism supplanted Gautama's original atheism. In some lands the Goddess of Mercy, the Hearer of the World's Prayers, came to hold a place akin to that occupied by the Virgin Mary in Roman Catholicism.

The enumeration of these points cries aloud at once for some qualification, for Mahayana Buddhism is subdivided into many sects and movements, comprising a gigantic syncretism of philosophy and popular superstition. 'Only the Buddha fully understands Buddhism', confesses its most prominent contemporary English protagonist.[1] While it is true that it sinks at times into fantastic and degrading forms, at others it soars aloft into vast realms of metaphysics and speculation. Its very novelty, its claim to intellectual insight and scientific accuracy, and its broadminded lack of dogmatic definition, have helped to give it power and attraction even outside the lands where it predominates.

2. The sects

The character and variety of Mahayana Buddhism may be illustrated by a brief reference to three of its most notable sects.

The Zen or Meditation Sect gets its name from the stress it lays on contemplation and meditation as opposed to study and all acquired knowledge. It teaches that Enlightenment may be attained in this life by a sudden comprehension of our true natures. Adherents of this sect would have little sympathy with many of the innovations of

[1] Christmas Humphries, *Buddhism*, p. 15.

Mahayana Buddhism listed above. From its independence of written texts it has been called 'the wordless sect'. The method of meditation employed has been thus described by an English Buddhist:

'The devotee takes up his position with his legs crossed and the soles of his feet uppermost (the lotus posture). His back is held straight, but not rigidly, the palm of his right hand facing upwards and its back contained in the palm of the left hand which rests, knuckles downwards, on his lap. His eyes are kept half-closed, his mouth slightly open and the tip of his tongue resting lightly at the base of his upper teeth. This position can be maintained for hours by those who have had sufficient experience, and there are even some who can maintain it for days.

'After taking up this posture, the seeker after Enlightenment allows a few moments for his thoughts to become calm, and then strives to put his mind into a condition to receive the intuitive knowledge which, it is believed, enters only when the mind is perfectly still and devoid of thoughts arising from the perception of external phenomena, or from the knowledge acquired from previous perceptions which has been stored up in the memory. People are said to differ greatly as to the amount of practice they require to perform this practice successfully, and the degrees of success range from the ability to keep the mind tranquil for a few moments to ecstatic contemplation lasting over a long period and leading to supreme Enlightenment. The intuitive knowledge which is the object of this practice consists in a complete realization of the individual's true nature.'[1]

The Pure Land Sect represents in many respects an attitude diametrically opposed to this. It is impressed with the difficulty of attaining Enlightenment in this life and teaches that by faith in Amita Buddha, said to have been a king who became a wanderer dedicated to attaining Buddhahood, we may obtain rebirth in a better world where there will be opportunities for grasping the truth. The Pure Land is not the goal, but a stepping-stone to the goal; it is not purgatory, for its essence does not consist in further purification but in receiving the fullest teaching under much more favourable conditions. According to this school, the Pure Land was created by Amita Buddha 'out of his infinite compassion and by the power of his accumulated merit' in order that those ensnared by desire, hatred and ignorance might be reborn there and have transferred to them the results of his

[1] J. Blofeld, *The Jewel in the Lotus*, p. 136.

excellent Karma. The Goddess of Mercy dwells in the Pure Land with him. There are said to be nine classes of rebirth in the Pure Land, the lowest of which is for those who repeat the name of Amita Buddha for ten seconds before death.

'As there is a danger that the moment of death may have such terrors that the dying man may neglect to repeat the holy name, members of the sect practice repeating it as often as possible, usually several thousand times in succession, and are exhorted to continue the practice mentally even when engaged in attending to the daily routine of their lives. They do this until it becomes such an ingrained habit that, even while they are eating or sleeping, the repetition goes on in their minds without conscious effort. Thus they trust that the habit will not fail them at the time of approaching death and that they will be thus assured of reaching the Pure Land. Many of them carry a rosary and allow one of its one hundred and eight beads to slip through their fingers with each repetition of the holy name.'[1]

The teachings of this sect are reckoned to be specially adapted to the intelligence of those who are unable to understand the more abstruse and philosophical Buddhist doctrines.[2]

The Esoteric Sect, so called from the high degree of secrecy its adherents observe, is the religion of Tibet, Mongolia, Bhutan, Sikkim and Nepal, often known as Lamaism. It is characterized by colourful pageantry and ritual which give it considerable attraction to those whose lives are dull and unromantic. The fundamental characteristic which distinguishes the sect is its belief that in the struggle for Enlightenment the help of Bodhisattvas can be enlisted by means of appropriate rituals. These rituals fall particularly into three categories, symbols (made by positioning hands and fingers in certain ways), formulas repeated in a special tone of voice, and attempts to visualize the form of the Bodhisattva whose help is desired.

'Devotees are expected to go through a period of preliminary training before any of the higher secrets are revealed to them. This consists of tens of thousands of full-length prostrations, the repetition according to certain rules of the commoner formulas, and the preparation of

[1] J. Blofeld, op. cit., pp. 145-6.
[2] However, its departure from the fundamental principles of original Buddhism is so marked that many Buddhist scholars refuse to recognize it as Buddhism at all.

symbolical offerings. In some cases a teacher may be prepared to allow his disciple to omit some of these preliminaries if he considers that the latter's development is already of a high order. When the time is ripe, he will begin to impart further knowledge in a series of carefully graduated stages, on the strict understanding that the essential details will never be divulged to anyone but the disciples whom the pupil will himself instruct in due course. Thus many of these details have never been committed to writing.

'Each Bodhisattva has certain symbols and formulas peculiar to himself. By forming these symbols and reciting the formulas in the proper tone of voice and, at the same time, visualizing the form of the Bodhisattva as being of a certain size, colour, appearance, etc., and having certain characteristics and particular ornaments and dress, the devotee is expected gradually to be able to identify himself with the Bodhisattva and so become one with him. Fiery letters and refulgent rays of various kinds also play an important part in these visualizations. The secret knowledge imparted to the disciples by their teachers consists of a knowledge of these symbols, formulas, visualizations, the ceremonies that are appropriate to their use, and, more rarely, of the metaphysical theories underlying this complicated ritual. There is hardly a single detail in the whole ceremonial which is not symbolical of something infinitely more profound than appears on the surface, though it may be doubted if all the instructors are aware of the true significance of what they teach.'[1]

A kind of baptismal ceremony, breathing exercises, and meditation are also practised, while by the same mysterious means magical powers, such as the ability to cover long distances at tremendous pace, are sought. This strange and influential system, in which religion is mechanized through prayer flags or wheels and vitiated by sorcery and devil dances, is a combination of Buddhism with magical and degraded elements of Tibetan superstition. It presents the world's most extreme development of monasticism and lends itself to grossly immoral practices.

In conclusion it should be stated that Buddhist psycho-ethical philosophy has made an appeal to some minds even in the West. Until the present century it was only an interest of a few scholars in English-speaking lands, who made translations of Buddhist scriptures. Since

[1] J. Blofeld, op. cit., pp. 154-6.

1906, however, there have been Westerners who were practising Buddhists. A Buddhist Society formed in 1924 exists today in London, for example. Its founder, Mr. Christmas Humphries, who still remains its President, has by his writings probably done as much as anyone to propagate Buddhism in the West. Although not apparently a large group numerically, this Buddhist Society possesses a library of some two thousand books and has published a considerable number of popular studies on different aspects of Buddhism as well as translations of selected scriptures and a quarterly magazine, entitled *The Middle Way*. Its official attitude embraces Theravada and Mahayana as complementary rather than contradictory aspects of the one teaching. Attracted principally by the philosophical doctrines of Gautama and their later amplifications by creative Mahayana thinkers, they maintain that Buddhism makes a unique contribution to world thought in teaching that the individual is complete in himself, needing neither God nor man to save him, and yet at the same time incomplete, as being part of the one life of all. In fairness to Buddhism we ought probably to judge it, not primarily by its wilder perversions and developments, but on the merits of such views as can be clearly traced back to the founder himself. Estimated in that spirit, we must think of it above all as a call to rigorous self-discipline, mind-development, and unselfish conduct, an appeal to work out one's own salvation by the use of faculties already latent in every human being.

CHAPTER VI

SHINTO

INTRODUCTION

SHINTO, the Way of the Gods, is a national religion. It is the worship or reverence paid to the gods of Japan. In pure Shinto it is inconceivable that anyone should follow the Way of the Gods without being a Japanese or wishing to become one.

Shinto literature speaks of the 'eight myriads of gods', implying that the number is unlimited. Shinto has no systematic doctrine, and no philosophy of its own. Its code of moral behaviour is an unwritten code, which in its modern expression owes much to Confucius and something to Buddhism. Pure Shinto does little to answer the questions or satisfy the needs of personal religion. It has only a very vague and shadowy conception of a life after death.

Yet in spite of these serious limitations, it is, or has been until very recently, a living religion, capable of inspiring great devotion and fanaticism, the only vital religion for the majority of the 80,000,000 subjects of the Emperor of Japan.

Before proceeding further, a few preparatory explanations are needed.

The greater part of what follows applies to Shinto as believed and practised in Japan before her catastrophic defeat in 1945. This must be understood except where direct reference is made at the end of this chapter to the post-war situation. The defeat of Japan is, at the time of writing, too recent for us to pronounce what permanent effect it will have on Shinto.

Our description, therefore, is of Shinto as it was maintained and practised at the height of its influence in the years immediately before the Second World War, and for that purpose a rough classification of the varieties of Shinto, as observed by the Japanese Government, is necessary. At that time the Government made a broad classification into *Shrine Shinto* and *Sect Shinto*. *Shrine Shinto* was controlled by a bureau of the Ministry of Home Affairs, and included as a subdivision some three hundred shrines of State Shinto, entirely maintained by the central Government, with a priesthood which was a branch of the civil service. It also included a vast number—fluctuating, but something above 100,000—of local shrines, large and small, maintained by local authorities and voluntary contributions. *Sect Shinto* is a development of the last two hundred years which stands in a position by itself. It bears the same relationship to the Japanese State as Buddhism and Christianity in that country, and like them was under the supervision of the Ministry of Education. It will very greatly help the understanding of Shinto if these distinctions are borne in mind, and it is realized that Shrine Shinto is the original Shinto, and State Shinto and Sect Shinto are modern developments.

Outside these divisions and not organized, but very influential, is the private Family Cult of Shinto, centred in the household 'god-shelf', where the spirits of the family ancestors are worshipped.

A final word of caution is necessary to the western student. The 'divisions' of Shinto are not mutually exclusive as in the various denominations of Christianity. They are divisions of function, just as in the wider sphere, Shinto and Buddhism are divisions of function, and not regarded by the average Japanese as in any way mutually exclusive. The same man can, without inconsistency, visit the State Shinto shrine as a loyal Japanese, the shrine of Inari, guardian of the goddess of fertility, to pray for a good harvest, the god-shelf in his home, to pay respect to his ancestors, the 'church' of a Shinto Sect for spiritual 'uplift', and a Buddhist temple for personal salvation and a propitious entry into the next life.

THE LAND OF THE GODS

One of the first things a foreign traveller will notice in Japan is the infinite variety and beauty of the landscape. He will see rocky islands with pine-clad cliffs; deep land-locked inlets of the sea; abrupt, forested mountains rising range upon range into the blue distance; and a few fertile plains. Before long he will notice an undercurrent of violence below the usually calm and lovely face of nature. Typhoons sweep across the seas and islands; earthquakes rock the land; the mountains are scarred with landslips; hot-springs bubble up from end to end of Japan; some of the most beautiful mountains are volcanoes, and the peerless Fuji herself is a heap of volcanic dust and lava. The climate throws over this fascinating landscape a variety of clearly defined moods—beautiful clear skies, hot sunshine, delicate mists skirting the mountain sides, torrential rain, hurricanes, and in some parts very deep snow.

These characteristics of nature have had a profound influence on the Japanese national character, and seem in some measure to be reproduced in it. It is as a part of this environment that Shinto has grown up and gripped the soul of the Japanese. Like his beautiful, volcanic land, the Japanese and his Shinto religion are subject to marked changes of mood and fashion, and possess an undercurrent of pent-up emotion ready to burst out in irrational violence.

The second thing which a traveller will soon come to recognize is the 'torii', the universal and most obvious symbol of Shinto, to be found before every shrine. The 'torii' is a simple gateway of wood, stone, or metal, consisting of two upright posts, gently slanting towards each other, joined overhead by two cross-beams, the upper one longer than the lower and projecting on each side beyond the uprights on which it rests. The 'torii' may be any size, from a model a few inches high to a towering structure of forty to fifty feet.

This gateway may be seen standing over the path leading to a shrine in a busy city, or in a quiet grove of trees in the country, or leading to the ascent of a mountain; or the 'torii' may stand before a waterfall, or odd-shaped rock, or even, as at Miyajima, in the sea at the approach to an island. There may be one 'torii' for a shrine or there may be several. The name in Japanese suggests that it has something to do with 'tori', birds, and hence 'bird-perch' is a commonly accepted meaning of the word; but the fact is that the meaning is lost in antiquity, and the 'torii' is simply accepted as the symbol of approach to 'holy ground'.

THE MEANING OF 'GOD' IN SHINTO

There is an immense variety in the nature of the objects of worship at the shrines. Sometimes it is a feature of the landscape—a 'sacred' mountain, island, tree, rock, or waterfall. To these there may or may not be a legend attached. Thus Mt. Takachihō in Kysühü is connected with the mythological history of Japan, while Mt. Fuji has its goddess of charming legend. At times the object of nature is directly worshipped; but more often worship is focused in a shrine, large or small.

Sometimes the object of worship is a mythological god or goddess; sometimes an animal-god, or plant, or even an article of domestic use. Sometimes the god belongs to popular folk-lore, and is regarded as a charm or 'luck-bringer', to be called on to give wealth or fertility to man, animal, or land. Sometimes it is an historical human figure: very occasionally a scholar or statesman, more commonly a warrior-hero, or in some few cases the departed spirit of an emperor. In the Family Cult it is the ancestors of the family. One of the most frequented shrines in recent years has been the Yasukuni Shrine in Tokyo, where the spirits of the war dead are enshrined from time to time in a solemn ceremony in the presence of the Emperor.

The Japanese noun has no plural termination, and its writing has no equivalent to our capital letters. The ideogram for 'God' is pronounced 'shin' in the so-called Chinese reading, and 'kami' in the pure Japanese of daily colloquial speech. It stands equally without distinction for 'God', 'gods', or 'god'. It is quite clear, however, that the 'kami', or 'shin' of Shinto is quite different from the God of monotheistic religions. As we shall see, many Shintoists have maintained that the worship paid to the 'kami' is fundamentally different from the worship paid to the God of Christianity, or Judaism, or Islam.

Is there anything that links together all these varied objects of 'worship' under the term 'kami'? And what is the meaning of 'worship' when it is directed to so diverse an assortment of objects as an ancient tree, a mythological god, a magical luck-bringer, an historical hero, the family ancestors, or the modern war dead? But before we try to answer that question we must know more about the origins and practice of Shinto.

THE ORIGINS OF SHINTO

I. *The Written Records*

The origins of Shinto are lost in the primitive child-history of the Japanese race. Quite clearly it started as a primitive tribal religion, just one among the many originating in the wide area of the islands of the Pacific. Apart from archaeology, our knowledge of the origins of Shinto is derived from a number of early written documents. Written records were not possible in Japan until Chinese writing and culture were introduced during the sixth and seventh centuries A.D. With Chinese culture came Buddhism, and with the alien religion the need to define and protect the ancient traditions by committing them to writing. The best known of these early documents are the *Kojiki* and *Nihongi*.

The *Kojiki*, or 'Chronicle of Ancient Events', was completed in 712 A.D. It records the traditional myths of creation, tells of the establishment of the Japanese Imperial Line, and emerging imperceptibly from myth to history, brings the story down to the end of the reign of the Empress Suiko (A.D. 628). The *Nihongi*, or 'Chronicles of Japan', is a compilation showing greater Chinese influence, completed in 720 A.D., covering the same ground as the Kojiki with some variations, but bringing the history down to A.D. 697

'Another document, the *Kujiki*, less well known, is reputed to belong to the reign of the Empress Suiko, A.D. 593-628, but received its present form much later than the Kojiki or Nihongi. Its historical sections add nothing to the other records, but in the earlier myths it gives important independent material.

Besides these chronicles may be mentioned the *Engishiki*, a collection of material relating to ancient court life, which contains twenty-six forms of prayer called 'norito' used on State occasions in services before the gods of the Shinto shrines. This collection dates from the first quarter of the tenth century A.D.

Finally, the *Manyōshū*, the 'Collection of a Myriad Leaves', is a collection of some four hundred poems compiled towards the end of the eighth century, giving the background and atmosphere of the period in which the Shinto records were compiled.

2. *The Myths*

These are very numerous, sometimes charming, often crude and childish, and some by western standards obscene. It is possible here only to pick out enough to make modern Shinto understandable to western students.

The creation myth starts with a pre-existing universe likened to an ocean of mud veiled in darkness. Three gods appeared from this—how, we are not told—Amé-no-minaka-nushi-no-kami (Divine Ruler of the August Centre of Heaven) and two other creation deities whose long names may be rendered High August Producing God and Divine Producing Goddess. These proceeded with the task of creation until heaven and earth were distinguished, but earth was still fluid like oil or foam on water. At this point the three deities retire and are never heard of again. A number of gods and goddesses appear and disappear without trace until we come to the divine couple, Izanagi and Izanami, the first god and goddess of any real significance in the Japanese Pantheon.

Izanagi, 'The Male who Invites', and Izanami, 'The Female who Invites', were ordered by the gods of heaven to descend to earth and create the land. They stood therefore on the Floating Bridge of Heaven, pushed down a jewelled spear and stirred up the brine until it curdled, whereupon they drew up the spear, and the drops which fell from it formed an island, stated to be the island of Awaji in the Inland Sea. They descended to this island and started their courtship there. They walked round the island in opposite directions until they met, whereupon Izanami exclaimed, 'O beautiful and attractive youth!' and Izanagi replied, 'O beautiful and attractive maiden!' Marriage was immediate and without ceremony, and from their union began to be born islands, plains, and the elements and forces of nature. But the first two to appear were failures. They realized that Izanami had made a mistake in speaking first. The courtship was repeated and on their meeting this time Izanagi exclaimed, 'O what a lovely and beautiful maiden!' and Izanami responded. After this all went well, and from their union the Islands of Japan and many nature deities were born—gods of rocks, of winds, of seasons, of seas, of trees, of mountains, and of food and fire.

When the fire-god was born, he scorched his mother and she died and went to the nether world of the dead. Izanagi killed the fire-god, and followed her to the underworld to try to bring her back, but found her in a state of filth and putrefaction, with eight thunder-gods born inside her. She tried to seize him and confine him to the nether world also, but he narrowly escaped after a fierce pursuit by furies. From the filth which he washed from himself were born numerous other deities, the most notable being Amaterasu-ōmikami, the Sun-goddess, who was born from the washing of his right eye. She is for all practical purposes the most important deity of the Shinto Pantheon, being the divine ancestress of the Japanese Imperial Line. From the left eye of Izanagi was born the Moon-god, Tsuki-yomi, and from his nostrils, Susa-no-o, the Rainstorm-god.

The story is then taken up with the adventures of Amaterasu and Susa-no-o. Izanagi having retired, the rule of the universe was divided between sister and brother. She ruled benevolently and instituted religious rites. He, however, being a storm-god, was arrogant and disobedient. He behaved so outrageously to his sister that she took offence and shut herself in the Rock-Cave-of-Heaven, whereupon the whole universe was thrown into darkness. There follows a story which is at the very centre of Shinto mythology, and one which reflects and has helped to preserve the ritual of the time at which it was recorded.

consternation at the darkness, the gods held a conference in the bed of the River of Heaven to discuss how she should be induced come out and give light to the world again. In the end a plan was greed upon. A mirror was made, jewels hung on the branch of a sakaki tree, a platform erected before the cave, and a goddess performed a lewd dance which so amused the assembled gods that they burst into loud and prolonged laughter. Amaterasu was overcome by curiosity and opened the door of her cave a little. She saw the reflection of her own brilliance in the mirror, and emerged a little further to examine it. Upon this, the god Strong-hand, who had been hidden in readiness, seized hold of her and pulled her out. Susa-no-o was barbarously punished and banished from heaven. In the course of his adventures on earth, however, Susa-no-o rescued a maiden from an eight-headed serpent and found a divine sword in the dead serpent's tail. The mirror, the jewels, and the sword became the three Imperial Treasures of Japan, and it is claimed that they survive to this day.

The next story of significance concerns Ō-kuni-nushi, Great Lord of the Land, one of the numerous sons of Susa-no-o. He ruled the province of Izumo on the Sea of Japan, facing the Asiatic continent, an ancient haunt of the gods. He is worshipped at the Great Shrine of Izumo (Izumo Taisha). Unlike his boisterous father, he ruled the land gently and beneficently and had many useful children such as the Harvest-god and the Food-goddess. But Amaterasu had decided that the rule over the land of Japan was to be given to her grandson, Ninigi-no-mikoto, and his descendants for ever in unbroken line. Ō-kuni-nushi humbly gave way to the wishes of Amaterasu and has been worshipped as the model of loyal and obedient self-sacrifice ever since.

When Amaterasu committed the government of the land to Ninigi-no-mikoto she is reported to have said: 'The Luxuriant Reed-plain Land of Fresh Rice-ears (Japan) is the land over which my descendants shall reign. Do thou, Imperial Grandson, go and rule over it, and the prosperity of the Imperial Succession of Heaven shall be as everlasting as Heaven and Earth."[1] This very important decision of Amaterasu is known among Shintoists as the 'Divine Edict' and is claimed as the divine sanction for the Imperial System of Japan.

Ninigi-no-mikoto married Konohana-sakuya-no-himé, daughter of a mountain-god, and herself the goddess of Mt. Fuji. One of their

[1] Quoted from *A National History for Middle Schools*, Tokyo, 1927, in D. C. Holtom, *The National Faith of Japan*, 1938, p. 82.

great-grandchildren was Jimmu Tennö, who is claimed to be the first historical human Emperor and founder of the Imperial Dynasty. A traditional date is given for his conquest of Yamato, the central province of Japan, and the foundation of his capital there in 660 B.C. This is regarded as the date of the foundation of the Empire of Japan, the 2,600th anniversary of which therefore was celebrated in 1940.

To Ninigi-no-mikoto and, through him, to Jimmu Tennö were entrusted the Three Sacred Imperial Treasures, or insignia of the throne, the Mirror, the Jewels and the Sword. The Mirror is said to be preserved at the holy of holies of Shinto, the Grand Shrine of Amaterasu-Ōmikami, the Sun-goddess, at Isé; the Jewels in the Imperial Household Shrine in the Imperial Palace in Tokyo; and the Sword at the Atsuta Shrine at Nagoya.

These myths have been quoted at some length as they are the foundation of Shinto, the source of authority for State Shinto, and provide the 'divine' sanction for the Japanese Imperial System. They are recorded in much the same form, though with some variations in the names, in both the Kojiki and the Nihongi, and are presented here approximately as they are taught to children in the primary schools throughout the Japanese Empire.

Students of anthropology and primitive religion will see much in these myths which can be paralleled elsewhere. Many of the stories of the gods attempt to explain or are influenced by the phenomena of nature, e.g. the descent of Izanagi to the nether world, and the retirement of the Sun-goddess. There is probably much symbolism in the grouping of deities and in their descriptive names. They reflect a very primitive state of Society in which nature is full of mystery and awe. There is little self-consciousness, and little attempt to philosophize or systematize. The gods are indistinguishable from the objects they represent, be they mountains, storms, products of the soil or animals; that is to say, they are not so much mountain-gods or rice-gods as god-mountains, god-rice, etc.

The myths represent a fairyland in which no limits exist and anything is possible. Later generations, as we shall see, have tried to explain and allegorize them, and make out of them a religious philosophy acceptable to modern men, but except along one line they have conspicuously failed. Pure Shinto was, and still remains, the very primitive nature worship of a simple but emotionally tense race. The one exception is that line of interpretation which sees in the myths of the

Kojiki and Nihongi the divine sanction for the Imperial Way of Japan and Japanese Nationalism. We shall return to a study of this later.

THE WORSHIP AND PRACTICE OF SHINTO

1. *Objects of Worship*

As has already been stated, the objects of worship at the shrines are by no means confined to mythological gods and objects of nature. Three other cases deserve mention, namely, the popular gods of folk-lore, the historical heroes whose spirits have been enshrined, and the family ancestors of the domestic cult. The popular bringers of good fortune need not delay us for long. One of the most popular is the goddess Uka-no-Mitama-no-kami, goddess of food and fertility, who is worshipped at the Inari, or Fox-shrines, for the prosperity of the crops. The Shichifukunin, or Seven Gods of Good Fortune, are a composite group derived from popular Buddhism, Brahmanism, and Taoism. They include in their number the very popular Ebisu, complete with fishing-rod, and riding on the back of a sea-bream, who is one of the numerous offspring of Izanagi and Izanami. The shrines of Ebisu are classified as Shinto by the State.

Again, historical human beings can be regarded as kami and be enshrined after death. Among the Government-sponsored shrines of State Shinto were to be found shrines erected to the spirits of three classes of historical characters: emperors, princes and subjects. It is often stated that 'Emperor worship' is a feature of Shinto, but that statement needs qualification. It is interesting to note that out of 123 emperors who are said to have reigned from Jimmu Tennö, 660 B.C., to Hirohito (Shöwa), at the time of writing, only twelve emperors and three empresses are worshipped by the public in some twenty State Shinto shrines out of a total of 183 shrines of this class, and many of these twenty shrines are of very recent foundation, notably the Meiji Shrine in Tokyo. The whole line of Imperial Ancestors is worshipped collectively in the Köreiden, the Hall of Imperial Spirits, which is the private shrine in the Imperial Palace in Tokyo. But there is strong evidence to show that though it was present, Emperor-worship was not a prominent feature of early Shinto.[1]

[1] Cf. C. C. Holtom, *Transactions of the Asiatic Society of Japan*, Vol. XLIX, Pt. II, 'The Political Philosophy of Modern Shinto', for a detailed study. The figures in this and the following paragraph are quoted from the above.

Some eleven Imperial princes are enshrined, usually for outstanding loyalty and devotion in military service. About thirty subjects of the emperors have been enshrined in State Shinto shrines, all but two having been military heroes of outstanding loyalty to the throne. One only is a scholar, Sugawara Michizane (845-903 A.D.), who is worshipped as Temmangu, the god of learning and calligraphy. The other is a legendary character who is said to have served five emperors in the early days of the nation.

These shrines can be continually added to, and the status of local cults raised to State Shinto rank, as indeed they are. Thus the Meiji Shrine in Tokyo was erected to honour the spirit of the Emperor Meiji who died in 1910, and the Nogi Shrine to the spirits of General Nogi and his wife who, with primitive loyalty, committed suicide together in the same year 1910 to follow Emperor Meiji to his grave.

Last but not least is the recently established and immensely popular cult of the war dead, dating from 1869, at the Yasukuni Shrine in Tokyo, where at periodic ceremonies in the presence of the Emperor the war dead were enshrined in their thousands.

It is this military and nationalistic aspect of Shinto which has been thrust into greatest prominence in recent years.

2. Shrines

The Shinto house of worship is ordinarily called a 'shrine' in English to distinguish it from the 'temple' of Buddhism and the 'church' of Christianity. Three corresponding words are always carefully distinguished in Japanese. The one exception is that the meeting-places of the modern Shinto sects are called 'churches' by the same word as is used for Christian places of worship.

Originally there seems to have been no building—only an enclosure of ground marked off as 'holy'. About the beginning of the Christian era, a building of very simple construction began to be added, and the same general form has prevailed to the present day. It is thought that this was the form of the ordinary dwelling-house of that period. It is always of wood, unpainted, with a bark, thatch or wooden roof. Occasional departures from this rule are a mark of Buddhist influence during the 'corrupt' period of amalgamation. The shrine is always small by western standards, as the building is not a hall for the assembly of worshippers, but merely a dwelling for the 'god'.[1] In the larger

[1] Cf. Chapter IV, Hinduism, p. 114.

K

shrines the inner sanctuary of the god has an outer 'hall of worship' in front of it, often connected by a covered bridge-gangway. In some cases, as at the Isé Grand Shrine of Amaterasu, the outer shrine is separated from the inner sanctuary by several miles. This 'hall of worship' is again small and not as a rule open to the general public. It is reserved for the performance of ceremonies by the priests, for the ritual dances and dramas of the shrine, and for the ceremonies attending the making of offerings by individuals.

The inner sanctuary contains no image or visible object of worship, but carefully wrapped up and hidden away is the 'shintai' or 'god-body', the emblem or symbol of the deity. It is also known as the 'mitama-shiro' or 'spirit-substitute'. It may be a mirror, as in the case of the great mirror of Amaterasu at Isé, a sword, spear, round stone, strips of consecrated paper, or human hair. In the case of nature-Shinto, the object of nature itself, in the open, may be considered the 'shintai'. This 'shintai' is usually kept strictly concealed, and terrible curses are believed to be incurred by those who pry into it. Even the priests are prohibited by law from viewing or handling it except by special permit.

But the 'atmosphere' of Shinto is attained as much by the surroundings of the shrine as by the shrine itself. The 'torii' marking the entrance to holy ground has been mentioned. There may be a succession of 'torii' and a number of precincts surrounding the innermost shrine. Trees are always associated with the shrines, and the atmosphere of still calm and ageless silence of a Shinto sanctuary is achieved by the grove of cryptomerias or other stately trees through whose cathedral-like aisles one approaches the shrine. The damp and mosses induced by the trees further enhance the air of hoary antiquity which takes the Japanese back in spirit to the primitive childhood of his race.

Such an awesome place cannot be approached without purification, and for this provision is made of running water in a trough or basin of stone. The worshipper must sprinkle the hands and wash out the mouth before appearing before the shrine. By the last 'torii' there are often two fantastic stone lions, one with open mouth, one with closed mouth. These betray Chinese influence and are indeed known as 'Chinese lions'. Sanctity is further ensured by a thick-plaited straw rope with strips of paper in a plait design woven into it, stretched across the more sacred objects or places. This, known as the 'shimenawa' or 'rope of demarcation', is supposed to keep off evil influences, and with the 'torii' marks off every haunt of a god-spirit. Finally, no shrine is complete without its 'gohei', which is a small pole or wand of choice wood or bamboo in which are inserted strips of paper or cloth folded in the plait design, and hanging down on either side. Its origin is obscure and today it is little more than a general symbol of divinity.

The greater shrines have other buildings in their precincts, e.g. a bell tower and a drum tower, buildings for the reception of votive offerings, for the sale of charms, or for the residence of priests, and sometimes even a sacred stable in which a living or model horse is kept for the pleasure of the god.

3. The Priesthood

The Shinto priesthood is usually hereditary, but it is not a sacerdotal caste, as in many other religions. The chief officials of ancient Shinto were divided into three hereditary families or clans, with distinct functions. The Nakatomi recited the prayers, or 'norito', at the rituals; the Imibe or Purifiers prepared the sanctuary and the offerings; and the Urabe or Diviners, like the Augurs of Rome, declared the will of the gods by divination. Divination continues to play a large part in modern Shinto.

The local shrines are in the charge of a Kannushi, i.e. Kami-nushi, or 'god-master'. They receive no special training, and have no pastoral responsibility for their parishioners, nor do they teach or preach. Their functions are to carry out ceremonies according to strictly prescribed forms, recite the prayers, and keep the shrine in repair, for this purpose administering Government funds, or receiving offerings and selling charms. The Kannushi is appointed but not 'ordained'. He wears no distinctive dress except when officiating, and he usually pursues some secular calling as well. The priesthood is no bar to marriage, and celibacy is not encouraged in Shinto.

The State Shinto shrines are served by priests who are Government officials in the same sense and with the same grades as the ordinary civil service. They were, until the end of the Second World War, directly controlled by a Government department. The Emperor was the chief-priest of Shinto, and performed the ritual before the Kōreiden, the Imperial Household Shrine in the Palace. He also paid State visits to other shrines, but as a rule delegated his religious functions.

In addition to the male priesthood there is usually at the greater shrines a corps of young girls appointed as dancers and attendants. They resign on marriage.

4. Worship and Ritual

The worship offered at Shinto shrines is not congregational. It is conducted entirely by the priests; and the general public, if present, are onlookers only. The sole exception to this custom is found in the comparatively recent practice of performing naming rites and celebrating weddings and funerals at the shrines. In these the families concerned play some part. On the greater national festivals and shrine anniversaries, public ceremonies will be held, purifications performed, norito recited, and offerings accepted. At the greater shrines, religious pantomime and dances will be presented on these occasions.

The public rituals of the Engishiki[1] and their modern adaptations usually take place at the appropriate festivals of the agricultural year, the equinoxes, the rice-planting, the first-fruits, the harvest, and the New Year. They are almost entirely concerned with the welfare of the crops and the prosperity of the Imperial House. The greatest of these is the Ŏ-nié or Great Tasting, equivalent to a coronation ceremony, when the new Emperor, in the eleventh month of the year of his accession, offers rice and wine to the gods, subsequently partaking of them himself with the court. All the preparations are subject to the most minute divination and most elaborately simple ceremony, performed in duplicate lest there be error or defect.

The annual rituals include appeasement of the gods who may injure the crops, the gods of blight and disease, of storm and wind and rain, and the propitiation of the gods of fertility in man, beast and soil. There are rituals for 'calming the august spirit of the Emperor', invoking the good will of the Imperial Ancestors, and praying for the long life and prosperity of the reigning Emperor.

Lastly there is the Ŏ-harai, or Great Purification, celebrated twice a year on the last day of December and the last day of June, for the ritual purification of the faults or mistakes of the people of the land.

At these ceremonies the priests, clad in the full and flowing white robes of ancient court dress, glide silently about with impressive dignity, waving branches of the sacred sakaki tree, sprinkling salt for purification, and reciting the norito, while the people look on.

At other times the worship is individual. When an offering is made, the priest will come out and accept it in a brief ceremony. Such offerings are usually foodstuffs or rice-wine. Otherwise the worshipper comes at his own convenience, purifies his hands and mouth

[1] See p. 140.

at the trough, advances to the front of the shrine, claps his hands as a sign of respect, says his personal prayer, bows and goes away.

In recent years, following the example of Buddhism and Christianity and sometimes copying their rites, the Shinto priests have instituted and encouraged ceremonies marking the major events of family life. Naming ceremonies are performed for new-born infants. Children are brought to the shrine to worship and make an offering on attaining the ages of three, five, and seven. Weddings and funerals are conducted according to Shinto rites. National, family, and personal events are 'reported' to the gods at the shrine. Again, the Shinto priesthood is called upon to perform cleansing and protective rites at the laying of foundations, the raising of roof-trees, the completion of buildings, the opening of bridges, or the launching of ships.

THE NEIGHBOURHOOD AND FAMILY CULTS

Interwoven with the public worship just described are the cults of the 'Ujigami' or patronal gods of neighbourhoods and families, and the cult of the family ancestors in the household 'kamidana' or 'god-shelf'. The 'ujigami' is usually the god of the local shrine who is the patron of the neighbourhood and of the families within it. His festivals are a corporate occasion for the local community or 'parish'. On these festivals the god is carried round the parish in a palanquin-shrine on the shoulders of a shouting and swaying tumult of young men to make his visitation and inspection. If any household has offended public opinion and incurred the displeasure of the god, the heavy portable shrine is dashed against the front of the house as a mark of censure, and is capable of causing considerable damage.

In many houses a god-shelf can be seen, high up in a corner of the wall, bearing a miniature model of a shrine in which the spirits of the family ancestors dwell and watch over the affairs of the family. Reverence is paid to them daily, and offerings of food placed before them, usually by the women-folk. The sense of the spirit ancestors is a very powerful bulwark of social convention and of the authority of the family over the individual.

THE RELIGIOUS VALUES OF SHINTO

From the above brief account it will be seen that the ideas of 'holiness', of purification, of offering and propitiation, and of petition enter into Shinto. But for the most part they remain at a very primitive and materialistic level. Purification, for pure Shinto, rarely rises much above the level of ritual purification for physical defilement, though the Family Cult and the rise of State Shinto have fostered ethical standards directed entirely towards the practice of obedience to the family and the service of the State. The defilements which the Shinto rituals are considered to cleanse are recorded in the ancient documents as contact with actual filth; incurring the wrath of the gods in sickness, earthquake, fire or other natural disaster; contact with corpses, blood, or leprosy; sexual intercourse; and a few ethical sins such as injury to rice-fields, removal of landmarks, or destruction of other men's animals.

No difference is recognized between accidental and deliberate defilement. This indicates a very limited sense of sin, or of the ethics of conscience. Prayer is also of the simplest nature, being confined almost entirely to petitions for material blessings and prosperity.

The Shinto sects have done something to encourage a more spiritual view of worship, and they emphasize purity of heart as a quality pleasing to the gods, but it is still possible for brothel-keepers and prostitutes to go to the shrine to pray for the prosperity of their trade. The methods of purification are bathing in water, particularly bathing in cold water in winter; pouring water over the hands, and washing out the mouth; sprinkling salt-water or salt; waving the sakaki branch or gohei; or a variety of substitutionary acts such as rubbing one's person with a human figure in paper and throwing it into a river or the sea. Human and animal sacrifice existed in early Shinto but was abandoned, probably under the influence of Buddhism. The idea of propitiation is very simple, being no more than the offering of a gift for which favours are expected in return.

Although the above account is true of pure historical Shinto, and of a large part of modern practice, there is the one great exception which has come to occupy the centre of the stage in modern times. This is the nationalistic State Shinto, for the understanding of which a brief historical survey is necessary.

HISTORY OF SHINTO TO THE MEIJI RESTORATION, 1868

Shinto held undisputed sway as the religion of the Japanese people until the introduction of Buddhism and continental culture from China. The arrival of the first Buddhist missionaries in 552 A.D. may be regarded as the opening date of this cultural invasion. Buddhism

by the power of its deeper philosophy and ethical standard, and the
higher culture and civilization which accompanied it, made its way
in the land, and with the help of imperial patronage was at the height
of its influence about the middle of the eighth century A.D., some two
hundred years after its introduction. The land was filled with great
Buddhist temples and giant Buddhist images.

About this time there started the process of assimilation of Shinto
and Buddhism under the title of Ryōbu-Shinto, or Dual-Shinto. It is
said that at the time of the casting of the great bronze image of Buddha
at Nara in 749 A.D. (still to be seen there), a Buddhist priest went to
the shrine of Amaterasu at Isé to enquire her opinion of the project.
To him it was revealed that the Sun-goddess approved, and that she
was in fact a manifestation of the Buddha Vairochana. The great
Buddhist leader, Kōbō Daishi (744-835 A.D.), founder of Shingon
Buddhism, carried on the process, declaring that the gods of Shinto
mythology were manifestations or earthly counterparts of the Buddhas
and Bodhisattvas of the Buddhist pantheon. From this time until the
nineteenth century Ryōbu-Shinto prevailed, and almost all Shinto
shrines, except the Grand Shrine of Isé and the Great Shrine of Ōkuni-
nushi in Izumo, were to a greater or lesser degree assimilated to Buddhism. Buddhist priests officiated with Buddhist rites at Shinto shrines,
and recited the sutras to Japanese gods under Buddhist names. Some
of this influence still remains after the forcible separation of the two
religions. It was felt, as it is generally felt today, to be no contradiction
for a Japanese to be a Buddhist as well as a follower of the Way of
the Gods. His untutored instinct and national spirit drew him to the
mysteries of Shinto, while his intellect and moral consciousness drew
him to the wider, deeper teaching of Buddhism. In public life he would
be a Shintoist, in private life a Buddhist.

For some sixty-five years from 1549, Christian missionaries preached
the Roman Catholic faith in Japan, enjoying considerable success and
gaining over a million converts, but in the reaction which followed
not only were missionaries and converts massacred and organized
Christianity driven out, but the Japanese nation turned in upon itself
and attempted to close the land to all foreign influences. An intensely
anti-foreign spirit was fostered during the 244 years of seclusion from
1624 to 1868 A.D.

It was in the eighteenth century, during this period of isolation, that
there arose a school of Shinto scholarship which had as its aim the

revival of pure and primitive Shinto, purged of all Buddhist and foreign accretions, as the religious faith of the Japanese people. It was in line with the reactionary and anti-foreign spirit of the age, but it is also notable as the first attempt to give a scholarly and reasoned expression to the primitive faith. Mabuchi (1697-1769 A.D.) prepared the ground for this 'Revival of Pure Shinto' by a study of Japanese history which represented the age before the introduction of Chinese and Buddhist culture as a Golden Age. Moto-ori (1730-1801 A.D.), the greatest of all Shinto scholars, and Hirata (1776-1843 A.D.) followed up this line of presentation by starting a movement to purify Shinto of foreign, especially Buddhist, influences, and re-convert the Japanese people to their own original religion in its primitive form.

They were, however, scholars and men of their own generation, and they could not forbear to interpret and rationalize the primitive faith which they tried to restore. Moto-ori, with a kind of inverted scholarship, was a thoroughgoing purist, and tried to remove all traces of interpretation, scholarship and philosophy derived from Buddhism, and return to the simple, unsophisticated and literal faith of pre-Buddhist days. Even the Nihongi was frowned upon because it showed traces of Chinese philosophic terms. He tried to meet criticism and scepticism by maintaining that the more improbable the myth the less likely it was to be invented. He explained that primitive Shinto had no ethics because the Japanese were by nature related to the gods, and that it was enough that they should follow their instincts. Corruption had not appeared in the nation until foreign influences had entered. This line of argument has had frequent public support in more recent times.

Hirata built on Moto-ori's foundation, but philosophized to the extent of claiming some unifying kami-force or principle behind the outward manifestations of the kami. He dotted the 'i's and crossed the 't's of Moto-ori's nationalistic xenophobia, claiming that Shinto was the purest form of worship in the world, that it was the only true religion, and that the Japanese people and their Emperor are by divine will unique, and should by divine right and by their inherent virtue rule the world.

This movement, although claiming to return to a pure Shinto of earlier days, in fact put its finger on the one element in primitive Shinto which was capable of development into a powerful religious force in a modern nation. This was the claim of the divine descent of the Imperial Line from Amaterasu, and all that went with it.

It is an element which was undoubtedly present in the earliest written records. But Hirata and his followers have exaggerated it far beyond the position which it had previously held. According to this view, Amaterasu becomes the supreme goddess. Her instructions to her grandson, Ninigi-no-mikoto, become the sanction and charter for the Imperial system; the submission of Ōkuni-nushi is the pattern of loyal renunciation, not only for Japanese subjects but ultimately for foreign princes and peoples; and the commission for world conquest is found in an obscure aspiration of the Emperor Jimmu Tennō, who looked forth from his palace at Kashiwara and said: 'Hereafter the Capital may be extended so as to embrace all the six cardinal points, and the eight cords may be covered so as to form a roof. Will this not be well?' This last passage is made the basis of the chauvinistic slogan, 'Hakko-ichiu', or 'Eight-cords, one-roof', i.e. unification of the world under the Japanese Imperial Throne.

In view of this development, it is not quite true to say that Shinto has no ethic. It has an exceedingly strict and exacting ethic, wholly concentrated on blind loyalty to the Imperial Throne, and the maintenance of the Imperial Way. And the nearest approach to a Shinto code of ethics is to be found in the code of Bushido, the Way of the Warrior, even though the latter owes something to Confucius and Buddhism.

For the time being the movement started by Moto-ori and Hirata met with little popular success. Popular Shinto was too closely enmeshed with Buddhism; and the element of instinctive nature-worship and ancestor-worship satisfied a people oppressed by a warrior caste and discouraged from thinking or taking any interest in public affairs. But the seed had been sown and bore fruit in the event known as the Restoration, in 1868, when the Tokugawa Shōgun, the hereditary dictator of Japan, was deposed, the military clans dissolved, and the Emperor Meiji brought out of his sacred but ineffectual seclusion in Kyōto to become the active monarch of a unified modern State.

MODERN SHINTO SINCE THE MEIJI RESTORATION, 1868

With the Restoration vast changes took place in every aspect of Japanese life, and not least in Shinto. That which Moto-ori had dreamed of came to pass. Buddhism received a severe blow; Ryōbu-Shinto was abolished, and the shrines 'purified' of Buddhist images, scriptures and decorations. Shinto was proclaimed the religion of the

State, and came under the control of a Government department which ranked as the highest among Government offices.

Since then, two apparently contradictory tendencies have been at work. The one has been the tendency to disown the religious aspect of Shinto and make of it a national ceremonial and sentiment, a secular buttress to the structure of government. The other has been the strong propagandist effort to stimulate the observance of Shinto as a religion, giving divine sanction to the claims of State Shinto, and trying to make them obligatory on all Japanese citizens, including the subject races of the Empire. The object of both these tendencies was really the same, namely, the strengthening of nationalistic Shinto.

After the first attack in 1868 Buddhism recovered some of its strength, and Christianity began to make its influence felt. The result was a modification of the position of Shinto as the sole State religion of Japan. In the Constitution of 1889, a clause was inserted granting liberty of conscience and religious observance to all Japanese citizens 'within limits not prejudicial to peace and order, and not antagonistic to their duties as subjects'. The first nationalistic reaction came ten years later when the officials of the Isé Grand Shrine petitioned the Government to be incorporated no longer as a religious body, but as an association for performing rites in honour of the Imperial Ancestors, and ceremonies of national significance. The effect was not to lower but to enhance the prestige of the Shrine, and by evading the conscience clause in the Constitution to widen the claim of the Shrine to the reverence of all Japanese, irrespective of their religious allegiance. This was the beginning of the claim frequently made in later years that Shinto was not a religion but a national obligation—with the implication obvious to every Japanese, but not to every Westerner, that therefore it had a prior claim over 'religious' allegiance, which was a merely personal matter. Modern Shintoists, while agreeing on the absolute claims of Shinto, are divided on this question. Some emphasize the obvious fact that Shinto is practised as a religion with rituals, prayers, offerings, divinations, and the sale of magic charms. Others, usually the sophisticated modern nationalists, sceptical on the religious side, but fanatical supporters of Shinto as an instrument of Imperial policy, maintain the secular and political claims of State Shinto. Government policy has on the whole followed the will of the latter party. Shrine laws have been passed which reduced the Department of Shrines to a sub-bureau of the Ministry of Home Affairs. Christians and Buddhists have been assured that they could attend the shrines without compromising their consciences, as an act of reverence to the Imperial Ancestors. The clear-cut distinction drawn between Shrine Shinto and Sect Shinto has been accompanied by a distinction on paper between State Shinto shrines and the other local shrines maintained by local government bodies and voluntary contributions. But in practice, little difference can be detected between the two classes of shrines, and from time to time a local shrine is 'promoted' to State Shrine status. The Buddhist and Christian bodies have accused the Government of being double-faced in securing compliance by declaring State Shinto shrines non-religious, and then in practice sending school children to any local shrine, however superstitious, which happened to be in the neighbourhood.

At the same time, however, State Shinto has been instilled into the people with all the influence that officialdom could command. It was taught in all grades of State schools under the headings of National History, National Ethics, Citizenship, and so forth, where officially religious teaching was not allowed. It was encouraged by the prestige enjoyed by the Isé Grand Shrine, the Meiji Shrine in Tokyo, and the stimulation of the official cult of the war dead at the Yasukuni Shrine in Tokyo. In 1940 a Religions Bill was passed for the control of all religious bodies, excluding Shrine Shinto. It is interesting to note that Sect Shinto, Buddhism and Christianity were recognized as 'religions' firmly rooted in Japan.

Such was the position at the outbreak and during the course of the Second World War. Events subsequent to the defeat of Japan, so far as they are known, deserve separate treatment below.

THE SHINTO SECTS

No account of Shinto would be complete without some reference to Sect or Denominational Shinto. This is a comparatively modern development, and has grown out of attempts to personalize and popularize Shinto, and supply the deficiencies of the ancient and official cult.

The sects differ from Shrine Shinto in having definite bodies of teaching and codes of ethics, a close-knit organization and clear-cut membership, and in maintaining, along with the ordinary shrine worship, buildings for congregational worship and assembly, known as 'churches'. As in English, the same word may be used either of the denomination or of the local building or congregation.

There are thirteen of these sects recognized by the Government. There have been others which have been suppressed for gross superstition or political fanaticism, e.g. Omotokyö. The thirteen sects are very diverse in character, but they can be classified under five headings: pure Shinto sects, Confucian sects, mountain sects, purification sects, and faith-healing sects.[1]

1. *Pure Shinto Sects*

There are three of these: Shinto Honkyoku, or The Main Bureau of Shinto, Shinri-kyö, and Taisha-kyö. They are the offspring of the movement of Moto-ori and Hirata, and seek to popularize and make a working religion of pure Shinto, based on the myths. They have opposed the Government policy of secularizing State Shinto, and in order to make Shinto adequate to meet the religious needs of modern men they have read philosophical and ethical interpretations into the ancient myths. Shinto Honkyoku, for instance, interprets the original creation-deity, Amé-no-minaka-nushi-no-kami, as the Absolute God of whom all subsequent gods are manifestations. Shinri-kyö teaches an esoteric doctrine said to be derived from the gods, claiming the absolute unity of the spiritual and physical worlds, and the disappearance of hardship and disease by the cleansing of the heart, and by moral conduct. Taisha-kyö is centred in the worship of Ōkuni-nushi, the great god of the Izumo Taisha, the model of benevolence and patriotic self-sacrifice.

2. *Confucian Sects*

There are two of these, which receive their classification because, on a Shinto background, they lay great emphasis on right conduct along the lines of the ethics of Confucius. One of these, Shüsei-ha, founded in 1873, takes as its watchword 'Improvement', and encourages its followers to leave every situation better than they found it. Its founder taught that Confucianism really originated in Japan.

3. *The Mountain Sects*

One of the most popular of Shinto developments has been that of the mountain-cults, two of them centering on Mt. Fuji and the third on

---

[1] The best account of the sects is in D. C. Holtom's *The National Faith of Japan*, to which the writer is indebted for most of this section.

Mt. Ontaké (or Mitaké). The Fuji sects claim that the gods are all manifestations of the one original creation-deity. Ontaké-kyö, like Taisha-kyö, looks to Okuni-nushi as its patron and example. All of them encourage pilgrimage to the summit of their patron peaks (Fuji, 12,300 ft.; Ontaké, 10,000 ft.) and communion with the gods there. The Fuji sects concentrate on 'Practical Ethics', particularly patriotism while Ontaké-kyö practises ecstatic communion with the deities through spiritualistic mediums and spiritual healing.

4. The Purification Sects

The two purification sects, adopting most of the characteristics of the other sects, lay particular emphasis on purification of the body and spirit from defilement. Shinshü-kyö recommends the method of spiritual self-culture by meditation, and washing with water, and includes among its ceremonies a 'fire-walking' and 'hot-water' cleansing. In the latter, boiling water is sprinkled over devotees for the purging of the body from all defilement. Misogi-kyö emphasizes deep breathing as a method of promoting health and control of the body, and teaches the repetition of a prayer: 'Ye distant gods, smile upon us, drive out evil, cleanse us we pray.'

5. The Faith-healing Sects

There are three sects which lay great emphasis on health as the fruit of a right spirit, and it is in these that we find the nearest approach in Shinto to western and Christian thought-forms. Kurozumi-kyö (founder: Kurozumi-Munétada, 1780-1850) regards Amaterasu-Omi-kami as the Supreme Deity, and every other form of existence as a manifestation of Amaterasu. Kurozumi himself recovered from serious illness after passing triumphantly through spiritual crises which convinced him that union of spirit with Amaterasu was the way of man's health and salvation. Faith, a cheerful optimism and a moral life were essential to this spiritual union with the deity, and some of the language used describing this union, and the new and eternal life resulting from it, is reminiscent of certain sayings of Christ in the Fourth Gospel.

Konkö-kyö (founder: Kawaté-Bunjirö, 1814-1883) is even more 'western' and less Shinto; in fact it has little claim to be called Shinto at all. Its teaching is monotheistic in practice; its founder repudiated all outward ceremonies and superstitious practices, taught belief in a God of Love, taught spontaneous extempore prayer in colloquial speech 'just as if you were talking to another human being', and was almost unique among the religious leaders of Japan in his modification of the claims of patriotism by the claims of universal human brotherhood. Konkō-kyō is classed as a 'Shinto' sect only for purposes of convenience, and it introduced three Shinto deities into its theology only to make its Shinto registration more plausible.

Tenri-kyō (founder: a woman, Maekawa-Miki, 1798-1887) calls itself by its title 'The Teaching of the Divine Reason', and has some resemblances to Christian Science. Its connection with Shinto is also remote, the foundress having been a devout Buddhist, and having taken Buddhist ideas and background into her system of religion. At the age of forty, when she and her family were ill, she became suddenly 'god-possessed' and was not released from the trance until she and her family complied with the demands of the god who possessed her. He claimed the title 'Commander of Heaven'. Against her will she was forced to renounce property, live a life of charitable works, and practise spiritual healing. When she obeyed the god of her trances all went well. When he was disobeyed, illness and misfortune dogged her and her followers. It was revealed to her that evil and disease were due to the eightfold 'dust' which settled on the human soul—the dusts of covetousness, meanness, undisciplined love, hatred, revenge, anger, pride and selfishness. In the rituals appointed to cleanse the heart of these dusts and to promote health, much use is made of dances, drum-beating and the incantation of 'psalms'. But these are only preparatory. The devotee must wait for 'the miracle' to happen, which brings spiritual and bodily health through god-possession. At Tambaichi, the central sanctuary of this sect, there is what is known as the 'Jiba' or 'Site', a holy place where an incomplete altar is in process of erection. This will be completed only when all mankind has accepted the Divine Reason and experienced 'the miracle'.

This sect has been described at some length as it is the most popular of the Sects, claiming a membership of 4,500,000, and is the only sect to show a missionary spirit, with missions in pre-war days in the United States and its territories and on the Asiatic continent.

POST-WAR SHINTO

All that has been said about Shinto hitherto applies to the situation up to the outbreak of the Second World War. Great changes have taken place as a result of the war. It is not yet possible to predict with certainty whether these changes will be permanent, or whether national Shinto will revive. Much will depend on the course of world history. State Shinto has received three crushing blows. The first is the defeat of Japan and the failure of the gods, the Imperial Way, and the god-inspired spirit of Japan to save her. There is evidence to show that even before the end of the war, as the Allied advance drew nearer to the shores of Japan, the influence of State Shinto declined very rapidly. It is a feature of Japanese psychology that 'nothing succeeds like success', and the opposite is also true. Japanese faith and morale had been built up on the legend of the invincibility of the Japanese spirit of absolute self-sacrifice and loyalty. Events have shattered this illusion for the time being, and have left a spiritual 'bomb crater', a people stunned and apathetic.

The second blow received by State Shinto is the repudiation by the Emperor in a broadcast on 1st January 1946 of the legend of his divinity. This is not so fundamental or far-reaching as might be imagined abroad. The Japanese have in practice always distinguished between the Emperor as an institution and the Emperor as an individual, and played off one against the other. It would be comparatively easy to repudiate any statement or action of the reigning Emperor as a personal lapse, not affecting the essence of the Imperial system. It would be in accordance with custom to lay the blame on the necessities of defeat, or on bad advisers. The outstanding fact, for good or ill, is that the Imperial House has survived the catastrophe and the Imperial Line is still unbroken.

A far more serious blow has been sustained by the disestablishment of the Shinto shrines in 1945 under an Allied Military Directive, whereby over three hundred State Shinto shrines were removed from all Government patronage and control, and all shrines of whatever class were put on a basis of voluntary support. Moreover the teaching of Shinto in the schools and all references to it in school textbooks were strictly forbidden. In the present mood of the people this has spelt economic disaster to the shrines and priesthood, for their popular support depended in no small degree on the prestige derived from Government backing, and on their function as the inspiration of aggressive nationalism. The great national shrines are almost deserted, the priests are in dire poverty or support themselves by secular employment, and shrine buildings, even in some cases the outer shrines themselves, are let to secular tenants.

Owing to the brief time that has elapsed since the changes have come about it is not possible to prophesy what will happen to Shinto in the future. It is unlikely that Shinto is dead. State Shinto is at present 'down and out', but it has left behind it a great vacuum in the hearts of the people. Much depends on what comes to occupy the vacuum. If nothing else takes its place there is every possibility, subject to the trend of world events, that nationalistic Shinto will revive and regain its hold on the Japanese people. Already there are indications that in some circles the defeat of Japan is being denied, and the surrender attributed to the peace-loving magnanimity of the Emperor.

In any case, Pure Shinto, the animistic worship of the forces of nature and of the beauty of Japan, and the worship of the ancestors of the family, will linger on—not as a vital faith, but as a superstition among the simple, or as an ancestral sentiment in the hearts of all classes.

Of the Shinto sects, those which approximate most closely to Pure Shinto and the former State Shinto will suffer the same decline as Shrine Shinto. Those, such as the Faith-healing Sects, which base their appeal on fundamental human needs and owe little to orthodox Shinto, are already flourishing widely and competing for the occupation of Japan's spiritual void.

(Handwritten annotations):

(MOST FEARED)
Mystical
Idealistic
Tao Chiao

CHINA
TAOISM
CONFUCIANISM

INDIA
BUDDHISM
A.D. 100
Fo Chiao
ARTISTIC
PHILOSOPHIC
(MOST LOVED)

Ju Chiao
ETHICAL
INTELLECTUAL
(MOST HONORED)

CHAPTER VII

CONFUCIANISM

OVER many centuries the cult of Confucianism has profoundly affected the thought and practice of the world's most numerous race. Although in the course of years its prestige has been assailed and weakened by the two rival systems of Taoism and Buddhism, not until recent times has the number of its adherents suffered any serious diminution.

Some scholars argue that Confucianism cannot be regarded as a religion, since the teaching of Confucius was almost entirely concerned with man's moral conduct and his social relations. But, in the opinion of J. K. Shryock, 'it is better to leave unanswered the question whether Confucianism is a religion, because of the difficulty of defining religion and because it is impossible to give a conclusive answer'. The term 'Confucianism', however, is usually understood to include not only the teaching of Confucius and of his leading disciples, but also that part of early Chinese religion subsequently absorbed by his system, together with the ritual which developed around his name after his death.

For six centuries Confucianism was rivalled by Taoism, the second of the two religions indigenous to China. Buddhism subsequently appeared from India in the first century of our era and, although for many years it bore the stigma of its foreign origin, eventually it became assimilated to the Chinese background, thus proving the truth of the proverb that 'China is a sea that salts every stream that flows into it'.

The *San Chiao*, Three Religions,[1] as they are commonly called, are not regarded by the Chinese as mutually exclusive systems, but are recognized moods of China's religious consciousness. The oft-quoted phrase, 'three ways to one goal', indicates the characteristic tolerance of the Chinese in religious matters. 'All three claim to teach *Tao*, or the order of the universe as it relates to mankind.' Without any sense of incongruity the services of any or all of the three religions are employed according to the occasion. An educated Confucianist, while

---

[1] In popular terminology, *Ju Chiao*, religion of the learned, i.e. Confucianism; *Tao Chiao*, religion of the Way, Taoism; *Fo Chiao*, religion of Buddha. The term *Chiao* is ambiguous, standing equally well for 'teaching' as for 'religion'.

normally professing disdain for Buddhism and Taoism, will readily lend his patronage to their temples and observances, to which, more frequently than not, his wife is a devout adherent.

Y. Y. Tsu describes the situation thus:[1] 'The accumulated influence of these three religions upon Chinese life cannot be separately defined. On the whole, Confucianism has contributed largely to the ethical and intellectual side of Chinese life, Buddhism to the artistic and philosophic, and Taoism to the mystical and idealistic. Judged by their present condition, Confucianism is the most honoured, Buddhism the most loved, and Taoism the most feared.'

THE LIFE AND TIMES OF CONFUCIUS

China, at the time of Confucius' birth, coincided approximately with the north-eastern quarter of modern China, with the Yellow Sea on its eastern fringe. The country was then ruled by the House of Chou, the third and longest historical dynasty (c. 1027-256 B.C.), and consisted of a collection of small and semi-independent States, each of which was governed by a ruler paying fealty to the central authority. The non-Chinese tribes living beyond the outer frontiers were regarded and referred to as 'barbarians'.

The political organization was feudal and aristocratic, and the States, while yielding nominal allegiance to the 'Son of Heaven', as the sovereign of the suzerain State was called, were often at war among themselves, each striving for the ascendancy, either for themselves or for their own particular clique of princes.

The founders of the House of Chou were constantly referred to by Confucius as supreme examples of political wisdom and moral integrity. But five centuries had passed since these traditional heroes flourished, and at the birth of the Sage the Chou kingdom had already passed its peak and was in process of decay. Immediately following his death, the dynasty was succeeded by the *Chan Kuo* or period of the Contending States (480-222 B.C.). So evident were the signs of Chou's political and moral decline that Nature is said to have expressed its abhorrence by an eclipse of the sun, which occurred on 29th August 776 B.C.

Into this troubled era Confucius[2] was born in 551 B.C. in the State

[1] *China Her Own Interpreter: Our Native Religions.*

[2] *K'ung* (Con) was the Sage's surname. 'Confucius' is the 17th century Jesuit missionaries' latinization of K'ung Fu-tzu (Master K'ung).

of Lu, the modern province of Shantung. The earliest biographical picture is that written by the historian Ssu-ma Chien five centuries later, time enough for embellishments and distortions of the first records. For further information about the Sage's personality we are dependent on the *Analects* or *Lun Yü*, 'Discussions and Sayings', collected by his disciples, but of unknown date.

From these sources there emerges a well defined and forceful personality, as sincere and selfless as his near contemporaries, Socrates (born *c.* 470 B.C.) and Buddha (died *c.* 480 B.C.). His mother was the second wife of his father, a military official who died three years after Confucius was born. Very little is known of his early life, but he says that at fifteen, though poor, he set his heart on learning. He married at nineteen, had a son named Li and at least one daughter. While acquiring an early control over himself, he observed an aristocratic dignity in all circumstances of life. As a young man he turned to teaching and politics, and is said to have filled several government appointments in his native State of Lu. Eschewing speculative thought he denied that he was 'an originator'. 'I am a transmitter', he affirmed, 'a believer in, and an admirer of, antiquity.' Self-depreciative, he was nevertheless deeply conscious of a sense of mission, and of being one whom Providence would protect for the sake of that mission. With creature comforts he was little concerned: 'With coarse food to eat and water to drink, and with no pillow but my bent arm, I can still find happiness. Riches and honour acquired by unrighteousness are to me as a floating cloud.'

The story runs that Confucius, when Minister of Justice, had his influence at court subtly undermined by an action of the neighbouring and rival ruler of the State of Ch'i. Dismayed at the growing prosperity in his rival's dominion, resulting from the counsel of Confucius, he sent the prince a present of singing girls and fine horses. The intrigue succeeded in turning the heart of the ruler of Lu away from public affairs to pleasure and self-indulgence. Confucius, finding his advice regarded no longer, reluctantly departed from the Court and never again held public office.

From this time he gave himself primarily to the group of disciples who gathered about him, after the manner of philosophers in Greece. For fifteen years he wandered through the States of Chou with those who could accompany him, often meeting with rebuff and disappointment. Few rulers gave heed to him: some affected to despise the solemn and ceremonious scholar, while others feared the result of his influence on their corrupt administration. At seventy he returned to his native state and spent the last five years of his life in teaching and literary work.

It was probably at this time that he wrote the *Spring and Autumn Annals*, or the *Annals of Lu*, covering the years 776 to 442 B.C. Besides these he is reputed to have collected and edited the ancient writings, afterwards known as the *Wu Ching* or Five Classics, being the earlier section of the Confucian Canon. In these is revealed the glorious age of the sage-kings, three notable rulers of the legendary period, namely, Yao, Shun and Yü, who are said to have flourished about 2200 B.C. and who, by the sheer force of their noble example, produced tranquillity throughout the land. The moral and social principles of these worthies, he was convinced, alone provided the means by which people of his country could survive as a truly ordered community.

Confucius' way with his disciples is illustrated by a characteristic remark. 'To him who has no enthusiasm,' he said, 'I shall not open up the truth, and I shall not help anyone who cannot express his ideas. If I have explained one side of a problem to someone, and he cannot deduce the other three sides, I shall not teach him any more.' His comment on a student found dozing in the day-time was: 'Rotten wood cannot be carved, nor a wall of dirty earth be plastered. This Yü fellow—what is the use of scolding him?'[1] On the other hand, Confucius was quick to appreciate the wholehearted disciple. Of Yen Hui, his favourite, he remarked, 'There is nothing that I say in which he does not delight.' Again: 'Such was (Yen) Hui that for three months there would be nothing in his mind contrary to perfect virtue. The others may attain to this on some days or in some months, but nothing more.'[2]

In personal habits he was simple, but precise and fastidious, insisting on the appropriate costume for the particular occasion, and the suitable sauce for each dish. The ceremonies of state and those connected with ancestor worship commanded his most punctilious observance. 'That man of ceremony' he was called in derision; but it was not the pomp and pageantry that moved him to regard these things carefully so much as the profound symbolism with which he appeared to invest them.

The death of Yen Hui in 481 B.C. plunged the now venerable Sage

[1] *Analects*, Bk. V. 9.   [2] Ibid., Bk. IX. 3 and Bk. VI. 5.

into the deepest grief, causing him to cry out, 'Alas! Heaven is destroying me! Heaven is destroying me!' The other disciples thought
that on this occasion his grief exceeded the bounds of propriety and
admonished him accordingly. Three years later he suffered the loss
of Tzu Lu, next in favour among the group. Towards his own end
he was under a cloud of despondency as to the triumph of his principles. Early one morning, says the record, he arose and, dragging
his staff, moved to the door, murmuring the words:

> 'The great mountain must crumble,
> The strong beam must break,
> The wise man must wither away like a plant.'[1]

In answer to an enquiry, he lamented, 'No intelligent ruler arises to
take me as his master. My time has come to die.' He took to his bed
and within a few days breathed his last. He was buried at Chüfou in
the province of Shantung and mourned at his tomb by some of his
disciples for three years. A temple was later built near the tomb in
honour of the Sage and sacrifices were instituted which continued to
be offered until the fall of the dynasty.

ANCIENT RELIGIOUS BELIEFS

Religious conceptions prevailing at the time of Confucius, furnished
by an ancient native religion, were expressed both in the early writings
and in the popular superstition. His 'religion' undoubtedly incul-
cates the worship of the forces of nature, or perhaps the spirits which
govern natural phenomena. These spirits, however, are all subject to
a personal, Supreme Ruler, who governs creation. As Shang Ti, He
is sacrificed to by the Emperor. As T'ien, or Heaven, in the impersonal
or less personal sense, all men are His generation and may cry to Him.
Filial piety demands also that the departed ancestors shall not be forgotten, but be worshipped in sacrifice.'[2] In other words, from oral
and written tradition, four main features emerge which were adopted
by the Confucian system. These were, first, the conception of Providence; second, the idea of Secondary Spirits; third, the cult of Ancestor
Worship; and fourth, the institution of the Imperial Sacrifice.

[1] J. Legge, *The Religions of China.*
[2] W. E. Soothill, *The Three Religions of China.*

1. *The Conception of Providence*

We learn from the classical writings, which bore the *imprimatur* of Confucius, that the sage-kings conceived of one personal Supreme Ruler, referred to as Ti (a ruling, deified being), or, more fully and more generally, Shang Ti (Shang: supreme, or upper, first), and that He rules the world in righteousness and requires righteousness from men. In the earliest of the ancient records, the *Shu Ching*, Book of History, it is interesting to note that the first reference to God is this term Shang Ti. In these writings 'we are ushered at one step into the presence of a religion in which there is One God supreme over all in heaven and earth, all other spirits being subordinate to Him. . . . The name bursts suddenly upon us from the first page of history without a word of warning.'[1]

This evidence from the earliest Chinese books is supported by inscriptions on the Oracle Bones. These are the earliest writings extant in China and date back to the Shang dynasty (*c.* 1523-1027 B.C.). According to F. S. Drake, of Cheloo University,[2] while the name for God—Ti—occurs some seven or eight hundred times, only a few traces of nature worship are contained in the inscriptions.

Chinese popular legends about the creation feature a mythological figure named P'an Ku, said to be the first living being on earth, whose chiselling brought the early chaos into shape. Over against this we read in the more sober records of the Chou dynasty the clear statement of Kuan Yin Tzu, 'Heaven and earth did not come of themselves; there was one who made them', while Tzu Hsia, a disciple of Confucius, in his commentary on one of the classical books, wrote, 'God (Ti) is the Lord the Creator: the maker (ancestor) of heaven and earth.'[3] Similarly, in one of the prayers used at the annual Imperial Sacrifice, the Chinese Emperor is quoted as saying, 'It is Thou, O Lord, who art the true parent of all things.'

'That God is no idle occupant of His throne is taught in a multitude of passages in the ancient books. The words of the young king Ch'ang, in the twelfth century B.C., are of general application:

[1] J. Ross, *The Original Religion of China.*
[2] *The Contribution of Chinese Religious Thought.*
[3] F. Rawlinson, *Some Chinese Ideas of God.*

"With reverence I will go
  Where duty's path is plain.
Heaven's will I clearly know;
  Its favour to retain
Is hard;—let me not say
  'Heaven is remote on high,
Nor notices men's way.'
  There in the starlit sky
It round about us moves,
  Inspecting all we do,
And daily disapproves
  What is not just and true." [1]

In the classics 'Shang Ti is always portrayed as majestic, glorious and personal. In the *Shih Shu*, Book of Odes, occur the following lines, "Great is Shang Ti, beholding this lower world in majesty." Again, "Shang Ti is with you, have no doubt in your heart." His distinct personality is shown in the passage, "The fame of King Wen ascended up to Shang Ti and Ti approved." Further, it is the Supreme Ruler who has implanted in man the sense of moral responsibility. The *Shu Ching*, Book of History, records the first sovereign of the Shang dynasty (1766 B.C.) as saying that, "The great Shang Ti has conferred even upon inferior people a moral sense." [2] These translated extracts are sufficient to show, observes Francis Wei, that 'the Chinese did have once a noble and lofty conception of the Lord of the Universe'.

Whether we are entitled on the available evidence to postulate that monotheism was the original religion of the Chinese or whether, as some would suggest,[3] the conception of the Supreme Ruler is but a stage reached in the development from a primeval form of religion basically animistic, is a matter of controversy. Some would say that it is an argument which can be determined only by reference to other and superior sources of knowledge.

The early philosophers of the Chou dynasty, however, evade direct reference to the supreme name for God, Shang Ti, and in their writings we find the notion of a personal Creator either absent or blurred. Confucius himself used the term Shang Ti only once in all his recorded

[1] J. Legge, *The Religions of China*, cit. *Book of Odes*, IV, i., Pt. 3, Ode 3.
[2] F. Wei, *Religious Beliefs of the Ancient Chinese*.
[3] Notably J. J. de Groot in *The Religious Systems of China*.

teaching. Chinese sages from this time increasingly used the more colourless term T'ien, Heaven, the impersonal Providence or Fate, as when Chu Yuan (332-295 B.C.), who flourished two hundred years after Confucius, wrote, 'Heaven is man's origin, and when oppressed with poverty he recalls his source. For when men are overwrought and worn out, who is there that does not cry to Heaven.' And yet in both earlier and later writers, Shang Ti and T'ien are sometimes used interchangeably and point to one Being. For example, H. A. Giles[1] quotes the account of a dream by the Emperor Yung Lo (1403-1425 A.D.), in which he relates that an angel appeared to him with a message from Shang Ti, upon which he remarked, 'Is not this a command from T'ien?'

2. The Belief in Secondary Spirits

If Shang Ti was the sole and supreme Ruler above, there were a host of spiritual beings associated with Him. These subordinate and secondary divinities were known as *Shen* (spirits or gods): that they were believed to move freely among mortals is shown by a quotation[2] from the ancient Book of Odes:

> 'Do not say, this place is not public;
> No one can see me here.
> The approaches of spiritual Beings
> Cannot be calculated beforehand;
> But on no account must they be ignored.'

The recognition of both orders of being, the Supreme and the Secondary, is illustrated by the record in which King Wu is said to be determined to punish Chou for his crimes. The announcement reads: '. . . I presume reverently to comply with Shang Ti to repress the ways of Chou. . . . And now, ye gods, grant me your aid. . . .' Indeed, all the ancient emperors are found sacrificing to Shang Ti, and to the host of gods.

The distinction between good and evil spirits was a rather later development, when the term *shen* came to refer to benevolent spirits and the term *kuei* to malevolent spirits. The power and influence of the spirits were manifested at such places as waterfalls, the rapids

[1] H. A. Giles, *Religions of Ancient China*.
[2] Translation by H. A. Giles in *Religions of AncienBot China*, cit. *ok of Odes*, III, iii, Ode 2.

of rivers, or indeed any remarkable object of nature, but, most of all, in association with the recurring seasons. They were the governors of natural phenomena and therefore it was deemed prudent to placate these divinities by appropriate sacrifice and ritual. These are all signs of the existence of an incipient nature worship which ran side by side with and threatened to corrupt the primitive monotheism. The worship of the *Tuti*, local god of the soil, by the common people predated and was approved by Confucius. In every field of the myriad farms of China, now as then, the Tuti has his mud shrine and receives the traditional offerings of its cultivators. Shang Ti was aloof and remote, but these divinities on every hand were for good or ill luck as the case might be.

It is remarkable that notwithstanding the animistic and polytheistic elements assimilated to the Confucian system, little or no idolatry is observed until the coming of Buddhism. Moreover, Confucianism, while allowing images of the Sage to be set up, never permitted an image to be made representing Shang Ti. But since the days of Confucius the worship of 'gods' and 'saints' in China has increased enormously, owing largely to the influence of Taoism and Buddhism. H. A. Giles refers to a single work, published in 1640, listing no fewer than eight hundred divinities.

3. *Ancestor Worship: its Ritual and Significance*

Most deep-rooted of all Chinese religious observances, however, is that of ancestor worship. It has the sanction of antiquity and the seal of China's greatest Sage, and would seem to have as its source an intuitive belief in life after death. The antiquity of this practice is illustrated by the *Shu Ching*, Book of History,[1] where referring to the great Shun (*c.* 2255 B.C.) it is stated, 'He presented a burnt offering to *Heaven* and sacrificed in order to the hills and rivers, and extended his worship to the host of *shen* (spirits). When he returned to the Capitol, he went to the accomplished *Ancestor*, and offered a simple bullock.' While other beliefs and practices have been shaken by the impact of western materialism, this custom, in one form or other, survives as the base of Chinese social and religious institutions. 'The real atheism in China is the refusal to worship at the ancestral shrine. Nearly everything else may be foregone and forgiven, but this never.'[2]

[1] Legge's edition, *Shu Ching*, Book of History, II, i. 8.
[2] W. E. Soothill, *The Three Religions of China*.

An experienced observer of things Chinese, writing on the subject, said: 'However much the Chinese may be divided in other matters, as religion, dialects, degrees of intelligence, wealth, etc., they form a unit in regard to this rite, both as to time and manner; and I believe it is the only point on which they are united. . . . It is a duty that takes precedence of all others, and, when faithfully performed, is a virtue that hides a multitude of sins. A man may discard any or all of the other forms of religion, but this he dare not. The perpetuity and prosperity of his family depend upon it. It is the one idea that excites in the Chinese mind a feeling of awe and reverence.'[1] By many educated Chinese the practice is deprecated, but seldom, if ever, dismissed. Like Shinto in Japan, it has modern apologists who deny the religious character of the ceremonial, and who for 'worship' substitute the terms 'homage' or 'veneration'.

The power and influence of this tradition is seen in the first act performed by the *Kuomintang*, Nationalist Party, when it regained power and formed a government in Nanking in 1927. Six million sterling was lavished on building the mausoleum for their dead leader, Sun Yat Sen.

(*a*) *The Ritual*. Where ancestor worship is practised each household possesses a small shrine, like a bookcase, where a wooden tablet is kept. This rests on a pedestal, upon which is written the name and dates of birth and death of the deceased. Those of the wealthy are gilded or highly ornamented. This tablet is called the *Shen Wei*, the Seat of the Spirits. It is usual to keep in the house of the ordinary family the tablets of the three previous generations. When a parent dies the eldest son does the honours for the family. At the grave he kneels and prays, 'Let the bones and the flesh return to the earth, and may the spirit reside with us in the tablet.' Later, at home, an official or scholar, or sometimes the eldest son, takes a red pencil and dots the *wang* (王) 'king' character, making it into *chu* (主) the character for 'lord', or 'to preside', thus making the disembodied spirit *present*, as a guest. After this the tablet takes its place at the family shrine. Before it the members of the family prostrate themselves (kow tow), at regular intervals, lighting candles and burning incense and making ceremonial offerings of food; or the head of the family may lead the worship while the members of the family stand in silence. Sacrifices to ancestors are offered monthly, quarterly and annually, and important events are announced

[1] M. T. Yates, *Ancestor Worship and Feng-Shuy*.

to them. The form and manner is the same as worship before idols, and the motive is similar. Those families able to do so maintain a separate Ancestral Hall and place the tablets there: this hall is the centre of the life of the clan. The Ancestral Hall is maintained from endowments, and bursaries are given to the promising scholar who will represent and honour the family in Government service.

(b) *The Theory.* 'While the worship is performed, the tablet is supposed to be occupied by the spirit specially interested in the service; and at the conclusion the spirit returns to his own place. . . . The Chinese regard ancestor worship as the highest duty evolving out of the principle of filial piety, and hold that the worship is not merely commemorative, but a pretended real intercourse with the world of spirit, pre-supposing that the happiness of the dead depends on the sacrifices of their descendants and that their departed spirits, on the other hand, have power to confer blessings or calamities on the living.'[1]

Filial piety thus finds in ancestor worship its chief expression and focal point. The ceremony, moreover, results in a family solidarity of amazing tenacity and endurance: this cult of the family or clan accounts in large measure for the continuing social stability of China and has provided a restraining and conserving influence on the Chinese people. Parental affection, self-love and fear together urge all concerned to provide for the continuity of the family, and, since sons alone are eligible to perform the rite of Ancestor Worship, it follows that every married man considers male issue to be of the first importance. To this imperious requirement is due the unhappy development of secondary wives and concubinage. Its importance is stressed in the *Family Instructions*, written for the ladies of the Imperial household by the Empress Jen Hsiao Wen, first wife of Emperor Ming Ch'eng Tsu (acc. 1402 A.D.). She writes: 'One of the most important things in life is marriage in order that the line of ancestry be not broken. It is, therefore, necessary that sacrifices be given to the ancestors. When the father pours out the marriage cup, as the son leaves to get his bride, he says, "Go and welcome your bride that we may have someone to sacrifice to the ancestors." '

It was over the question of ancestor worship that the Vatican fell foul of the Imperial Court of K'ang Hsi in the seventeenth century A.D. When the Roman See, on the advice of the Dominicans, but contrary to that of the Jesuits, declared against the practice, the Emperor,

[1] J. Legge, *The Religions of China.*

hitherto well disposed to the Roman priests, proceeded to bitter enmity and open opposition. Most Protestant Chinese Christians have no difficulty in deciding that it is a ceremony belonging to their pagan background, and as such to be repudiated.

In the opinion of Francis Wei[1] the present-day observation of the rite is a perversion of the true classical tradition. He says: 'Ancestor worship among the Chinese of today is not the ancestor worship represented in the classics. The intense filial piety and affection, the sincere reverence, are no more to be found in the performance of the ceremonies. Nothing but the tedious formality is left. With the spread of Taoism and Buddhism, it has been clothed with appalling superstitions, while its true meaning is known within only a narrow circle. It is no longer classical, for it has been taken captive and enslaved by Taoism and Buddhism.'

4. The Imperial Sacrifice

From earliest times the keystone in the religious system of the State was the Imperial or Grand Sacrifice made by the Emperor at the Altar of Heaven in Peking. The day of the sacrifice was the morning of the day of the winter solstice. On this day the sun reaches its southernmost point and begins its journey northward. The altar is a white marble dais, circular in form (answering to the circle of heaven) and of proportions and simplicity that have inspired the admiration of men from every land.

The stately ceremony was enacted by the Emperor, when as representative of his people he offered in sacrifice a red-brown calf and prostrated himself before a tablet bearing the inscription *Huang T'ien Shang Ti*, The Supreme Ruler of Imperial Heaven. In sacrifice and prayer to Shang Ti he expressed his sense of the nation's obligation to and dependence upon the Higher Powers. The sacrifice was not offered in expiation, but was the homage of the nation in the person of the chief prince and the only legitimate approach to Shang Ti which was permitted by Confucian teaching. On that day no funeral, mourning dress, or weeping was to be seen or heard in public. Worship was also paid to the great dynastic ancestors, but at a side altar.

There were two notable and significant omissions from the ceremony: first, the absence of any form or image to represent the Supreme Ruler and the host of spirits worshipped; and, second, the

[1] *Religious Beliefs of the Ancient Chinese.*

absence of sacerdotalism. No professional priest was present: an
official performed all necessary acts in assisting the Emperor and served
in that capacity as one chosen from among the body of worshippers
and only for that single occasion. The *Li Chi*, Book of Rites, stressing
the exalted nature of the ceremony, says: 'The sacrifice to the Ti . . .
is the highest expression of reverence; only the holy man (i.e. the
Emperor) is capable of making an offering to the Ti'—a privilege
jealously guarded through the centuries. Referring to the intrusion
upon the ceremony by a certain Empress, another ancient record says
that on one occasion at the Grand Sacrifice 'the Empress poured the
libation and then assisted with cups and salvers'. But the commentator
observes with barely concealed disdain: 'We must remember that the
great Spirit of Heaven and Earth is most majestic and it is not per-
missible to make a *libation* to Him. Besides, He is worshipped without
ostentation. Hence it may be seen that the libation of the Empress was
to the lesser spirits and not to the august Shang Ti. There is no need
for cups and salvers in His service."[1]

In the seventeenth century A.D., towards the end of the Ming
dynasty, the Imperial authorities having determined to make a change
in the ascription to Shang Ti at the Solstitial Sacrifice, occasion was
taken to compose a series of prayers for presentation by the Emperor
at the Altar of Heaven. While these prayers portray Confucianism at
its best, the State worship is almost, if not entirely, 'a material worship
for material benefits' and the spiritual element is largely absent. The
following are a few short extracts from Legge's translation:[2]

When the great day arrived, the Emperor greeted the real though
invisible approach of Shang Ti thus:

'Of old, in the beginning, there was the great chaos, without form
and dark. The five elements had not begun to revolve, nor the sun
and moon to shine. In the midst thereof there presented itself neither
form nor sound. Thou, O Spiritual Sovereign, camest torth in Thy
presidency, and first didst divide the gross from the pure (i.e. the ethereal from the material). Thou madest heaven; Thou madest earth; Thou
madest man. All things got their being, with their reproducing power.
. . . I, Thy servant, presume reverently to thank Thee, and, while I
worship, present the notice to Thee, O Ti, calling Thee Sovereign.'

[1] Evan Morgan, *The Meaning of the Term Shang Ti*.
[2] J. Legge, *The Religions of China*.

Silks and jade were then presented with the following address:

'Thou hast vouchsafed, O Ti, to hear us, for Thou regardest us as our Father. I, Thy child, dull and unenlightened, am unable to show forth my feelings. I thank Thee that Thou hast accepted the intimation. Honourable is Thy great name . . .'

A thanksgiving followed in these words:

'When Ti, the Lord, had so decreed, He called into existence the three powers (heaven, earth, and man). Between heaven and earth He separately disposed men and things, all overspread by the heavens. I, His small servant, beg His (favouring) decree, to enlighten me, His vassal; so may I ever appear before Him in the empyrean.'

At the second drink-offering it was said:

'. . . All living things are indebted to Thy goodness, but who knows whence his blessings come to him? It is Thou alone, O Lord, who art the true parent of all things.'

Finally:

'We have worshipped and written the Great Name on this gem-like sheet. Now we display it before Ti, and place it in the fire. These valuable offerings of silks and fine meats we burn also, with these sincere prayers, that they may ascend in volumes of flames up to the distant azure. All the ends of the earth look up to Him. All human beings, all things on the earth, rejoice together in the Great Name.'

ATTITUDE OF CONFUCIUS TO THE RELIGIOUS TRADITIONS

In all things Confucius deferred to the tradition of the ancients, including the main religious elements enumerated above. If he himself stressed practicalities this was in revolt against the puerile and profitless superstitions into which, in his day, the popular religion had sunk. He was usually reticent regarding the disciples' enquiries about the supernatural and whatever transcends earthly existence. Some have interpreted this attitude as evidence of his fundamental agnosticism; for once, when questioned, he urged his disciples, 'While respecting spiritual beings, to keep aloof from them.'[1] To Chi Lu, one of his disciples, who asked about death, he answered, 'While you do not understand life, how can you know about death?'[2] The Sage, says the same record,[3] also avoided speaking about spirits. But this seemingly sceptical view, together with an unwillingness to commit himself on

[1] *Analects*, Bk. VI, 20.   [2] Op. cit., Bk. XI, 11.   [3] Op. cit., Bk. VII, 20.

points about which he had no certain knowledge, were probably because he revolted against the burdensome multiplication of objects worshipped and feared. He saw no way of directing the common people to Shang Ti and so aimed at continuing their worship to their ancestors.[1]

Confucius certainly believed in the reality of the spiritual world, and his frequent references to Heaven show belief in a supreme power, governing and controlling the destinies of men. 'There is Heaven; it knows me,' was his reply[2] to certain false insinuations; again, 'If I have acted improperly, may Heaven reject me!'[3] If a man sinned against Heaven then, Confucius declared, he had nowhere left for prayer.[4] When Huan Ti, Minister of War in the Sung State, sought his hurt, the Sage asserted that since his teaching was from Heaven his opponent was powerless.[5] 'Nevertheless, the fact remains that his supreme interest was not in religion. He was not a prophet, anxious above all that the nation should stand in right relation with God. He was essentially an ethical teacher with a political aim.'[6]

BOOKS OF THE CONFUCIAN CANON

After the death of the Sage the Confucian tradition was perpetuated by the activity of several eminent followers, and by the influence of those writings which came to form the Confucian Canon, generally known as the *Wu Ching*, Five Classics, and the *Ssu Shu*, Four Books. Some modern scholars question whether Confucius was responsible for compiling or editing any of the early classical works—the Five Classics. For our present purpose the point is immaterial. The fact to remember is that this body of literature was increasingly regarded as the standard of Confucian orthodoxy.

Most important and most interesting of the classical writings is the *Lun Yü*, or Analects, one of the Four Books. This small volume gives

---

[1] A strange system of divination, employing the shell of a tortoise and stalks of a kind of grass, was an inheritance from the earliest past. Confucius is said to have given it attention and credence, but it forms no part of his teaching. Soothill says that he is unaware of any instance where divination was used to ascertain the will of God: its use appears to have been limited to seeking direction from ancestors.

[2] *Analects*, Bk. XIV, 37.

[3] Op. cit., Bk. VI, 26.   [4] Op. cit., Bk. XIII, 2.   [5] Op. cit., Bk. VII, 22.

[6] B. S. Bonsall, *Confucianism and Taoism*.

a collection of the Master's sayings on a variety of subjects: it is the nearest approach to a systematic presentation of his teaching and gives the most authentic account of his personality. The Analects gain in importance when it is remembered that before Confucius there evidently existed no recorded system of thought on the problems of man and his place in society. As regards the other writings it is sufficient here merely to add that the remaining three Books are: the *Ta Hsüeh*, Great Learning, attributed to the Sage, with an appended commentary by a disciple; the *Chung Yung*, Doctrine of the Mean, compiled by a disciple, probably Tzu Ssu, the grandson of Confucius; and the *Meng Tzu*, or (works of) Mencius, who came to be known as the Second Sage.

The Five Classics, to which reference has previously been made, were for the most part documents in existence before the time of Confucius. There is the *Yi Ching*, or Book of Changes, a book of divination based on the *pa kua*, a series of whole and broken lines, the various combinations of which are supposed to yield a mystical and moral interpretation. The book is barely intelligible. The *Shu Ching*, or Book of History, covers the period approximately from 2300 to 600 B.C. in terse and elegant prose. This is the oldest known Chinese book, in which the first term for God used is 'Shang Ti'. This work is chiefly concerned with the words and doings of the sage-kings in the golden age. The *Shih Ching*, or Book of Odes, contains ballads and religious songs, much admired by Confucius, who declared that their faithful study would produce a mind without a single depraving thought. The *Ch'un Ch'iu*, or Spring and Autumn Annals (Annals of the State of Lu), written by Confucius, contains a bare record of events, but is accompanied by an important commentary known as the *Tso Chuan*. Finally there is the *Li Chi*, or Book of Rites, which is a collection of treatises on ceremonial usages, both secular and religious.

LEADING IDEAS OF CONFUCIUS' TEACHING

Confucius passed on no inherited system of thought, nor did he formulate one himself. The record of his sayings in the Analects, however, shows as the dominant characteristic an ethical-utilitarian strain. In accord with this pragmatic bent we find 'the advocacy of the golden mean in conduct, the avoidance of merely speculative issues, and a utilitarian gospel of common sense and homely virtues . . . Confucian literature is all shot through with this ethical quality . . . and learning is in order to moral ends . . . its philosophy, history and poetry are all alike suffused with moral purpose.'[1] The Sage's avowed aim was to reform the corrupt kingdom of Chou by means of the moral principles of the ancient worthies. A chosen method of instruction was to picture the Chun-tzu, the Superior Man or Gentleman, and to describe the way in which he would behave in his private and public relationships. Confucius had much to say about the Chun-tzu, but over and beyond the individual there is always his 'castle in the air'—the ideal social community, a mental projection drawing its inspiration from all he read of the golden days of antiquity. Into this ideal society he put his ideal man, a person actuated by high moral standards and punctilious in his observance of the conventions of family and state.

The ideal person is not a challenging, heroic figure, although if he is true to himself, as a Superior Man, he will suffer no emergency to drive him from his principles, and will maintain his course when bad principles prevail. Bonsell contests the frequent assertion that Confucian morality is merely external by saying that the inwardness of morality is recognized in the distinction which the master makes between fear of punishment and the sense of shame as motives to conduct, as well as in his insistence that the whole worth of filial piety lies in the feeling which accompanies service to parents. Moreover, the Sage went deeper than the surface when he observed, 'If a man be without virtues proper to humanity, what has he to do with the rites of propriety?'[2]

Although Confucius set a high moral standard, he had yet to confess, as he looked about him, that it was rarely even approached. 'Those who know virtue,' he says, 'are few.'[3] 'I have not seen one who loves virtue as he loves beauty (or sensual pleasure).'[4] 'A good man it is not mine to see.'[5] 'I have not seen one who could perceive his faults and inwardly accuse himself.'[6] 'I have not seen a person who loved virtue, or hated what was not virtuous. He who loved virtue would esteem nothing above it.'[7]

The Sage perhaps reached his highest level in the doctrine of *Jen*—Goodness or Charity, a word 'embracing all those moral qualities

[1] Leighton Stuart, *The Chinese Mind and the Gospel.*
[2] *Analects*, Bk. III, 3.   [3] *Analects*, Bk. XV, 3.
[4] Op. cit., Bk. IX, 17, and XV, 12.   [5] Op. cit., Bk. VII, 25.
[6] Op. cit., Bk. V, 26.   [7] Op. cit., Bk. IV, 6.

which should govern one man in his relations with another'. It was when expounding the meaning of this word that he gave expression to the Golden Rule. 'Is there any one word,' asked Tzu-Kung[1] the disciple, 'which may serve as a rule of practice for all one's life?' The Master replied: 'Is not *Jen* such a word? What you do not want done to yourself, do not to others.' And elsewhere he says, 'The way of the Gentleman is to offer first to others what one requires of them.'

The so-called *Wu Ch'ang*, or Five Virtues, including *Jen*, Goodness or Charity, are: Righteousness, Propriety, Knowledge, and Sincerity. In addition to possessing moral virtues, the Gentleman, it should be observed again, is distinguished by punctilious conformity to *Li*, or 'propriety', a code of formal behaviour precisely defining personal and social relationships. Ceremony and ritual had its appropriate time and place, and only a 'small man' would be insensible to its importance and significance. Naturally the family is regarded as the first scene for the display of these virtues. 'It is not possible,' reads The Great Learning, 'for a man to teach others who cannot teach his own family . . . for from the loving example of one family the whole state becomes loving . . . while from the ambition and perverseness of one man, the whole state may be led to rebellions, disorders . . . Such is the nature of influence.'

The five moral qualities, moreover, should be manifested in the so-called *Wu Lun*, or Five Relationships, which are: Prince and Minister, Father and Son, Husband and Wife, Elder Brother and Younger Brother, Friend and Friend. Good conduct and good government consist in maintaining and regulating these relationships.

Confucius diverges from the Christian ethical standard in his principle of recompensing private injury with justice—not with mercy or forgiveness. His retort to disapproval was: 'Then with what will you recompense kindness?'[2] He moreover tones down the rule of entire truthfulness, as when he sends word to an unwelcome visitor that he is 'indisposed',[3] and allows for prevarication if this seems necessary in order to save another from embarrassment—especially if the other person were a parent, since then his doctrine of filial piety would be involved. 'Do the dead have knowledge of our service and worship?' one of his disciples asked. 'If I say "Yes",' was the answer, 'filial sons

---

[1] *Analects*, Bk. XV, 23.   [2] *Op. cit.*, Bk. XII, 36.
[3] *Op. cit.*, Bk. XVII, 20.

and grandsons will ruin themselves in such services and offerings. If I say "No", the unfilial will leave the dead unburied.' Commenting on this passage, Leighton Stuart[1] writes: 'Such pragmatic treatment has resulted in the most radical defect, not only of Chinese character but of their mental processes as well, not only of their moral indifference to truth but their illogical indifference to fact. There is an elusive sense of unreality playing over everything Chinese; they manifest a perverse lack of interest as to whether a given doctrine or fact is historically or objectively true. All that matters is whether or not it functions well.'

'The dead hand of the Master,' Dr. Stuart goes on to say, 'is felt again in his insistence on outward rites, the performance of which he claimed would not only reveal, but would prompt and preserve the proper state of the heart. But while this theory has fixed a morality of externals, it largely explains the Chinese "saving of face"; it has made them a nation of Pharisees, rigidly scrupulous and zealous but deficient in any disturbing sense of sin or eager seeking for salvation. Indeed, with the sole exception of Hsün Tzu and his school, Chinese moralists postulate the natural goodness of man. One other defect in Confucianism is its failure to touch the deeper springs of life. A religion of common sense and regulated propriety paralyses the imagination. Common sense is only a rough register of common experience. Even in material progress the Chinese have paid heavily . . . and have remained static.'

THE PERIOD OF THE GREAT PHILOSOPHERS

The Chou dynasty in its latter phase was a time of intense intellectual activity against a background of political chaos. The teaching of the Confucian classics was reinforced and learnedly expounded and discussed by successive leaders of thought: probably all the great and formative thinkers of China lived during this period. 'It is of more than passing interest,' writes Neville Whymant, 'that this same period saw the full flowering of Greek philosophical and oratorical genius half a world away.'

Best known of the post-Confucian philosophers to western students is Mencius (372-289 B.C.), who flourished one hundred years after Confucius, and who was the first of the great Confucian disciples to

[1] *The Chinese Mind and the Gospel.*

develop a reasoned exposition of Confucian teaching. He was a brilliant and vigorous writer, but more than a thousand years were to elapse before his works were included in the Confucian Canon. Like his master he habitually employed the impersonal term 'Heaven' and left on record only one direct reference to 'Shang Ti', where he says that even an evil man, if he mourns and purifies himself, may serve Shang Ti.

Like other Chou philosophers, Mencius was mainly concerned with the problem of man's nature which, more explicitly than his master, he asserted to be intrinsically good. 'Its tendency to good,' he declared, 'is like that of water to flow downwards.' Evil is the result of ignorance and of the lack of good example and vigilant cultivation of Heaven-bestowed instincts. 'The heart of the infant,' says Mencius, 'is naturally so inclined toward good as to exclude all evil.' It naturally follows that 'those who are great among men are those who, throughout their lives, do not lose their childlike heart.'

In this view he was vigorously opposed by a teacher of equal brilliance, Hsün Tzu (298–238 B.C.), who in his great essay, *That the Nature of Man is Evil*, asserts that only by the imposition of laws and the guidance of teachers can man be directed into reasonable and right conduct, and that without these he would by nature tend to a state of savagery.

Notwithstanding these philosophical polemics about man's fundamental nature, the two rivals were in agreement as to the fact that moral evil was widespread, if not universal. From this point the Confucian school takes up the problem of its rectification, and to this problem the Confucianist gives one answer. He affirms that it is chiefly a question of education and training: if erring man can be shown the right path he will automatically incline to it. 'If *you*, sir, were not covetous,' once said Confucius to a perplexed prince, '*they* (the thieves) would not steal.'[1]

Mo Tzu was one of the most outstanding of the Chou philosophers and was born (c. 470) about the time of Confucius' death. His principles were opposed to the Confucian system, the extravagant ceremonialism of which he denounced. In his view only the principle of Universal Love was the adequate answer to the mutual hate that characterized mankind. But he was a utilitarian, exalting Love, but as the only means to the desired end of human happiness. 'Doctrine',

[1] *Analects*, Bk. XII, 18.

he said, 'which cannot be translated into conduct should not be taught.'[1] For a time his system presented a serious challenge to the teaching of Confucius.

Yang Tzu (c. 320–235 B.C.) was another heterodox and independent thinker. 'China's first professional hedonist,' he advocated a species of individualism and anarchy. 'What is this life of man, what pleasure is in it?' is his summing-up of life beneath the sun. 'While alive (it may not be for long), therefore, let us hasten to make the best of life. What leisure have we to be thinking of anything after death?'

The teaching of Mo Tzu and Yang Tzu was vigorously opposed by Mencius and the orthodox; and, notwithstanding the fact that during this period the various schools flourished with such spontaneity and vigour, within a few years the system of Confucius alone survived, to be the standard for China's scholars.

CONFUCIANISM COMPARED WITH TAOISM

As the disciple Tzu Kung once remarked, Confucius in his discourse chiefly confined himself to consideration of the 'externals of culture'. Moreover, as we have seen, it was the Sage's practice largely to confine his teaching to a limited audience of enquirers and disciples belonging to the ruling class. In this way the religious range of the common people was restricted to the worship of their ancestors and to the crude animism of the time.

Such was the situation which gave rise to the growth of Taoism. As time went on, this, the second indigenous religion, was drawn upon to supply the deficiencies of Confucianism, not only by the common people but also and increasingly by the literati, some of whom felt that Confucianism had become inflexible, too detailed, and the source of much hypocrisy. At different times in the course of the centuries Taoism was destined seriously to rival the more sedate and disciplined way of Confucius. More than once it was first in favour at the Imperial Court, although Confucianism was always employed as needed, especially to meet the requirements of State ritual.

Taoism had two main manifestations: it is seen as a mystical philosophy, pervading a great deal of later Chinese literature, and also as a popular and superstitious religion.

[1] *Mo Tzu*, Chapter 46.

Taoist philosophy was enshrined in the *Tao Tê Ching*,[1] 'the Canon of the Tao and the exemplification thereof'. This brief book of little more than five thousand Chinese characters was for long attributed to Lao Tzu, but is now generally regarded as a composite work embodying some of Lao Tzu's utterances, 'mixed up with the hocus-pocus of later Taoism, and may safely be assigned to the Han dynasty (206 B.C.-221 A.D.).'

Lao Tzu, meaning 'the Old Philosopher' (604 B.C.), if we accept the account of Ssu-ma Chien, was an elder contemporary of Confucius. A discounted tradition says that the two once met and discussed the subject of ceremonies. Lao Tzu is said to have been for a time keeper of the Royal Archives. Beyond this we learn practically nothing of him, save that a story is told of how the Tao Tê Ching came to be written. While residing at the seat of Government, he grew weary of the ways of society and decided to become a recluse. As he was entering the pass of Hsien Ku on his way to the north-west, he was stopped by the warden of the pass who, hearing of his purpose, implored him to leave a record of his teaching: the response to this was the Tao Tê Ching. 'He then went away, and it is not known where he died. He was a superior man who liked to keep himself unknown.'[2]

The theme of the Taoist classic briefly is that man in his quest for the good life should cease from preoccupation with 'externals' and from fretful effort. He should relax and let Nature have her way. Nature, or the Universal Principle, perhaps best translates the elusive concept of *Tao* as used in the Tao Tê Ching. The way of the Tao expresses itself in a natural spontaneity: everything is accomplished by not striving for anything—'a perpetual accommodation of self to one's surroundings, with the minimum of effort'. Taoism, in terms of the Tao Tê Ching, is the Chinese brand of mystical quietism. It was the adopted philosophy of some of the more famous poets and the writers of fairy tales. Supplying the colour and romance, for which men crave, it provided something which the rigid, cold externalities of Confucianism could never give.

A story told by a Taoist writer gives a picturesque illustration of the Taoist contempt for fuss. He says, 'There was once a man who was

[1] *Ching*: Canon or Classic. *Tê*: Behaviour, virtue, principles exemplified in action. *Tao*: Road, the Way, the true Path. Arthur Waley translates the book's title as 'The Canon of the Way and its Power'.
[2] Ssu-ma Chien's History.

so afraid of his shadow and so disliked his own footsteps that he determined to run away from them. But the oftener he raised his feet the more footsteps he made, and though he ran very hard his shadow never left him. From this he inferred that he went too slowly, and ran as hard as he could without resting, the consequence being that his strength broke down and he died. He was not aware that by going into the shade he would have got rid of his shadow, and that by keeping still he would have put an end to his footsteps. Fool that he was.'[1]

As Legge points out, there is no inculcation of religion in the Tao Tê Ching. At most we meet with a few references to Heaven and the idea of a First Cause, 'the first of the first . . without a name . . . the beginning of heaven and earth'. Since no name is known it is called Tao. The exalted virtues are gentleness, economy and absence of self-assertion. Water is the favourite emblem of the Tao with the author, for 'it occupies the low place, which all men dislike'.

The second great name in Taoism is that of Chuang Tzu (b. 330 B.C.), whose brilliantly written essays elucidating the teaching of Lao Tzu are the most widely read of Taoist literature. His conception of Tao is substantially the same as that of the Tao Tê Ching. What Mencius was to Confucius, Chuang Tzu was to Lao Tzu.

The second main manifestation of Taoism arose naturally out of the early popular religion, but it is not until a considerable time after the Christian era that we find it existing as a religion. In course of time new and superstitious developments occurred which radically changed and debased it. The early Taoist mystics practised breathing and posturing. Somewhat later search began to be made for the elixir of life and the 'Isles of the Immortals'. To this, in due course, was added the practice of alchemy. It was an easy transition from these to magic and exorcism, which had the dire result of bringing the Chinese people into bondage to demons. 'Then came Buddhism with its attractive ritual and its manifold consolations, and put an end once for all to the "ancient glories" of the teachings of Lao Tzu . . . still, it was not until the third or fourth centuries of our era that Buddhism began to make itself appreciably felt. When this came about there ensued a long and fierce struggle between the Buddhists and the Taoists, resulting, after alternating triumphs and defeats on both sides, in that mutual toleration which obtains at the present day. Each religion began early

[1] W. E. Soothill, The Three Religions of China.

to borrow from the other. In the words of the philosopher Chu Hsi of the eleventh century, "Buddhism stole the best features of Taoism; Taoism stole the worst features of Buddhism".[1]

THE RELIGIOUS CHARACTER OF CONFUCIANISM

While Taoism and Buddhism were undergoing religious changes, Confucianism began to take on the forms of religion also; it had had a marked influence on the other two cults and was to be influenced by them in turn. The Imperial authorities of successive dynasties seemed to vie with their predecessors in doing the Sage honour and in surrounding his person with the air of mystical sanctity. Some features of Confucianism which reveal the gradually acquired religious aspects are:

(1) Confucian classical literature contains prayers and enjoins offerings to Shang Ti, the Supreme Ruler.

(2) The Sage accepted and endorsed the 'religion of the state' as set forth in the Book of History and the Book of Odes, and as manifested in the annual Imperial Sacrifice to Shang Ti.

(3) Confucius attached great importance to the sacrificial rites associated with the worship of ancestral spirits. 'These offerings are made for the special purpose of conciliating the spirit . . . this is the essential feature of the rite and this it is which makes the rite an act of worship pure and simple.'[2]

(4) Worship of the Sage is conducted in Confucian temples, erected in the chief cities throughout the Empire. In them is placed the tablet of the Sage, and on either side those of his more famous disciples. On the tablet of Confucius is written, 'The divine seat of the great completer, the most holy, ancient teacher Confucius', and on the entrance gates are inscriptions such as, 'The teacher and example for ten thousand generations'. Early in the Christian era, more than five centuries after his death, a new direction was given to the worship of Confucius by the offering of animal sacrifices at the vernal and autumnal equinoxes.

In Imperial China schools observed a ceremony of homage twice a month as well as on special occasions. Incense and candles were burnt, when the master with his pupils prostrated themselves before the tablet of the Sage. At the turn of the present century the same cere-

[1] H. A. Giles, *China and the Chinese.*
[2] H. A. Giles, *The Civilization of China.*

mony was held on the first day of each month in the hall specially set apart in each school for the purpose. At the present day, in modified form, the ceremony is observed only on his birthday, 27th August.

The worship of Confucius reached its climax in his elevation to a position of equality with *T'ien*, Heaven. The Imperial Edict of 1907 reads: 'In view of the supreme excellence of the great sage Confucius, whose virtues equal Heaven and Earth, and make him worthy of the adoration of a myriad ages, it is the desire of her Imperial Majesty the Empress Dowager Tzu Hsi, etc., that the great Sage shall in future be accorded the same sacrificial ceremonies of worship accorded Heaven and Earth when sacrifice is paid by the Emperor.'

CONFUCIANISM IN HISTORY

1. *Some Early Historical Developments*

The course of history went against Confucianism for four hundred years. The Sage had died under a shroud of gloom, and his death was followed by the Age of Polemics during which rival schools of thought, some for and some against his principles, struggled in wordy contest for the supremacy. The Confucian tradition barely escaped obliteration when Shih Hwang Ti, the first Emperor of the shortlived Ch'in dynasty, provoked by opposition from the scholar-class, committed all copies of their classical books he could find to the flames (213 B.C.).

It was not until the period of the Han dynasty (221 B.C.-206 A.D.) that Confucianism was firmly established, and even so some of the more powerful of the early Han emperors cherished a private predilection for Taoism.

A powerful scholar-class arose and these made Confucianism the cult of the State and dominant at Court. A fresh and close study of the classics at this time synchronized with the invention of printing; furthermore, the interpretation in the commentaries they wrote provided the first 'definitive' edition of the Canon for a thousand years. All this took place at the time when Buddhism began its deep and widespread penetration of Chinese life.

With the advent of the great T'ang dynasty (618-906 A.D.), a period Elizabethan in its creative activity, Confucianism was restored to the supremacy from which Buddhism had temporarily ousted it. Temples to Confucius were built everywhere and the Emperor himself sacrificed to the Sage. In 631 A.D. Confucian classics were made the sole literary subject for examination of aspirants to the civil service, a system which helped further to sustain the life of Confucianism, and which continued for the duration of the Empire. By process of elimination at the Imperial examination, the flower of literary scholarship was selected and brought to an unrivalled place of honour in the service of the State. B. S. Bonsall points out: 'It was the conservatism and arrogance of the scholar-class, which believed that all the wisdom of mankind was stored in the Confucian literature, and the power which the system of education, culminating in the examination for Government positions, placed in the hands of that class that made China so slow to adapt itself to the new situation created by the opening-up of intercourse with the other great nations of the world.'

2. Renaissance in the Middle Ages

Both Taoism and Buddhism reached their zenith in the T'ang period (618–907 A.D.), but neither was ever to regain fully the position then attained: on the other hand, the period of greatest influence and power still lay before Confucianism.

During the three hundred years of the Sung dynasty (960–1279 A.D.) the Sung School of Philosophers arose. This age of intellectual activity gave birth to a notable renaissance of Confucian learning. One result among others was a re-interpretation of the classical texts, the doctrine so expounded being referred to as 'Neo-Confucianism'. The most notable of the new commentators was Chu Hsi (1130–1200 A.D.), whose interpretation of the Five Classics and Four Books set for succeeding centuries the standard of Confucian orthodoxy, so that one scholar remarked, 'No more writing is needed: what is left to us is practice.' In the Confucian temple the name of Chu Hsi heads the 'Twelve Men of Genius', whose names are inscribed on tablets of the second category, those of the first category being the 'Four Associates', three immediate disciples of the Sage and the philosopher Mencius.[1]

---

[1] The Confucian temple faces south. The chief feature is the tablet to Confucius, placed at the northern end. Ranged immediately on its left, east, is the tablet to the favourite disciple, Yen Hui; and then that to Yüan Ssu, 'noted for his pursuit of truth, and carelessness of worldly advantage'. Immediately on the right of the central tablet, west, is placed that of Tseng Tzu, a disciple famed for devotion to his parents. He composed the *Classic of Filial Piety* and wrote a commentary on the *Great Learning*. Next stood the tablet of Mencius, the man 'to whose genius and devotion may be traced the final triumph of Confucianism'.

Neo-Confucianism, as it left the hands of the Sung scholars, was not unaffected by Buddhist and Taoist ideas. Making some use of these borrowed elements, Chu Hsi and his companions added to the old politico-ethical teaching of the *Analects* a newly devised metaphysical system. This reaffirmed the doctrines of man's innate goodness, the Middle Course, and the moral or natural law. But Chu Hsi, who was somewhat of a rationalist, tended to empty of their original meaning the theistic terms of the ancient writings and instead gave currency to the idea of a Universal Reason. 'Confucianism was modernized, stripped of its religious character, and left as an ethical system divorced from supernatural sanctions.' Only in recent years have Chinese scholars tended to dissociate themselves from the interpretations of the Sung School and revert to the original character of the classical texts.

In 1530 all temple images to the Sage and other Confucian worthies were destroyed on command of the Ming Emperor. Only the wooden tablets inscribed with names and titles were left for veneration.

In subsequent centuries both Mongol and Manchu conquerors of China were diligent to uphold the orthodox Confucianism of the State and thereby secure the support of Chinese officials. The Mongol Kublai Khan in 1306 erected a temple to Confucius in Peking, while the Manchu Emperor K'ang Hsi issued the Sacred Edict in which he inveighed against the heterodoxies of Buddhism, Taoism and Roman Catholicism, and extolled the virtues of Confucianism.

3. *Confucianism in Modern Times*

The fall of the Manchu dynasty in 1911 was associated with a great change for the worse in the status of Confucianism. A reference has already been made to the last despairing attempt, made in 1907, to rehabilitate the monarchy in the eyes of the official class by the issue of an Imperial Edict according the Sage a position equal in honour to that of Shang Ti.

The abolition of the old State examinations removed one of the chief incentives to the study of Confucian books, which are written in the archaic literary style. Moreover, the new leadership came not from the class of Confucian scholar-officials but from the modern, western-trained students, highly critical of traditional thought and traditional ways. The ceremony of the Imperial Sacrifice was discontinued with the abdication of the last of the Emperors, and there was no longer one recognized cult of the State: it was the 'twilight of the gods'. Yuan Shih-kai, first president of the new republic, in an ill-advised moment, sought to found a new dynasty, and at the famous Altar of Heaven went through a modified form of the Imperial ritual. But this ambitious sacrilege, as it was in Chinese eyes, served only to hasten his downfall.

The process of disintegration was artificially arrested when a group of the more zealous spirits attempted a Confucianist revival. During the ten years following the collapse of the Imperial throne their efforts took these forms:

(1) The establishment of a Confucian Association in the interests of the cult's revival. This was partly in order to preserve the morality of the people, for old sanctions had been severely shaken.

(2) An endeavour to have Confucianism adopted as the State religion and to have this so stated in the Constitution of the Republic.

(3) A further attempt a few years later to secure in the Constitution government sanction for Confucianism as the basis for moral education in the schools.

(4) The publication of *The Confucian Association Monthly* by Dr. Chen Huan-chang. This closed down after a run of two years. Another start was made in 1924, but this also met with failure.

(5) The maintenance of old-time birthday ceremonies in the temple at Chufou in Shantung, the Sage's birthplace. This birthday, on 27th August 1949, marked the 2,500th year since the Sage's birth.

These vain efforts were summarily written off in 1934 by Hu Shih, China's foremost scholar, when he declared: 'The spiritualization of our national character cannot be restored by superficial observances and the shouting of a few slogans.' However, in 1936, in a general survey one observer wrote: 'On the whole the non-Christian religions are in a stronger position than they were thirty years ago. They are adjusting themselves to a growing nationalism which holds on to certain customs because they are native.' More recently there have been evidences of the readiness of Confucianism to assimilate the principles of Christianity—in the old characteristically eclectic spirit.

Since the death and subsequent glorification of Sun Yat Sen, founder of the Republic, the prestige of Confucius has been somewhat obscured. Nevertheless, Confucianism in some places still finds its expression in the older forms and still permeates the thinking of the Chinese people; for, in the minds of many Chinese, Confucius stands for the whole of the ancient Chinese civilization. It is interesting, however to note the view of a Communist Government observer. Dealing with the present religious situation in the country, he expressed himself as follows: 'Five religious philosophies—Confucianism, Buddhism, Taoism, Muhammadanism and Christianity—make up the currents of religious life in China today. Of these, two—Confucianism and Taoism—are regarded as antiquated religions which are rapidly dying out and for which there is no place in New China, both religions having been deeply associated with the feudal era which has come to an end. As both Taoism and Confucianism are unorganized religions, it is impossible to give any statistical information on the extent of their influence, except to mention the thoroughgoing hold of Confucianism or neo-Confucianism as a feudalistic code of life typified in the rule of Chiang Kai-shek. Unlike Buddhism, which still has a considerable following among the common people, Taoism has lost touch with the people and for all practical purposes has degenerated into a code of superstitious and mercenary practices.'

T HE study of comparative religion, fascinating though it is, leaves many with a sense of bewilderment. Such diverse beliefs are held by multitudes whose sincerity cannot be questioned that the student may easily fall into the logical absurdity of wondering whether any ultimate truth exists in matters of religion, or into the resigned pessimism of doubting whether any certain knowledge in such matters can be attained by man. Should not all religions be discarded, then, as profitless attempts to solve the insoluble or, alternatively, be regarded as different roads to one grand but distant goal? Admittedly, most of the world's faiths seem to the unprejudiced enquirer a patchwork of good and bad, or at least of the desirable and the less desirable: but cannot the mind which eschews fanaticism accept the postulate which seems in some sense common to all, that there is a Force or a Person beyond and behind the material universe, which to recognize, or whom to worship, meets some craving of the human heart? As for the rest—the details of dogma and worship—may not each individual work out for himself an eclectic faith chosen from what seems best in all the great religions?

To the Christian this is an impossible attitude. He will, of course, be vitally concerned with what millions of his fellow creatures believe, and their convictions will command his interest, study and respect. More, he will find much in those who follow other religions which will rebuke, instruct and inspire him, as, for instance, the Muslim's fidelity in prayer and fast, the Buddhist's dignified self-discipline, and the Sadhu's detachment from the things of time and sense. But these things concern matters of observance rather than teaching, of practice rather than dogma, noble though some non-Christian dogma undoubtedly is. In regard to the content of his faith, the Christian will neither want nor dare to meddle. This is partly because his religion satisfies both heart and mind and leaves no longing except for a deeper apprehension and response. But fundamentally it rests on something less subjective and individualistic than this, for he knows that his faith is not man-made but God-revealed, and therefore of universal validity: and he bases this conviction on the deity, authority, and exclusive claims of the historic Christ.

The early disciples, being convinced Jews, were as ardent monotheists as the modern Muslim. They began, therefore, by regarding their Master as nothing more than a great teacher. But as they lived with Him for over three years, as they heard His teaching, as they saw His miracles and, above all, as they watched the supreme wonder of a sinless life, they came to realize intuitively that this could be no mere man. More, they heard the astounding claims which fell quietly and confidently from His lips: 'I am the light of the world: he that followeth Me shall not walk in darkness, but shall have the light of life';[1] 'I am the bread of life; he that cometh to Me shall never hunger; and he that believeth on Me shall never thirst';[2] 'I am the way, the truth and the life; no man cometh unto the Father, but by Me.'[3] Surely One who made such claims, not merely for His teaching but for Himself, could be only an impostor, a megalomaniac, or God Himself: and to those who lived with Him neither of the first two alternatives were possible.

Even so, it would stagger the imagination of any company of men to realize that one with whom they ate, walked and talked was none other than the Eternal God come to live as Man among men. It is scarcely surprising, then, that the disciples, in spite of all the evidence, had apprehended this in flashes of intuition rather than as reasoned conviction when the worst happened, and He was crucified. Their bewilderment and despair throughout the Friday and Saturday stand vividly portrayed in the Gospel story. But on the first Easter morning the women who visited the tomb found it empty (a fact which no anti-Christian theory has ever adequately explained) and for forty days the disciples held intermittent but intimate converse with their risen Lord. Now at last they knew beyond a doubt that He and His Father were one,[4] and that His words and teaching could be trusted implicitly. And the witness of the Gospel narratives, with their decisive evidence for the unique Person, atoning death, and bodily resurrection of the historic Christ, has been confirmed by Christian experience all down the ages.

What, then, is the Christian's attitude to these other religions? We have seen that for him any suggestion of a synthesis is impossible; but can he regard them as forerunners and harbingers of the full revelation in Christ? Clearly, such a view is literally applicable only to the revelation of the Old Testament, for the other pre-Christian religions are inherently hostile to Christ's exclusive claims, while Islam, coming after Him, specifically denies them. Even in the case of those animistic beliefs and practices which are commonly regarded as representing

[1] Jn. viii. 12.   [2] Jn. vi. 35.   [3] Jn. xiv. 6.   [4] Cf. Jn. x. 30.

the first stepping-stone in man's progress towards true religion, the fact that animists seem everywhere to recognize the existence and pre-eminence of the Creator (although they largely ignore Him in practice in their desire to propitiate lesser but more immanent spirits) strongly supports St. Paul's assertion that paganism represents not the first step in an ascent to true worship, but the fatal result of withholding worship from a God once known.[1] The question remains, however, whether the other 'revealed' religions can be thought of as in any sense from God, or whether the Christian must regard them either as products of that religious instinct which is inherent in mankind or as 'inspired' indeed, but by him whose primary purpose (as both the Bible and human experience reveal) is to keep men from the true knowledge of God and to delude them with any kind of substitute.

In any final analysis, it is clear, everything that is good and true and beautiful has its origin in God, mediated to men through that living Word who has been from eternity the Revealer of the Godhead. Did He not say, 'I am the truth',[2] and is He not the 'light that lighteth every man'?[3] The Christian, then, can trace all that is best in non-Christian religions to its ultimate source and origin, and give Him thanks. Similarly, all that is evil, false and unlovely comes from below, for 'God is light, and in Him is no darkness at all'.[4] These other religions, then, like so much else in the world of men, are made up of elements whose ultimate origins are diverse. But in so far as these diverse elements have been welded into systems which serve only to divert and keep men from that way of salvation and life which cost God Himself the incarnation and the cross, the Christian must regard them as Satanic substitutes, however good they may be in parts. This intolerance, if intolerance it be, is not that of a sectarian and insensitive spirit, but is necessarily inherent in the nature of the Christian message. It is, therefore, to the essential of that message that we must now turn.

Great religious teachers have commonly claimed to bring God's message to men, but Christ was (and is) Himself the message. Others have taught men about God, and tried to tell them how to climb to heaven; but in Christ God came down to earth and revealed Himself to men. On some such revelation, moreover, a man must necessarily depend, for although human reason can build up a strong case for the existence, 'personality' and love of God, the final initiative must lie

[1] See p. 22.   [2] Jn. xiv. 6.   [3] Jn. i. 9.   [4] I Jn. i. 5.

with Him, and man must await His self-revelation. But if God is a living, beneficent Person who loves His creatures, it seems neither unreasonable nor presumptuous to expect some such revelation.

But how could He convey any real knowledge of His infinite Godhead to finite human minds? Something, certainly, can be learnt from nature, which is why St. Paul categorically described as 'without excuse'[1] those who have failed to deduce His eternal power and Godhead from the wonders of His creation. More still can be gleaned from the utterances and writings of men and women into whose hearts He has breathed His messages. Such were the Old Testament prophets. But there could be no full and final revelation unless He would deign to reveal Himself as a Man among men; for man can never really know God as pure Spirit, but only as His heart and nature are revealed in terms of human life. It is surely a deep-rooted instinct that such a revelation alone could suffice which has prompted men of many religions and mythologies to postulate some theophany or incarnation. But in Christ alone we find a human life lived in the light of history which not only compelled His first followers to cry, 'My Lord and my God', but has had the same impact on millions all down the ages; for the closer man gets to Him, the more conscious he becomes that He was none other than God 'manifest in the flesh'.[2]

In Christ, then, we have the final answer to the fundamental question of all religion, 'Can I know God, . . . What is He like?' Baffling problems confront the would-be worshipper, for phenomena are not lacking which seem inconsistent with either the goodness or omnipotence of God. Can we be sure that He is good, that He sympathizes with man's sorrow and suffering, that He cares about man's sin, and that He can bring victory out of seeming defeat? For the Christian, the final answer has been given in the life and death of the Lord Jesus Christ. He went about doing good; He could never meet human suffering without that deity, which He usually kept hidden, blazing out in healing and succour; He was the friend of sinners. And at last He, the Almighty, willingly went to that cross where the humble worshipper finds the fullest revelation of the heart and nature of God (and, incidentally, the key to the enigma of suffering and pain). God knows, cares and loves—and He can meet every need.

For that same cross provides the only answer to the second most

[1] Rom. i. 20.   [2] I Tim. iii. 16.

N

fundamental problem of religion: how can I, a sinner, find forgiveness and acceptance with God? The more lofty the revelation of God, the more profoundly does man feel this need. To this instinct even the sacrifices offered by animists to propitiate malignant spirits bear their distorted witness, while in many non-Christian religions sacrifices are clearly associated with sin and the need for atonement. Commonly, however, the concept is one of man trying to placate or appease an angry Deity. It is only in the New Testament (and Old Testament foreshadowing) that we find a propitiation which has its very origin in the love of God and His longing to save sinful men—a propitiation which from first to last is God-provided. 'God was in Christ, reconciling the world unto Himself.'[1]

In the cross of Christ three supreme facts stand revealed: the nature of sin in the sight of a holy God, His measureless love for the sinner, and how alone He can righteously extend a full and free forgiveness to the penitent. Sin is so black to Him who sees it in its true nature, possibilities and implications, that even He could deal with it only by bearing it to the cross: while His love for the sinner was so infinite that He was willing to go to this incredible length to win him back to Himself. This is the subjective side of the atonement: it is the realization of the guilt of sin and of the matchless love of God which prompts repentance and leads to conversion. But there is also a deep objective significance: for the God who, being Himself the Fount and Origin of the moral order of the universe, could never ignore nor excuse the foul fact of sin, came and identified Himself in Christ with sinful humanity and bore that sin, with its consequences and penalty, 'in His own body on the tree'.[2] In that mystery of mysteries, when He who was eternally one with the Father had to cry, 'My God, my God, why hast Thou forsaken Me?',[3] God's judgment and condemnation of sin were finally revealed and the way of forgiveness and acceptance was opened wide to the penitent believer. The moral order was vindicated, God's righteousness manifested, and His redeeming love made free for all. No wonder that to the Christian Calvary, rather than Bethlehem, is the focal point of history; for even the most perfect revelation of the character of God avails us little until the barrier of sin which inevitably separates us from Him is removed, and we can enjoy fellowship with the One so revealed.

It is just here, again, that Christianity is unique. Other religions

[1] 2 Cor. v. 19. [2] 1 Pet. ii. 24. [3] Mk. xv. 34.

teach a way of life which must somehow be attained by man. By the observance of the rites of religion, by the performance of deeds of beneficence, or by the achievement of ethical conduct, merit must be accumulated and 'salvation' won. As in the problem of revelation, it is man who must scale the heavens. Christianity, by contrast, brings the 'good news' of a salvation which is wholly God-provided: man can do nothing to earn it or achieve it, but can only accept it as a gift. Where every other religion teaches what man must *do*, Christianity alone tells what God has *done*.

To many, this may sound dangerous. The Christian, it would seem, has only to accept a salvation provided by Another and he can then behave as he likes. The paradox is that in fact the preaching of 'justification by faith' produces a moral transformation which no amount of pious exhortation could ever evoke. This is because the 'faith' which 'justifies' the Christian is no mere mental assent to a dogma but vital trust in a Saviour, a Saviour who does not save men in their sins but from them. It is the glory of the gospel that God receives the ungodly, the sinful and the depraved; but only in order to make them godly, holy and upright. He never relaxes His moral demands. Unlike the devotees of many of the world's great religions, the Christian must show a transformed moral personality in all the relationships of human life, or else his religion is counterfeit. The Saviour who died to redeem by His death rose again to save by His life; and He does this not only by the external inspiration of His presence and companionship, but by the internal mediation of His own life by His Spirit. The Christian has only one moral goal, to be Christ-like: and he hopes to reach that goal not by the laborious and hopeless imitation of an unattainable ideal, but by the supernatural reproduction of that ideal in the life where the divine Spirit is given unrestricted sway.

But it must not be thought that the Christian message and revelation are purely individualistic. Of necessity they bring their challenge first to the individual, but only to demand of all who experience Christ's saving power that they should pass on the good news to others. To this the unique, although still totally inadequate, world-wide mission-ary enterprise of the Christian Church, with all its devotion and sacrifice, bears convincing testimony. More, all true believers are united in the fellowship of that Church which transcends all de-nominational barriers and is called in the New Testament the very 'body of Christ'—partly because its high calling is collectively to show forth His life and proclaim His message to the world He came to save.

The Christian believes that God is not only Creator but Sovereign of the world He made. True, His fair creation has been marred by sin, and His proper sovereignty flouted not only by human self-will, but also in the spirit realm. Yet the Christian is no dualist, for he knows that the power of Satan is limited and temporary; more, victory over all the power of darkness was won at Calvary's cross,[1] and Christ is already seated at the right hand of God waiting 'till His enemies be made His footstool'.[2] Every detail of life concerns Him. For the present He seems to let men (and Satan) go their way, although always within limits; but a day is surely coming when He will again intervene, and the Christ who came to suffer will come again to reign. The Bible is crystal-clear on this point; He is coming, both for salvation and for judgment. Now is the Christian's opportunity to evangelize: not to preach an ethic, however lofty, but to tell the whole world the good news of what God has done in Christ for sinful humanity and will work out in any individual heart by His Spirit.

In conclusion, may we urge every student of comparative religion to turn afresh to the New Testament? The eternal God did not come to live as a Man among men and go to the cross of Calvary for nothing, nor did He leave future generations in any uncertainty regarding His actions and their meaning. As St. John puts it, 'These (things) are written, that ye might believe that Jesus is the Christ, the Son of God; and that believing ye might have life through His name.'[3] One of the express purposes for which the Holy Spirit was sent was to bring to the disciples' remembrance the things which Christ had said to them,[4] and to guide them into all truth[5] concerning the meaning of what they had seen and heard. And the records so inspired remain for all to read.

Surely there can be no more vital issue. In the nature of things there can be only one life which is eternal in both quality and duration—the life of God Himself. But the burden of the New Testament is that God has given us to share that life in His Son.[6] It inevitably follows that 'he that hath the Son hath life; and he that hath not the Son of God hath not life'.[7]

---

[1] Cf. Col. ii. 15. Heb. ii. 14.   [2] Heb. x. 13.
[3] Jn. xx. 31.   [4] Jn. xiv. 26.   [5] Jn. xvi. 13.
[6] Compare 1 Jn. v. 11; 2 Peter i. 4; Jn. xiv. 19; Col. iii. 4, etc.
[7] 1 Jn. v. 12.

BIBLIOGRAPHY

COMPARATIVE RELIGION

Comparative Religion. A. C. Bouquet. Pelican Books. 1941.

The Christian Message in a Non-Christian World. H. Kraemer. Edinburgh House Press. 1938.

The History of Religions. E. W. Hopkins. Macmillan. 1928.

The Gospel in the World. G. E. Phillips. Duckworth. 1939.

The Originality of the Christian Message. H. R. Mackintosh. Duckworth. 1920.

An Introduction to the Study of Some Living Religions of the East. Sydney Cave. Duckworth. 1921.

Christianity and the Religions of the World. A. Schweitzer. George Allen & Unwin. 1923.

The Living God. N. Soderblom. Oxford University Press. 1933.

ANIMISM

The Golden Bough. Sir J. G. Frazer. Macmillan & Co. 13 vols. £9 3s. 6d. Abridged Edition in one volume. 24s. 714 pp.

An Introduction to the History of Religion. F. B. Jevons. London. Puts forward the thesis of a universal Totemism, preceding all other forms of religion.

The Making of Religion. Andrew Lang. 1898. Suggests the hypothesis that the existence of 'High Gods' in primitive culture may point to an original Theism which later became debased.

Primitive Culture. Sir E. B. Tylor. 1871. The author gave the name 'Animism' to primitive spirit worship.

West African Religion. Geoffrey Parrinder. The Epworth Press. 1949. 10s. 6d. 215 pp. A factual study of West African tribal religion, suggesting that the terms Polytheism or Polydemonism better describe their primitive beliefs, and abolishing the title of Fetishism as misleading.

The Living Forces of the Gospel. Joh. Warneck. Oliphant, Anderson and Ferrier. 1909. 308 pp. A scholarly work written entirely from the Christian standpoint, as the result of a lifetime of experience among primitive Indonesians. The best study of Animism in existence from this standpoint.

Jesus Christ and the World's Religions. William Paton. Edinburgh House Press. 1916. 19th Impression, 1941. The first chapter contains a useful summary of some characteristics of primitive religion.

Encyclopaedia of Religion and Ethics. Edited by James Hastings. Articles on *Animism* (Goblet d'Alviella, 3 pp.), *Ancestor Worship and Cult of the Dead* (Introduction by W. Crooks, 8 pp.) and *Magic* (Introduction by H. R. Marett, 77 pp.), *Fetishism* (by W. G. Aston, 12 pp.), *Totemism* (by E. Sydney Hartland, 14 pp.).

JUDAISM

The Essence of Judaism. Leo Baeck. London. 1936.

A Short History of the Jewish People. Cecil Roth. The East and West Library. Oxford. 1943. 169 pp.

Everyman's Talmud. Dr. A. Cohen. London. 1943.

Communion in the Messiah. Lev. Gillet. Lutterworth Press. 1942. 242 pp.

The Jew in the Christian World. Kosmala and Smith. S.C.M. Press. 1942. 173 pp.

A History of Palestine. James Parkes. Victor Gollancz. 1948. 21s.

The Jewish People and Jesus Christ. J. Jocz. S.P.C.K. 1949. 446 pp.

Hostages of Civilization. Eva G. Reichmann. Victor Gollancz. 1950.

Learning Laughter. (A Journey through Israel.) Stephen Spender. Weidenfeld & Nicolson. 1953.

The Church and the Jewish People. A Symposium edited by Göte Hedenquist. Edinburgh House Press. 1954.

The Parting of the Ways. Dr. A. Cohen. London, Lincolns-Prager. 1954.

ISLAM

The Arabs, A Short History. P. K. Hitti. Macmillan & Co. 1948. 207 pp.

Literary History of the Arabs. R. A. Nicholson. Cambridge University Press. 1930. 2nd Edition. xxxi + 506 pp.

Introduction to the Koran. Richard Bell. Edinburgh University Press. 1953. x + 190 pp.

The Koran. Translated by J. M. Rodwell. Williams & Norgate. 1861.

The Koran as Scripture. A. Jeffery. New York, Russell S. Moore. 1952. 103 pp.

The Life of Mohammad. Sir William Muir. New edition. J. Grant. Edinburgh. 1923. cxix + 556 pp

Mohammed. D. S. Margoliouth. Blackie & Sons. 1939. vi + 151 pp.

Mohammed: the Man and his Faith. Tor Andrae (trans. T. Menzel). Allen & Unwin. 1936. 274 pp.

Mohammed and the Rise of Islam. D. S. Margoliouth. G. O. Putnam. 1927. xxvi +481 pp.

The Traditions of Islam. A. Guillaume. Clarendon Press. 1924. 184 pp.

The Caliphate: Its Rise, Decline and Fall. Sir William Muir. New edition. Edinburgh. J. Grant. 1924. xix +633 pp. and maps.

The Early Development of Mohammedanism. D. S. Margoliouth. Williams & Norgate. 1914. ix +265 pp.

Mohammedanism. C. S. Hurgronje. New York, Putnam. 1937. 154 pp.

Islam, Beliefs and Institutions. H. Lammens. (Translated from the French.) Methuen & Co. 1929. ix +256 pp.

Development of Muslim Theology, Jurisprudence and Constitutional Theory. D. B. Macdonald. New York, C. Scribner's Sons. 1903. xii +386 pp.

Aspects of Islam. D. B. Macdonald. New York, Macmillan. 1911. xiii +375 pp.

Religious Attitude to Life in Islam. D. B. Macdonald. University of Chicago Press. 1909. xvii +317 pp.

Mystics of Islam. R. A. Nicholson. G. Bell & Sons. 1914. vi +178 pp.

Origins of Muhammadan Jurisprudence. J. Schacht. Oxford University Press. 1950.

Dictionary of Islam. T. P. Hughes. 2nd Edition. W. H. Allen & Co. 1935. vi +750 pp

Encyclopaedia of Islam. 4 vols. and supplement. Leyden, E. J. Brill.; London, Luzac & Co. 1913-38. (Also published in French and German.) Many articles.

Encyclopaedia of Religion and Ethics. Edited by James Hastings. Various editions. 13 vols. New York, C. Scribner's Sons; Edinburgh, T. & T. Clark. 1925-32. Various articles.

Whither Islam? H. A. R. Gibb. Victor Gollancz. 1932. 384 pp.

The Christian Approach to the Moslem. J. T. Addison. Columbia University Press. 1942. x +365 pp.

The Influence of Animism in Islam. S. M. Zwemer. New York, Macmillan & Co. 1920. viii +246 pp.

The Rebuke of Islam. W. H. Temple Gairdner. London, U.C.M.E. 1920. xvi +367 pp.

How to Lead Moslems to Christ. G. K. Harris. The China Inland Mission. v +122 pp. 1948.

Islam and Modernism in Egypt. C. C. Adams. Oxford University Press. 1933.

Modern Trends in Islam. H. A. R. Gibb. Cambridge University Press. 1947.

Le Dogme et la Loi de l'Islam. I. Goldziher (trans. F. Arin). Paris, Paul Geuthner. 1920. 315 pp.

HINDUISM

Hinduism. Sir M. Monier Williams. S.P.C.K. 1911. 238 pp.

Hinduism. A. C. Bouquet. Hutchinson's University Library. 1948. 171 pp.

Outline of Hinduism. F. Harold Smith. Epworth Press. 1934. 135 pp.

Primer of Hinduism. J. N. Farquhar. Oxford University Press. 1912. 222 pp.

Crown of Hinduism. J. N. Farquhar. Oxford University Press. Madras. 1915. 469 pp.

The Religions of India. E. W. Hopkins. Ginn & Co. 1895.

Modern Religious Movements in India. J. N. Farquhar. New York, Macmillan. 1915. 471 pp.

Introduction to the Study of the Hindu Doctrines. Réné Guenon. (Translated.) Luzac. 1945. 351 pp.

Rites of the Twice-Born. Sinclair Stevenson. Oxford University Press. 1920. 474 pp.

Redemption, Hindu and Christian. Sidney Cave. Oxford University Press. 1919. 263 pp.

Christianity and Some Living Religions of the East. Sidney Cave. Duckworth. 1929. 221 pp.

Popular Hinduism. S. S. O'Malley. Cambridge University Press. 1935. 246 pp.

Living Religions of the Indian People. N. MacNicol. S.C.M. Press. 1934. 324 pp.

Ancient Faiths and Lore of India. C. S. Milford and W. R. Garrad. Press and Publications Board of the Church Assembly. 43 pp.

Hindu Manners, Customs and Ceremonies. Dubois and Beauchamp. Oxford University Press. 1906.

Mystics, Ascetics and Saints of India. J. C. Oman. Fisher Unwin. 1903.

Brahmans, Theists and Muslims of India. J. C. Oman. Fisher Unwin. 1907.

Cults, Customs and Superstitions of India. J. C. Oman. Fisher Unwin. 1908.

A Hindu View of Life. S. Radhakrishnan. George Allen & Unwin. 1928. 133 pp.

The Heart of India. L. D. Barnett. John Murray. Wisdom of the East Series. 1924. 122 pp.

The Heart of the Aryavarta. Zetland, Earl of Ronaldshay. Constable. 1925. 262 pp.

The Christian Message to the Hindu. A. G. Hogg. S.C.M. Press. 1947. 104 pp.

India and the Christian Movement. Bishop V. S. Azariah. Christian Literature Society for India. Madras. 1936. 126 pp.

India on the Threshold. L. W. Bryce. Edinburgh House Press. 1948. 152 pp.

Things as They Are. Amy Carmichael. Marshall Morgan & Scott. 1905. 304 pp.

A History of Sanskrit Literature. A. A. Macdonald. Heinemann. 1913. 472 pp.

Sakuntala, Meghaduta, Bhagavadgita. English translations. Scott Library.

India in Outline. Lady Hartog. Oxford University Press. 1944. 110 pp.

Living India. Lady Hartog. Blackie & Co. 1935. 200 pp.

India, Pakistan and the West. Spear. Oxford University Press. 1949. 232 pp.

BUDDHISM

What is Buddhism? Compiled and published by the Buddhist Society. 1928. Reprinted 1947. 216 pp. A reasoned exposition of the principles of Buddhism written for Westerners.

Buddhism. Christmas Humphries. Penguin Books. 1951. 250 pp. The handiest survey of the whole subject available in English.

Buddhism. Vol. I. Hinayana. C. H. S. Ward. The Epworth Press. 1948. 143 pp. Primarily for scholars but readily understandable, full of useful quotations, and with a valuable bibliography.

Thus Have I Heard. Christmas Humphries. The Buddhist Society. 1948. 73 pp. The teaching, application, and some scriptures of the Southern School of Buddhism.

The Path of the Elders. E. E. Power. The Buddhist Society.

The Jewel in the Lotus. John Blofeld. Sidgwick & Jackson. 1948. 193 pp. An outline of present-day Buddhism in China. A well-written, frank and illustrated study of Mahayana Buddhism by an English Buddhist.

Truth and Tradition in Chinese Buddhism. K. L. Reichelt. The Commercial Press, Shanghai. 1927. A study of Chinese Mahayana Buddhism.

Introduction to Mahayana Buddhism. McGovern. Kegan, Paul, Trench, Trubner & Co. 1922.

Buddhism as a Religion. H. Hackmann. London. Probsthain & Co. 1910. Strongly recommended.

Buddhism in Translations. H. C. Warren. Harvard University. 1922.

Buddhism. T. W. Rhys-Davies. S.P.C.K. 1912.

Buddhism: Its History and Literature. T. W. Rhys-Davies. Putnam's Sons. 1926.

Buddhism. Sir M. Monier Williams. Murray. 1889.

The Three Religions of China. W. E. Soothill. Hodder & Stoughton. 1913. 324 pp.

The Gospel of Buddha. Paul Carus. Chicago. Open Court Publishing Co. London agents: Kegan, Paul, Trench, Trubner & Co. Ltd. 1917.

The Essence of Buddhism. D. T. Suzuki. The Buddhist Society.

The Creed of Buddha. Holmes. The Buddhist Society.

Karma and Rebirth. Christmas Humphries. The Buddhist Society.

SHINTO

Shinto, the Way of the Gods. W. G. Aston. 1905. The standard work in English on the subject.

Shinto, the Ancient Religion of Japan. W. G. Aston. 1921. A brief abridgment of the previous work.

Article on Shinto in *Encyclopaedia of Religion and Ethics.* Edited by James Hastings. W. G. Aston.

History of Japanese Religion. M. Anesaki. 1930. An excellent scientific study.

A Study of Shinto. G. Kato. 1927. A Japanese defence of Shinto.

Shintoism, the Indigenous Religion of Japan. A. C. Underwood. 1934. A useful outline.

The Political Philosophy of Modern Shinto. D. C. Holtom. 1922. Being the Transactions of the Asiatic Society of Japan. Vol. XLIX, Part 2. A scholarly study of modern tendencies in Shinto.

The National Faith of Japan. D. C. Holtom. 1938. The most recent scholarly survey of the whole field of Shinto.

Modern Japan and Shinto Nationalism. D. C. Holtom. 1943. Re-edited with two chapters added on the post-war situation. 1947. A well-documented account.

Japan Past and Present. E. O. Reuschauer. 1947. Brief but balanced outline of Japanese history.

CONFUCIANISM

Confucianism and Taoism. B. S. Bonsall. Epworth Press. 1934. 127 pp. A compact but adequate summary of the two religions.

China. Edited by H. F. MacNair. University of California Press. 1946. 573 pp. Contains articles on *Chinese Thought, Confucianism, Neo-Confucianism* and *Taoism* by modern Chinese and American scholars of the first rank.

The Three Religions of China. W. E. Soothill. Hodder & Stoughton. 1913. 324 pp. Readable and comprehensive.

The Religions of China. James Legge. Hodder & Stoughton. 1880. 310 pp. By the translator into English of the Chinese Classics and first Professor of Chinese at Oxford. From an unrivalled knowledge of the subject he compares Confucianism and Taoism with Christianity.

The Chinese: Their History and Culture. K. S. Latourette. Macmillan. 1934. Vol. I, 506 pp.; Vol. II, 390 pp. Confucianism seen in the main stream of Chinese history.

Chinese Philosophy in Classical Times. E. R. Hughes. Dent (Everyman's Library). 1942. 36 pp. Translated extracts from leading Confucian and Taoist writers.

The Analects of Confucius. Arthur Waley. George Allen & Unwin. 1938. A translation with an introduction embodying modern critical views of authorship and interpretation.

A China Manual. Edited by Neville Whymant. Chinese Government Information Office. 1948. Contains short but authoritative articles on the Classics and Philosophy.

Chinese Religious Ideas. P. J. Maclagan. S.C.M. Press. 1926. A Christian valuation of China's three religions.

China Moulded by Confucius. F. T. Cheng. Stevens & Sons. 1947. A modern Chinese apologia for Confucianism.

INDEX

204

Tendancies in Islam 95f
                        64